LETTERS

OF

ISAAC PENINGTON,

AN

EMINENT MINISTER OF THE GOSPEL

IN

THE SOCIETY OF FRIENDS,

WHICH HE JOINED ABOUT THE YEAR 1658.

From the Second London Edition.

PHILADELPHIA:
FOR SALE AT FRIENDS' BOOK-STORE,
No. 304 ARCH STREET.

PREFACE TO THE LONDON EDITION.

THE editor of the present volume, having been much instructed in perusing "Letters of Isaac Penington," &c., (published in the year 1796, by John Kendall of Colchester, and now, for a considerable time out of print,) was induced to turn his attention towards reviving them. In this object he was further encouraged, by the circumstance of having access to a large number of manuscript letters of the same author, some of which were originals.

When the greater part of the materials now before the reader were nearly prepared for the press, it was ascertained, that the work above mentioned was compiled from an extensive collection of Isaac Penington's papers in the possession of John Kendall, which he eventually presented to the Society of Friends. This important document (copied with much assiduity and care by the son of I. P.) has been by permission examined; and those letters of the former publication, which are retained in the ensuing, (thirty-three in number,) have been revised and corrected by it; a few others being introduced from the same source. It will also be proper here to state, that slight verbal alterations, not affecting the sense of the author, have been adopted, where perspicuity seemed to require; and that some portions of the letters have been occasionally excluded, when they appeared to bear too close a resemblance to other passages, or to be adapted rather to the circumstances of those times than the present.

On producing from obscurity these valuable records, for the perusal of the Society of Friends and others, the editor cannot well refrain from stating, that his concern and intention has been, to promote, if it be ever so feebly, the spiritual edification, harmony, and enlargement of our Divine Redeemer's Church Universal; his desires having been much in unison with the expressions of the apostle Paul,— that, "speaking the truth in love," we may "grow up *into* Him in *all* things, which is the Head, even Christ." For we are further assured, it is *from Him* alone, that "the whole body" can be "fitly joined together, and compacted by that which every joint supplieth, according to the effectual working in the measure of every part," and thus be known an "increase of the body, unto the edifying of itself in love." Ephes. iv. 15, 16. The very weighty and confirming character of these letters, their quickening tendency, — the clear doctrine, and deep experience throughout evinced, must, it is apprehended, if perused with desires after spiritual good, prove salutary in various ways to most classes and states of Christian believers. They are not the product of a speculative imagination or of uncertain reasonings; they comprehend many of the plain positions of Scriptural faith and practice, conveyed in simple but forcible, nay, pathetic appeals; indeed, they are evidently dictated under a very deep sense of the inestimable value of heavenly things, refined and proved by no ordinary exercises of spirit, as well as by manifold outward sufferings.

And here, it may with deference be suggested, that this particular description of ministerial communication, (for such it is,) will be likely to prove more beneficial, if but a few, or even a single letter be read at one time, and a sufficient interval be allowed for the mind to reflect on and appropriate their contents. In order to this, and with a view that the reader may be in some degree apprized of the topics before him, the editor has attempted, (however imperfectly,) at the head of each letter, and in the Table of Contents, to give some brief account of the subjects of it; the advantages of which plan will, he trusts, be evident.

To the Society of Friends, it is presumed, little need be said by way of information respecting the author of these letters — his life, character, sufferings for the testimony of a good conscience, or services in the church of Christ. Such readers as have not had the privilege of access to his collected works, of which there have been several editions, may be referred to his "Life," &c. by Joseph Gurney Bevan; wherein, besides a detailed and interesting memoir, they will find extracts from his writings. Our historian, Gough, has also given a biographical sketch of him. It may, however, still be desirable to insert some particulars of this excellent man; that, in conjunction with these specimens of his labours of love, may be held up to view his lively, consistent, and blessed example. This Preface shall therefore be followed by a brief notice of Isaac Penington, being, with some slight variations, the testimony of his contemporary, William Penn.

JOHN BARCLAY.

ALTON, Fifth Month, 1828.

TESTIMONY OF WILLIAM PENN, CONCERNING ISAAC PENINGTON.

AS 'the memory of the just is blessed,' so to me there seems a blessing upon those, that have a right remembrance of them; wherefore, to the memory of this just man, my dear Friend and relation, Isaac Penington, I do, with a sincere and religious affection, dedicate this ensuing testimony.

"He was well descended as to his worldly parentage,* and born about the year 1617, being heir to a fair inheritance; his education was suitable to his quality among men, having all the advantages the schools and universities of his own country could give, joined with the conversation of some of the most knowing and considerable men of that time. His natural abilities, the gifts of his Creator, excelled; he was a man quick in apprehension, fruitful in conception, of a lively wit and intelligence, but adorned with an extraordinary mildness and engaging sweetness of disposition.

"His father's station in public business, gave him pretensions enough to share of this world's greatness; but he, with blessed meek Moses, refused the Egyptian glory of it, and chose rather a life dedicated to an inquiry after God, and holy fellowship with him and his despised Israel.

"Very early did the Lord visit him, with more than ordinary manifestations of His love; and it had such an

* He was the eldest son of Isaac Penington, of London, many years an Alderman, and for two years successively Mayor of the city, also a noted Member of the Long Parliament.

effect upon him, that it kept him both from the evils and vain worships of the world; he became the wonder of his kindred and familiars, for his awful life and serious frequent retirements, declining all company that might interrupt his meditations: by thus giving himself over to a life of mourning and pilgrimage, he was as unpleasant to those of the world, as they were to him. Nor did this sorrow flow from a sense of former vice, for he was virtuous from his childhood: but, with holy Habakkuk, from the dread he had of the majesty of God, and his desire to find a resting-place in the great day of trouble. Nothing in these exercises gave him ease or comfort, but the smiles of God's countenance upon his soul, and *that* he thirsted after with a continual solicitation; first, 'How shall I appear?' and then, 'O that I may appear before God!'

"His inward exercises and enjoyments being of a very peculiar nature, made him take little comfort in any of the religious societies then known to him. He was as one alone; for he saw so much of that uncircumcised and uncrucified flesh, which is as grass, professing the mysteries of the heavenly kingdom; — I mean, people under but ordinary convictions, who had never known Jacob's troubles, nor the fear and trembling with which salvation is to be wrought out; — and that, in religious duties, the spirit and abilities of man took up so great a share among them, and the Spirit of the Lord so little. With such he was often burdened, and pressed in spirit to lay open their carnal state under a Christian profession. For, though they held the notions of Truth, it was not in the precious experimental sense of the holy virtue and life of it; insomuch, that he found it his duty to endeavour to break their false peace, and bewilder their lofty wisdom and profession: rather approving of a state of humble doubting, than hypocritical confidence. For, the Lord's coming in spirit, without sin, to the salvation of the soul, is to be waited for; that people may truly know him and his work, and, *from thence*, speak forth his praise to others; rather than profess the enjoyments of *other* saints, which have been obtained through great tribulation, while *they* have never known this *in themselves*, and so, can have no true sense of an acceptable sacrifice of God's preparing.

"Such views drew reproach upon him from the worldly professors, as a man singular and censorious; yet those who with him waited for the consolation of Israel, and the coming of the Son of man in power and great glory, found him out, valued and honoured him; and sweet was *their* fellowship to him, who boasted in nothing more, than that they had nothing to boast of, while the Laodicea of their age thought she wanted nothing. In that emptiness, they waited to be filled of Him, who filleth all things at his coming and kingdom, that they might be the witnesses of his resurrection and appearance. Some of them died before that blessed time came; some saw it, and were glad, and with good old Simeon departed in peace; others lived to see that blessed day both dawn and break forth upon them, to their admiration and comfort; among whom, my dear father-in-law, Isaac Penington, was not the last, nor the least of note.

"About the year 1657, it pleased the Lord to send him a Peter, to declare to him, that a time of pouring forth of the Holy Spirit, and breaking forth of a heavenly work of God in the souls of men and women, was come; and many Aquilas and Priscillas came after, who instructed him in the way of God more perfectly. Though he was advanced above many in his knowledge of Scripture, and had formerly received many heavenly openings of Truth's mysteries; yet, did the Lord's way of appearance disappoint his expectation. And when the light broke forth in his heart, which his sincerity longed for, he found in himself a great mixture; and that he had much to lose and part with, before he could become that blessed little child, that new and heavenly birth, which inherits the kingdom of God: this, indeed, made him cry, 'Narrow is the way, and strait is the gate that leads to life.'

"But, to the glory of the living God, and praise of this just man's memory, let me say, — neither his worldly station, (the most considerable of any, that had closed in with his way of religion,) nor the contradictions it gave to his former conceptions, nor the debasement it brought upon his learning and wisdom, nor yet that reproach and loss which attended his public espousal of it, did deter him from embracing it. With an humble and broken spirit, he fell before this holy appearance of Jesus, — that true Light of men whose power and life he felt revealed within him, to the saving of his soul; and boldly confessed this spiritual coming of the great Messiah, who was able to teach him all things; to His name his knee truly bowed, and with Nathaniel he could cry, 'Thou art the Son of God, thou art the King of Israel.' Now, he saw clearly between the precious and the vile *in himself*, between that which was truly *of God*, in his former exercises, and that which was merely *of man:* he was not stiff nor stout in defence of his own building, and former apprehensions; no, but sold all for the 'pearl of great price,' and became willingly 'poor in spirit,' that he might enter 'the kingdom of God.' Thus, parting with all he had not received of God, he received a new stock from heaven, wherein the Lord prospered him; the dew of heaven rested upon his branch and root, he grew rich and fruitful in all heavenly treasure; full of love, faith, mercy, patience, and long-suffering; diligent in the work of the Lord, and his duty to God and men. Insomuch, that I may say, he was one of a thousand; zealous, yet tender; wise, yet humble; a constant and early attendant at meetings, watchful and reverent in them; one that ever loved *power* and *life*, more than *words;* and, as it was for *that* he waited, so would he be often deeply affected with it,—even, enabled to utter such testimonies, as were greatly to the help of the poor and needy, the weary and the heavy-laden, the true sojourners and travellers to eternal rest. To this, his writings as well as ministry tended; wherein, it will be easy for the reader to observe, his peculiar and mighty love to the great professors of religion in these kingdoms; whom carnal apprehensions or unjust prejudices, have hindered from closing with the blessed Truth, as it is known and felt among us. His fervent labour to remove these obstructions, was with such tenderness, yet great clearness, that I may venture to style him their apostle; for, as in almost every meeting, so in every book, the bent of his spirit was towards them: — that those who made a more than ordinary profession of God,—not without some ancient touches of the divine grace, and experience of his heavenly visitation, (though much extinguished by human and worldly mixtures,) — might come to know what *that* was they once tasted of, how they lost it, and which is the way to recover the living and full enjoyment of it,—even, the inward knockings and appearance of Jesus, the Saviour, to the salvation of their souls. I pray God, they may answer his love; for, he was much spent on their account; that so his ministry, writings, travels, and tears, may not be matter of charge and evidence against them in the day of judgment.*

---

* Some account of his sufferings is here added, given by Thomas Ellwood, who was well acquainted with him. "And, as it was given him to believe in Christ, so he had also to suffer for his sake; his imprisonments being many, and some of them long; which he underwent with great constancy and quietness of mind. He was first imprisoned in the year 1661, in Aylesbury Gaol, for worshipping God in his own house; and endured great hardships for seventeen weeks, in a cold, incommodious room, without a chimney, great

"As his outward man grew in age, his inward man grew in grace, and in the knowledge of our dear Lord and Saviour Jesus Christ, for the excellency of which, he had justly counted all things else but as dross and dung. For it was observable, among them that rightly knew him in his declining time, when the candle of his natural life burnt more dim, his soul waxed stronger, and, like a replenished lamp, shined with greater lustre; and truly, he had a double portion of the Spirit upon him, being anointed with judgment and zeal for the Lord, which appeared in two eminent respects.

"First, he was very urgent, that all those who knew any thing of the heavenly gift of ministry to others, would always wait in their several exercises, to be endued with matter and power from on high, before they opened their mouths in a testimony for the Lord. And that, at all times, as well out of meetings as in them, they might live so near the Lord, as to feel the key of David opening the mysteries of the heavenly kingdom; and, by experiencing the depth of the heavenly travail, and the trials, deliverances, and consolations of it,— with that dominion and victory that, in the end, by perseverance is obtained,— they might be as true saviours on mount Zion, the salt and lights of the world, thoroughly furnished unto every good word and work, and master builders in God's house:— that a pure and living stream of ministry, might be continued and conveyed to the generations to come,— that *they* might not only hear, but taste of what *we* have

part of the time in winter; from which usage, his body contracted so great a disorder, that, for several weeks, he was not able to turn himself in his bed. He was imprisoned five times after this, on account of his religious profession; and being of a tender constitution, was in danger of losing his life from the hardship he endured. Thus, through many tribulations did he enter the kingdom, having been long exercised, tried, and approved of the Lord."

known of the Word of life and work of redemption in our age.

"But, his excellency in the second respect, was his fervent love to the heavenly union of brethren; whatever struck at that, though under ever such specious pretences, he no sooner perceived, however subtle the mischievous workings thereof, than with deep wisdom he detected, and with his whole might opposed it. For, though by nature he was long suffering, to a degree of letting his mercy to others, almost wound his own soul; yet, so deeply did his love to the Lord and his people, and to that comely order in which God had settled them, engage his soul; that he was bold as a lion, yea, warlike as a champion against that spirit, that went up and down to sow jealousies, to smite and reflect upon the holy care of the brethren, interpreting their tender love and great pains, as if what was done by them were not intended for the edification of the body, but for the exaltation of some particular persons over it. This ingratitude and injustice his soul abhorred, and often he mourned for such as were so seduced; as if it were the design of those, that had from the beginning laid themselves out in the service of God and his people, to bring them at last to a blind and unwarrantable subjection, that they themselves might the better exercise dominion over them. This evil eye he helped to put out; and, in his opposition to this wandering and destroying spirit, that ever leads out of the love and unity of brethren, he approved himself a valiant of Israel, a Phinehas for the God of his salvation; — and the rewards of heaven were poured into his bosom; for his holy ministry manifestly increased in life and power, and his peace flowed as a river, and many were witnesses of his enlargements. Let those that have lost their first love, and are gone from their ancient habitation, 'rage, and imagine vain things,' if they will; surely, the travails and testimonies of this blessed man will be a witness against them, that will not easily be silenced, and a burden upon their backs, that will not readily be taken off. Yet, because he desired not their destruction, but prayed earnestly to the last for their return, let me not, whilst I am writing his character, fall short of his compassions: no, I pray God also, with my whole spirit, that they may repent, be contrite in heart, and faithfully return; at which, if the angels in heaven rejoice, certainly the spirits of the just, that dwell in heavenly places, will abundantly rejoice too.

"These two cares were chiefly and almost continually before him. And as he was, in these respects, a light in the church, so he was a blessing to his own family; a loving husband, a very tender and prudent father, a just and kind master,—I will add, a good neighbour, and a most firm friend: of all unapt to believe ill, never to report it, much less to do it to any; a man that ruled his tongue, swift to hear, slow to speak; but when he did speak, he was serious, yet sweet, and not uncheerful. What shall I say more? for great and many were the gifts God honoured him with, and with them he truly honoured his profession.

"Being thus fit to live, he was prepared to die, and had nothing else to do, when that summons was served upon him, which was in the 63d year of his age; at which time, it pleased the Lord, he fell very sick, under a sharp and painful distemper, which hastened his dissolution. However, to internal peace so well established, the anguish of that bitter exercise could give no shock; for he died, as he lived, in the faith that overcomes the world; whose soul, being now released from the confinements of time and frailties of mortality, is ascended into the glorious freedom and undisturbed joys of the just; where, with his holy brethren, the patriarchs, prophets, apostles, and martyrs of Jesus, he forever blesseth and praiseth the God and Father of the righteous generations by Jesus Christ, God's Lamb, and our heavenly Redeemer — to whom with the Father be all honour, glory, might, majesty, and dominion, through every age of his church, and forever. Amen.

"WILLIAM PENN."

"WESTMINSTER,
"12th of Twelfth Month, 1680–81."

CONTENTS.

Letter | Page

I. On the pure, living, spiritual Food. — To the Friends at Chalfont in Buckinghamshire 21

II. Christ the Root of all True Religion, &c. — To Thomas Walmsley 22

III. Of a growth in Grace, amidst distressing Exercises of Spirit. — To Bridget Atley 25

IV. On the State of the Puritans, and of Friends . . . 27

V. The Compassions of the Shepherd of the Flock towards the Weak, &c. How they should follow Him. — To Friends 30

VI. On Searching for the hidden Treasure, and Selling all for it. — To Catherine Pordage 31

VII. A Christian Salutation. — To Elizabeth Walmsley . 34

VIII. On Christ being manifested within, and the Sprinkling of his Blood inwardly. — To Thomas Walmsley . 35

IX. The Way of God's Redemption is above the ways of Man's Wisdom 36

X. On the Gospel, and on Preaching it; also on the Scriptures, &c. 39

XI. The Duty of being Content with what is made known 41

XII. Of Faith in the healing Power of Christ 42

XIII. Advice to One respecting the dark Suggestions of the Enemy 44

XIV. On Obedience, spiritual Growth, Establishment, and Victory, in and through our Lord Jesus Christ . . 46

XV. The least Messenger of the Gospel is not to be despised. A Change of Heart is to be sought, rather than a Sign 51

XVI. Advice on Reading the Scriptures 52

XVII. On the Righteousness which is of Christ. On the Manhood and Godhead of Christ. — To the Friend of Francis Fines 53

Letter Page

XVIII. On the religious Care of Children. — To a Parent 59

XIX. A Day of Calamity. — To a Friend in London: supposed to be written on occasion of the Plague . 61

XX. The spiritual Life is to be cherished. — To Friends of Truth in and about the two Chalfonts . . 62

XXI. On true Judgment, and on Prejudices; also on the variety of Gifts and Stations in the Church. — To Friends of Truth in and about the two Chalfonts 64

XXII. To a Couple about to marry 67

XXIII. The Day of God's Power and Love. — To John Mannock 69

XXIV. On Simplicity of Faith and Dedication. — To John Mannock 73

XXV. The Blessedness of Suffering for Christ's sake. — To Elizabeth Walmsley 75

XXVI. Exhortation, chiefly, on Rev. xiv. 7, "Fear God, give glory to Him," &c. — To Widow Hemmings . 78

XXVII. Advice and Sympathy under Trial. — To Elizabeth Walmsley 83

XXVIII. Of Obedience in confessing Christ; also on the Light of Christ. — To Elizabeth Stonar 84

XXIX. On the Life, inward Sense, and power of the Spirit; also respecting the Scriptures, and the Church, &c. — To Nathaniel Stonar 86

XXX. Of Truth in the inward Parts. — To Widow Hemmings 91

XXXI. Deliverance from spiritual Enemies by Christ, &c.; also of Offences 93

XXXII. Encouragement to Faithfulness under apprehension of Sufferings. — To Widow Hemmings . . 96

XXXIII. Exhortation relative to the Christian Life and Travel. — To Dulcibella Laiton 97

XXXIV. On Decay of "first Love," and a hardened State "through the Deceitfulness of Sin." — To George Winkfield 99

Letter Page

XXXV. Propositions relating to the Truth and Substance of Religion. — To Sir William Drake (so styled) 101

XXXVI. Concerning the Seed of the Kingdom. — To S. W. 105

XXXVII. Comfort and Counsel under Affliction. — To the Lady Conway 107

XXXVIII. On the benefit of Chastening by Afflictions. — To the Lady Conway 109

XXXIX. On being ingrafted into Christ, being preserved alive in Him, and growing up in Him in all Things. — To S. W. 112

XL. Counsel to One tossed as with Tempests . . 116

XLI. Encouragement under Trials incident to bearing the Cross of Christ 117

XLII. On being offended with those who fall into Temptation 118

XLIII. The Mind may be stayed in Peace amidst the Enemy's Accusations. — To Widow Hemmings 120

XLIV. On resisting, and on receiving God's Spirit; also on Redemption by Christ Jesus. — To Nathaniel Stonar 122

XLV. Respecting some Snares of the Adversary to distress the Soul. — To Bridget Atley . . . 125

XLVI. Weighty Counsel. — To Sir William Armorer (so styled) 126

XLVII. On an unfaithful profession of the Truth. — To Abraham Grimsden 129

XLVIII. Christ, the Resurrection and the Life. On His Appearance in the Flesh, &c. 130

XLIX. To One who sent a Paper of Richard Baxter's . 132

L. Of the Gospel State in general, and of the State of Believers in particular 133

LI. On shunning the Cross. — To Catherine Pordage 136

LII. On Love, Meekness, and watching over each other. — To Friends in Amersham . . . 137

LIII. On the Spiritual Appearance of Christ . . 138

Letter Page

LIV. To One under Divine Visitation 139

LV. The Kingdom of God within. Of the new Covenant. Professors of the day. Trial of Spirits. Exhortation to wait for and walk in the Spirit . 140

LVI. Encouragement to look up to the Lord, amidst his Chastenings, and the Smitings of the Enemy . 144

LVII. Of the Gospel Dispensation, and of the States of its Professors. — To Colonel Kenrick 146

LVIII. On the Lord's Supper with Believers. — To Widow Hemmings 150

LIX. Respecting the Payment of Tithes. — To James Eeles 152

LX. On Election, and on Falling Away. Of our own Righteousness, and of Christ's in us. — To Ruth Palm r 154

LXI. To his Brother Arthur, who became a Roman Catholic 159

LXII. Respecting his Brother, a Roman Catholic. — To Joseph Wright 163

LXIII. On Baptism by Water. — To William Rolls . . 165

LXIV. On unreserved Obedience. — To Bridget Atley . 166

LXV. To the Poor among Friends, who are relieved by the Charity and bowels of Love, which God opens in other Friends towards them 168

LXVI. Afflictions may work out a weight of Glory. — For Friends in Scotland 170

LXVII. Against Earthly Reasonings and Expectations. — To Sarah Bond 172

LXVIII. An Invitation to Heavenly Substance . . . 175

LXIX. Exhortation to walk in the Truth. — To Friends at Lewes 177

LXX. Consolation for a Mother on the Death of her Child. — To Sarah Elgar 178

LXXI. Advice respecting Church Discipline. — To the Women's Meeting of Friends, at John Mannock's 179

LXXII. On Prayer in Families, &c. Also on the State of Professors of the Day 182

Letter Page

LXXIII. Of Preservation and a Growth in the Heavenly Life; its power over the Earthly Nature.—To Friends in and about the two Chalfonts . 185

LXXIV. The Holy Scriptures not the Primary Rule.—To Nathaniel Stonar 190

LXXV. On true, living, heavenly Knowledge.—To the Lady Conway 193

LXXVI. On Disputation; and on hearing Wisdom's voice. Also respecting the Puritan State.—To E. Terry 196

LXXVII. Advice as to Self-deceit. On the Unity of the Spirit. The younger are to submit to the Elder.—To Miles Stanclif 198

LXXVIII. The Loving-kindness of the Lord.—To Elizabeth Walmsley 200

LXXIX. On Confessing Christ before Men, &c.—To Elizabeth Stonar 201

LXXX. Observations on the Ministry.—To a near Relative 206

LXXXI. Of Love, Humility, and Order among Friends. Also of Persecution.—To a near Relative . 208

LXXXII. Danger of Self-complacency.—To Catherine Pordage 212

LXXXIII. Against Self-exaltation; and on the Cross of our Lord Jesus Christ.—To Catherine Pordage . 214

LXXXIV. To such as Drink of the Waters at Astrop Wells 217

LXXXV. To One who sent a Message to him from Astrop Wells 219

LXXXVI. Acknowledgment of Christ's Manhood.—To Richard Roberts 221

LXXXVII. Postscript to some Considerations respecting the Gospel Church.—Addressed to the Independents at Canterbury 222

LXXXVIII. The Way to Life narrow; hard things made easy to the Obedient. Also some Answers to Objections on Prayer, &c.—To Catherine Pordage 225

Letter Page

LXXXIX. The Scriptures exceedingly precious. The Gospel a Ministration of the Spirit of Life in Christ Jesus. The Liability of losing the Sense and Savour of this 230

XC. On abiding in the Root of Life. — To Friends in and about the two Chalfonts 234

XCI. The unsearchable Riches of Christ. Believers may partake thereof through Obedience, and be preserved from every Harm. — To Friends of both the Chalfonts 235

XCII. On the Fear of God. To those persons that drink of the Waters at Astrop Wells 241

XCIII. Some Doubts answered respecting Prayer. — To Widow Hemmings 243

XCIV. On Drinking of the Fountain of Living Waters. — To Widow Hemmings 247

XCV. Considerations relative to the Church; with some Cautions to Christian Professors. — To my Friends at Horton and thereabouts 250

XCVI. Hints on Steadfastness in the Truth and its Testimony; on forsaking Assemblies for Divine Worship, and on slighting Gospel Ministers. — To Thomas and Ann Mudd 254

XCVII. On hating Reproof. — To Catherine Pordage and another 257

XCVIII. Of "Fleshly Wisdom." — To Francis Pordage . 259

XCIX. Advice on Church Discipline. — To the Women Friends that meet at Armscot in Worcestershire 261

C. An Expostulation and Warning. — To the Earl of Bridgewater 264

CI. Faithful Dealing between Brethren recommended 267

CII. On dwelling with the lowly Seed of Life in all Conditions. — To M. Hiorns 269

CIII. On Prejudices against Anointed Ministers. — To his Brother 271

CIV. Of the Church and Ministry. In reply to an Answer of I. H. to somewhat written on behalf of Truth 276

Account of Lady Conway 279

LETTERS

OF

ISAAC PENINGTON.

LETTER I.

On the Pure, Living, Spiritual Food.

TO THE FRIENDS AT CHALFONT, IN BUCKINGHAMSHIRE.

O FRIENDS! Feed on the tree of life; feed on the measure of life, and the pure power thereof, which God hath revealed, and manifesteth in you. Do ye know your food, do ye remember the taste and relish of it? Then keep to it, and do not meddle with that which seemeth very desirable to the other eye, and very able to make wise. O abide in the simplicity that is in Christ, in the naked truth that ye have felt there! and there, ye will be able to know and distinguish your food, which hath several names in Scripture, but is all one and the same thing:— the bread, the milk, the water, the wine, the flesh and blood of Him that came down from heaven, &c. John vi. 51, &c.,— it is the same, only it is given forth weaker and stronger, according to the capacity of him that receiveth it; and so hath different names given to it accordingly.

O keep out of that wisdom, which knoweth not the thing; for that is it, which also stumbles about the names. But keep to the principle of life — keep to the seed of the kingdom — feed on that which was from the beginning. Is not this meat indeed, and drink indeed! flesh indeed, and blood indeed! The Lord hath advanced you to that ministration of life and power, wherein things are known above and beyond names; wherein the life is revealed and felt, beyond what words can utter. O dwell in your habitations; and feed on the food which God brings you into your habitations; which is pure, living, spiritual, and will cause your souls and spirits more and more to live in and to God, as ye eat and drink thereof. So, be not shaken or disquieted by the wisdom of the flesh; but feel that which settleth and establisheth in the pure power.

And the Lord God preserve you, and give you to watch against, and to feel victory and dominion over, all that is contrary to Him in any of you; and which stands in the way of your fellowship with Him, and of your joy and peace in Him.

This sprang unto you in the good will of your Father, from the life and love of your brother in the Truth,

I. P.

AYLESBURY GOAL,
18th of Fifth month, 1667.

LETTER II.

Christ the Root of all True Religion, &c.

TO THOMAS WALMSLEY.

DEAR FRIEND.— There is somewhat on my heart this morning to write to thee, in the same love wherein I have hitherto written, which I feel to be pure, of God, and unfeigned towards thee and all men; though it also putteth a difference between those that are renewed by him and bear his image, and those who have only a form of religion, without the power and life thereof, which sanctifies and redeems up to God, wherever it is received.

That which was on my heart to thee, in true, pure, and tender love, is this which follows:

All true religion hath a true root; and that religion, profession, worship, faith, hope, peace, assurance, &c., which groweth not from the true root, is not true.

Now, this root is near, and must be felt near, bearing the branch, and causing it to bring forth fruit. It is not enough to hear of Christ, or read of Christ; but this is the thing,—to feel him my root, my life, my foundation; and my soul engrafted into him by him who hath power to ingraft. To feel repentance given me by him, faith given me by him, the Father revealed and made known to me by him, by the pure shinings of his light in my heart; God, who caused the light to shine out of darkness, causing it to shine there; so that, in and through him, I come to know, not the Son himself only, but the Father also:—and then, to come out of the darkness, out of the sin, out of the pollutions of the spirit of this world, into the pure, holy fellowship of the living, by his holy guidance and conduct; and so, to feel all my prayers, all my comforts, all my willingness, all my ability to do and suffer for God and the testimony of his Truth, to arise from this holy, pure root of life, which gives daily strength against sin and death, to all who wait in true humility, and pure subjection of soul and spirit, upon him:—here, is unspeakable comfort and satisfaction given by him to the soul, which all the reasonings of men, with all the devices of Satan, cannot damp. For, He who gave it, preserves and maintains it, over all the strength that can assault it.

O Friend! I beseech thee, mind this; come, O come to the true root! come to Christ indeed! Rest not in an outward knowledge; but come to the inward life, the hidden life, and receive life from him who is the life; and then abide in and live to God in the life of his Son. For death and destruction, corruption and vanity, may talk of the fame of Christ, who is the wisdom of God; but they cannot know nor find out the place where this wisdom is revealed; they cannot come at the true, pure fear, which God puts into the hearts of his; this is the beginning of the true wisdom, which cleanses darkness and impurity out of the hearts of those to whom it is given. For light expelleth darkness; life expelleth death; purity expelleth impurity; Christ, where he is received, bindeth and casts out the strong man, taking possession of the heart. And if any man be truly and really in Christ, he comes to witness a new creation, even the passing away of old things, and all things becoming new.

Christ is faithful in all his house, ("whose house are we," saith the Apostle, "if we hold fast the confidence, and the rejoicing of the hope, firm unto the end," Heb. iii. 6,) — faithful as a Son, who comes in the name and authority of the Father, to do whatsoever is to be done in the heart — faithful in discovering whatever is contrary to God there — faithful in engaging his power against it. And shall not his power prevail? and where it doth prevail, and the good pleasure of God's goodness is fulfilled, and the work of faith with power, is not the name of the Lord Jesus Christ glorified there? Read 2 Thess. i. 11, 12, and consider. Did Christ overcome the devil in that body of his flesh, and shall He not overcome him in the hearts of his children by the power of his Spirit, which he received of the Father to comfort them, and carry on his work gloriously in them? What shall become of those that do not fight under Christ, and overcome through Christ? Read Rev. iii. 21. I would not have thee deceived of thy soul, or of that religion which saves the soul, which religion stands not in word, but in power. Therefore, wait to feel the Spirit and power of Christ, saving thee from that, which nothing else can save thee from ; and bringing that down in thee under his feet, which nothing else can bring down.

This is from the true desire which my soul hath, after the eternal salvation and satisfaction of thine. I. P.

28th of First month, 1670.

LETTER III.

Of a growth in Grace, amidst Distressing Exercises of Spirit.

To Bridget Atley.

My dear Friend,— If thy heart come to feel the seed of God, and to wait upon him in the measure of his life, he will be tender of thee as a father of his child, and his love will be naturally breaking forth towards thee. This is the end of all his dealings with thee, to bring thee hither, to make thee fit and capable of entering and abiding here. And he hath changed, and doth change thy spirit daily; though it be as the shooting up of the corn, whose growth cannot be discerned at present by the most observing eye, but it is very manifest afterwards that it hath grown. My heart is refreshed for thy sake, rejoicing in the Lord's goodness towards thee; and that the blackness of darkness begins to scatter from thee, though the enemy be still striving the same way to enter and distress thee again. But wait to feel the relieving measure of life, and heed not distressing thoughts, when they rise ever so strongly in thee; nay, though they have entered thee, fear them not, but *be still awhile, not believing in the power which thou feelest they have over thee,* and it will fall on a sudden.

It is good for thy spirit, and greatly to thy advantage, to be much and variously exercised by the Lord. Thou dost not know what the Lord hath already done, and what he is yet doing for thee therein. Ah! how precious it is to be poor, weak, low, empty, naked, distressed for Christ's sake, that way may be made for the power and glory of his life in the heart. And, O learn, daily more and more, to trust him and hope in him, and not to be affrighted with any amazement, nor to be taken up with the sight of the present thing; but wait for the shutting of thy own eye upon every occasion, and for the opening of the eye of God in thee, and for the sight of things therewith, as they are from him. It is no matter what the enemy strives to do in thy heart, nor how distressed thy condition is, but what the Lord will do for thee, which is with patience to be waited for at his season in every condition. And though sin overtake, let not that bow down; nor let the eye open in thee, which stands poring at that: but wait for the healing through the chastisement, and know there is an Advocate, who, in that hour, hath an office of love and a faithful heart towards thee. Yea, though thou canst not believe, yet be not dismayed thereat; thy Advocate, who undertakes thy cause, hath faith to give: only do thou sink into, or at least pant after the hidden measure of life, which is not in that which distresseth, disturbeth, and filleth thee with thoughts, fears, troubles, anguish, darknesses, terrors, and the like; no, no! but in that which inclines to the patience, to the stillness, to the hope, to the waiting, to the silence before the Father: this is the same in nature, with the most refreshing and glorious-visiting life, though not the same in appearance; and if thy mind be turned to it, not minding but overlooking the other, thou wilt find some of the same virtue springing up in thy heart and soul, at least to stay thee.

In and through these things, thou wilt become deeply acquainted with the nature of God, and know the wonderful riches and virtue of his life, the mightiness of his power, and the preciousness of his love, tenderness of his mercy, and infiniteness of his wisdom, the glory also, and exactness of his righteousness, &c.: thou wilt be made large in spirit to receive and drink in abundantly of them; and the snares of the enemy will be so known to thee and discerned, the way of help so manifest and easy, that their strength will be broken, and the poor entangled bird will fly away singing, from the nets and entanglements of the fowler; and praises will spring up, and great love in thy heart to the Forgiver and Redeemer. O wait, hope, trust, look up to thy God! look over that which stands between; come into his mercy! let in the faith which openeth the way of life, which will shut out the distrusting and doubting mind, and will close up the wrong eye, that letteth in reasonings and temptations, the wrong sense, and death with them.

Thus mayest thou witness, in and through thy Redeemer, the abundance of his life and peace. I. P.

LETTER IV.

On the State of the Puritans, and of Friends.

THE Lord God of heaven and earth, who searcheth the heart and trieth the reins, knows, that we, who are called Quakers, have no secret things or hidden principles among us to win people to; but, as we have ourselves been won to the simplicity and plainness of Truth, as it is in Christ Jesus, and walk therein, so it is the single desire of our hearts to bring men thither, where they may have the demonstration of God's Spirit, and hear the true witness speaking truth in their own consciences. And indeed, it was great matter of satisfaction to our hearts, when the Lord turned us to his Truth, that we found it to be no new thing, but that which we had witnessed and experienced in the days of our former profession. For, we well remembered, that we had been acquainted with it then; and God now gives us the true and certain sense, that all the prayers, and knowledge, and understanding of the Scriptures, faith, love, zeal, meekness, patience, humility, and whatever we then had, which was dear unto us, and precious in the eye of God, came from this Spirit of life, this principle of life, which God hath now manifested to us, and turned our minds unto. And, O, that they, who yet speak against it, knew it, as the Lord hath given us to know! surely they could not then either think or speak so hardly of it as they do. But Christ was the Son of God in his appearance in flesh, whatever the wise men and professors of that age judged and spake of him. And this is the appearance and manifestation of *the same Christ* inwardly, even the same virtue, life, and power, which appeared in that body of flesh, whatever the professors of this age think or speak concerning it; and they are not guiltless before the Lord, but deeply guilty for rising up against it.

There was a precious appearance of God, among that sort that were called Puritans, before there was such a rent among them, by falling into several ways of worship. There was among them great sincerity, and love, and tenderness, and unity in that which was true; minding the work of God in themselves, and being sensible of grace and truth in one another's hearts. Now, to desire to know the true worship, this was good; but, every one that had this desire, was not acquainted with the Spirit of the Lord, nor did wait aright on him, to be led by him into the true worship, but followed the apprehensions and conceivings of their own minds upon the Scriptures. Now, had these known the true Leader, they would never thus have wandered, nor have been so scattered from the Puritan state, which was better than any of these. For, is it possible, if the Spirit of God had been the Leader of these, they could thus have wandered from the truth, life, love and sense, into a barren dead state in comparison of that? It is true, there was a sincerity and simplicity in many of them; but was not that sincerity and simplicity betrayed, and drawn out to seek the living among the dead, among dead forms, ways, and worships? For, though they carried some life with them into their forms, yet by degrees the form grew, and the virtue and power of godliness decreased, and they were swallowed up in high esteem of, and contendings, each sort, for their forms; but themselves had lost what they were inwardly to God, and had inwardly received from God in the days of their former zeal and tenderness. O that they could see this! O that they could return to their Puritan state, to the sense they then had, the love and tenderness that was then in them, to the feeling of the principle of life, which they then felt, and which then wrought in them! though, they then distinctly knew it not, yet they loved that which gathered their minds to God, and in which they felt ability to pray, and which opened the Scriptures and the things of God, and warmed their hearts truly and livingly in some measure. O that they were but there again! they might soon come further. O that they knew their state, as it is known in the light of the Lord, and by the Spirit of the Lord! The Lord open the true eye in them, and give them to see therewith.

I. P.

Reading Gaol,
19th of Seventh Month, 1670.

LETTER V.

The Compassion of the Shepherd of the Flock towards the weak, &c. How they should follow Him.

To Friends.— He that is weak and foolish among the lambs, continually ready to wander, both out of the pastures and from the fold, and thus to betray his life into the hands of the enemy; — he who is continually scattering and squandering away what the Lord in mercy gathers for him, and freely bestows upon him; who, through drowsiness and carelessness, hath lost the benefit of, and forfeited the sweet and tender visitations of the Most High, and is now become dry, dead, barren, thick, earthy;— O my God! let *that* soul feel the stirrings of the springs of life, and find some encouragements from thee, to hope in the free and large mercies of the Shepherd of Israel, who casteth not off his sheep because of their wanderings, because of their backslidings, because of their infirmities, because of their diseases, nay, not because of their hardness; but pursues them with his love, findeth them out, visiteth with his correcting hand according to their need, woundeth with his sword, and melteth in his fire, until he hath made them tender and pliable, and then he pours in the fresh oil of his salvation and sweetly healeth them.

O my Friends and brethren in the pure life! be faithful to the Lord in returning him all the incomes of his Spirit; follow on in every drawing of his love, while any of the virtue of it lasts upon your spirits. Walk with him all the day long, and wait for him all the night season. And, in case of erring from him, or sinning grievously against him, be not discouraged; for he is a God of mercies, and delighteth in pardoning and forgiving much and very often. What tender mother can be more ready to forgive and embrace the child, that appears broken and afflicted with her sore displeasure! Yea, *He* gives brokenness, *he* melteth the heart, that he may be tender towards, and embrace it in his arms of reconciliation, and in the peace of his Spirit.

O my dear companions, and fellow-travellers in spirit towards the land of the living! *all* the motions of the life are cross to the corrupt [part] — dwell [in the life,] draw the yoke close about your necks, that ye may come into unity with the life, and the corrupt be worn out. Take the yoke, the cross, the contrariety of Jesus upon your spirits daily; that that may be worn out which hinders the unity, and so, ye may feel your King and Saviour exalted upon his throne in your hearts: this is your rest, peace, life, kingdom, and crown forever. I. P.

LETTER VI.

On Searching for the Hidden Treasure, and selling all for it.

To Catherine Pordage.

Friend, — Thy estate and condition hath been pretty much with me, since I last saw thee. I am sensible how hard it is for thee, to give up to be reached by the seed and power of life; how readily and easily thy ear and heart is opened to another, and the adulterer entertained, who hunteth after the precious life. This word of advice hath been much in my heart to thee this morning: Sit down and count the cost of ploughing up thy field, and of searching after the hidden treasure of pure and true wisdom, and consider seriously, whether thou canst sell all for it, both inward and outward riches; that, if thou do set thy hand to the plough, thou mayst not look back after anything else, within or without, but mayest be content and satisfied with the pearl of true wisdom and life alone.

Now, if thou be truly willing in God's sight thus to do, thou must singly give up to follow the Lord in the leadings of his Spirit, out of all the ways of thy own wisdom and knowledge, out of all things wherein thou hast a life and delight out of him; thou must not determine what thou hast a life in, but the Lord must search thy heart, and he will soon show thee (if thy heart be naked and open before him, willing to hear and learn of him,) somewhat in thy heart, somewhat in thy ways, somewhat in thy words, thoughts, &c., which is contrary to his pure life and Spirit; and then, that must be denied and given up immediately. And afterwards, perhaps the Lord will soon discover to thee another lover, which hath had more of thy heart than thou hast been aware of; and so, thou must part with one after another, until thou hast parted with all: and this will prepare thee for the bosom of thy Beloved, who is a jealous God, and seeth not with the eye wherewith man seeth. But, if thou be not thus singly given up, though thou should put thy hand to the plough, thou wilt be looking back some time or other: and that wisdom which draweth aside from the Lord, will blind thy eye and deceive thy mind, and draw thee from the simplicity and nakedness of Truth, into some image or other of it, so that instead of the pure Truth itself, thou wilt believe and embrace a lie.

Thou hast travelled long in the heights above the seed; O! consider, if that be not yet standing in thee, which could not have been found standing, if thou hadst known the true seed, and travelled therewith. This enhances the price of Truth as to thee, that thou must part with more for it, than will be required of many others; yet, if thou be faithful to the Lord, and diligently follow him in the simplicity, Truth will at length recompense thee for all thy labours, sorrows, and travels. But a thorough work will the Lord make in thy earth, if thou singly give up unto him, and faithfully follow; and many devices wilt thou meet with, to turn thy mind out of the way, and to cause thee to shun the bitterness of the cross, and to kindle and nourish a hope in thee, that thou mayest find a more easy way to the same life and everlasting substance. The Lord hath reached to thee, and the Lord is willing to search thy heart, to find out the deceiver and enemy in his most secret lurking-places; but, when the Lord hath found him out, thou must give him up to God's stroke, and not suffer him to find a shelter in thy mind to save him therefrom. For he is very subtle, and will twist and twine all manner of ways to deceive thee and save himself; nor art thou yet acquainted with, or able to discern his devices. The Lord alone can help thee — and he will help thee, if thou be not hasty to join with the enemy, nor give up thy judgment to believe what he represents, and seems inwardly to represent to thee as true; but abide and dwell in the sense of thy own inability to judge, waiting to feel that which is true, pure, and living of God, judge in thee, not so much in demonstrations of wisdom, as in tender and secret drawings of the beginnings of a new nature, away from what is of an earthly nature. For, thou must come out of the spirit of this world, if thou wilt come into God's Spirit; and thou must come out of the love of the things of this world; if thou wilt come out of the spirit of this world; for, in the love of the things of this world, the spirit of this world lodgeth and dwelleth, and thou canst not touch the unclean thing, but thou also touchest somewhat of the unclean spirit. Therefore, said John, from a true and deep understanding, "Love not the world, neither the things of the world," (if thou love the things of the world, thou lovest the world,) for, "if any man love the world, the love of the Father is not in him."

The day of God's mercy and visitation is upon thee, who is visiting that spirit in thee which hath led thee aside, even with the judgment proper for it; that Zion in thee might be thereby redeemed, and thy soul converted to, and truly brought forth in righteousness. I. P.

11th of First Month, 1670.

LETTER VII.

A Christian Salutation.

To Elizabeth Walmsley.

Dear Friend,—My heart was exceedingly melted within me at the reading of thy precious and tender lines; yea, indeed, I was quite overcome, and was fain several times to break off, the freshness and strength of life in them did so flow in upon me; and I said, again and again, in my heart, It is the very voice of my Father's child, whose sound did deeply reach to, and refresh my very soul. And this my heart saith, Blessed be my God, for his tender mercies to thee, in visiting, leading, and preserving thee to this day, and for teaching his seed thus to speak in thee. Oh! let his praise live and abound in thy breast forever. And in the flowings and streamings of this life, remember me at the throne of my Father's mercy, by which alone I live, and have hope before him.

May the mercies, blessing, and pure presence of my God, fill thy soul, and rest upon thee forever! Amen! Amen!

Thus prayeth for thee thy unfeigned Friend, and dear lover of the pure seed of life in thee, I. P.

Mind my dear love to thy sister, whose inward welfare and prosperity I desire, even that she may be one with thee in the seed and life of God.

Aylesbury Gaol,
19th of Eighth Month, 1665.

LETTER VIII.

On Christ being Manifested Within, and the Sprinkling of His Blood Inwardly.

To Thomas Walmsley.

Friend T. W.,—God is love: and he giveth love, and teacheth to love; and with the love which my God hath given me, and wherewith he hath taught me to love, have I loved thee, and sought the everlasting good of thy soul, even as of my own.

This morning, the consideration of thee was strong upon my spirit, how that thou wast stricken in years, and must shortly pass out of this world, and give an account to God; and this earnest desire was in my heart, that thou mightst be fitted and rightly prepared, to give such an account, as the Lord, the great, righteous, and impartial Judge, might own and approve of, to thy eternal joy; for which end, two things were upon my heart to propose to thee, to be rightly considered by thee.

One is, whether thou canst truly say, as in God's sight, that thou hast known and experienced *Christ within*, redeeming thee from sin *within?* Hath Christ indeed brought salvation home to thy heart? Hast thou known his inward living power, breaking the strength and power of Satan within thee? Hast thou known Him stronger than the strong man inwardly? Hast thou first known Christ knock at the door of thy heart, and opened to and let him in; and afterwards experienced *what* he doth in the heart, where he is let in? Or hast thou had only a notional knowledge and belief concerning Christ *without*, and never known what it was to have the Son *revealed in thee?* Oh! that thou mightst know, and experimentally understand this Scripture, before thou go hence and be no more seen,—"If Christ be in you, the body is dead because of sin;"—and this other also,—"He that is Christ's hath crucified the flesh with the affections and lusts." The Lord God make thee truly weighty and serious, and rightly considerate, and give thee true, unerring judgment; that thou mayst not be deceived about this thing, which is of such deep and everlasting concernment to thy soul!

The other is, whether thou dost experience the sprinkling of the blood of the Lord Jesus upon thy conscience? The Jews were saved by the sprinkling of the blood of the lamb outwardly. The Lamb of God taketh away the sins of the world, by the sprinkling of his blood inwardly. Now, I beseech thee, consider: hast thou only a notion of Christ's blood as it was shed without, or dost thou also know the sprinkling within in thy own heart? Hath God made that new covenant, the everlasting covenant with thee, wherein the blood of sprinkling is felt, and the precious effects of it experienced? for then, indeed, iniquities are forgiven, and sin remembered no more; but the soul comes to witness real justification from sin, and that peace which passeth understanding, which no man can give or take away; neither doth any man know what it is, but he that hath it. O that thou mayst know the righteousness of the Lord Jesus Christ, and be clothed with it, that thou mayst stand justified in God's sight forever, at that great day! I. P.

12th of Eleventh Month, 1677.

LETTER IX.

The Way of God's Redemption is above the Ways of Man's Wisdom.

My dear Friend,—This then is the way of redemption; to wait to feel the appearance of the light of the

Spirit in the heart; and, at its least or lowest appearance, to be turned from the darkness towards it. Oh! feel the redeeming arm in thine own heart, and know the love which stretcheth it forth, and take heed of being prejudiced against its inward visitations to thee: for, there is that near thee which would darken thee, and keep the seed of life in bondage. I know there is that in thee, which pants and is not satisfied, somewhat that thirsts after the living waters. The Spirit of the Lord saith, Come, come to the fountain of eternal life; drink, and live.

O Lord my God! discover to the thirsty souls, what it is that withholds them from the living waters; that they may not labour and spend their strength in vain, in duties and ordinances invented by man, for that which may lull asleep for the present, but can never quiet the cry of the living seed, nor ever satisfy the soul.

I know thy snare: there is a building in the earthly wisdom, a knowledge which thou holdest in the comprehension, out of the living feeling of that light, from which the true knowledge springs, and in which alone it is held. Thou must know the rasing of this building, the confounding and scattering of this knowledge; that the true heir of the true knowledge may spring, and thou mayst feel the babe raised, to whom God reveals the mysteries of his kingdom; which he hides from the wise professors and teachers in this age, as he hath done in all ages. Thou art very wise; but thou must sell all that, and become a very fool, if thou wilt have the riches and everlasting treasure of the kingdom.

And, if thou wouldst draw near and find access to God in prayer, thou must wait to feel the birth pray, and take heed of putting up requests in thy own wisdom, and according to thy own will; for these are the prayers of the false-formed child, or counterfeited birth, and not of the right seed; and the Father knows not, nor regards this voice. This is our religion: to feel that, which God begets in our hearts, preserved alive by God; to be taught by him to know him, to worship, and live to him, in the leadings and by the power of his Spirit: and, in this religion we have the comforts and appearance of his Spirit; which are past all the disputings and questionings of man's wisdom, yea, and of our own hearts also, being demonstrated and made manifest to our spirits in a higher principle.

I found my heart in great love drawn to write these things to thee; and my soul pursueth them with breathings to the Lord my God, that hereby, or by what other means he shall see good, thou mayst be drawn into true unity and fellowship with the spring of eternal life; and not be deceived from the precious enjoyment of the God of thy life here, or of the salvation of thy soul forever. The path of life is living; and thy feet must be guided into it, and walk faithfully in it to the end, if thou wilt sit down in God's eternal rest and peace.

I have been long desolate, and a great mourner after my God, and know how to pity and weep over wandering souls; though I cannot but rejoice at this great day of salvation and powerful visitation of God's Spirit, wherein he hath sought out and gathered many into the fold of his pure rest, where he is become their living Shepherd, and daily ministers of his life unto them. And he is seeking out many more: — happy are they, that know and return at the Shepherd's voice, when he calleth after them.

I remain thy true, entire, faithful, loving Friend, in the love and good-will of the Lord, wishing to thy soul as to my own. I. P.

LETTER X.

On the Gospel, and on preaching it; also on the Scriptures, &c.

THERE is a question ariseth in my heart to thee, which is this:

How is the everlasting gospel (wherein Christ is truly made known, and salvation really witnessed in the hearts of those that receive it,) preached at this day? How hath the Lord appointed it to be preached, and how is it preached, and how many men come to hear it, that their souls may live? Are not they blessed that hear the joyful sound thereof? Are not they wretched, and miserable, and blind, and naked, who mistake and miss concerning the sound of it, which it pleaseth the Spirit of the Lord to give forth in this our day? O Friend! I beseech thee, consider it, and do not think it strange that I propose it to thee; for he that would find the gospel, must search where it is hid; and it is hid in them that are lost, who go astray from the life and power of it.

It is a wonderful thing, to those whom the Lord hath made truly sensible, to consider how the Truth, the gospel, the life, the power which saves, is one and the same in all ages and generations, and yet, still hid from the wise, prudent, professing eye in every age and generation. O Friend! that thou didst thoroughly know that wise and prudent eye in thyself, from which the Lord hides it, and that eye, which perhaps thou wilt not call prudent, to which the Lord opens it.

Now, Friend, let me speak a few words to thee, not only from what I have felt in my heart, but have also read in the Scriptures of truth.

The gospel, after the apostacy, is thus to be preached,

"Fear God, and give glory to him; for the hour of his judgment is come; and worship him that made heaven, and earth," &c. Rev. xiv. 7. If thou knowest the Preacher that preached this, if thou hast heard this preached in thine own heart, if thou hast met with that fear there, which God's Spirit teacheth and giveth, if thou hast known the hour of God's judgment, and had the axe laid to the root of the tree; and if thou hast been taught by the Son to worship the Father in Spirit and truth; thou hast, without doubt, met with the gospel, the everlasting gospel; and if God require of thee, and assist thee by his Spirit and power to preach this to others, thou art a preacher of the everlasting gospel, and an able minister of the New Testament, not of the letter, but of the Spirit. But, I beseech thee, take heed of preaching thine own formings and conceivings upon the letter, as too many do in this day; for that falls short of true preaching the letter. O let these things be weighty with thee! that thou mayst learn aright to search and understand the Scriptures, and know how the Father hath revealed the Son in this day, and how to come to him, to receive life from him. For many, through ignorance, mistake in this matter; and so run on in their own wills, wisdom, and comprehension of things, and miss of the drawings of the Father; and thus, come not aright to the Son, but only according as they imagine and apprehend, according to what they have gathered and conceived upon the Scriptures.

Friend, God who caused light to shine in this outward world, hath judged it necessary to cause the light of his Spirit to shine inwardly in the heart; and *this* gives the knowledge of the Scriptures, and the true sense and discerning of inward and spiritual things. Yea, *here* the Son is known, and his blood felt cleansing; which, without *this*, the Scriptures do not make manifest; but, in *this*, the Scriptures are a clear and faithful record of and testimony to them. O take heed *how* thou readest, and *how* thou understandest the Scriptures,—in what light, in what spirit! for, it is easy erring; and without the presence and guidance of God's Spirit herein, thou canst not walk safely. And truly it is great presumption in any man to read the Scriptures boldly, and without fear and reverence to Him who penned them, or to put any of his own meanings and conceivings upon God's words; which it is hard for him to forbear to do, who reads them in the liberty of his own spirit, out of the light of God's Spirit, which is the limit and yoke of the true readers, and of those who understand the Scriptures. I. P.

4th of Fourth Month,—

LETTER XI.

The Duty of being Content with what is Made Known.

The enemy kindles a great distress in the mind, by stirring up an earnest desire, and a sense of a seeming necessity, to *know*. When a motion ariseth, how shall I do, to know whether it be of God or no? For, if it be of God, it ought to be obeyed; and, if it be not of God, it ought to be resisted; but what shall I do, who cannot tell what it is? I must of necessity fall, either into disobedience to God's Spirit, or into the snares of the enemy. Thus the enemy raiseth up a strength in the reasoning part, even unanswerable there. But, what if it be better for thee, at present, to be darkened about these things, than as yet to know? Can that possibly be? will the strong reason readily say. Yes, that it may, in many respects. There is somewhat else would live and be acting in thee, if the clear and heavenly knowledge were given; and thou wouldst be centering in self, that which thou receivedst from God; yea, thou wouldst miss of the way of true knowledge, and never learn in every state to be content, nor know the pure way and actings of life in such a state. Truly, this is not the way of the child's knowing; but the child knows, in resignation and subjection of its very knowledge; and if there appear ever so great a necessity of knowledge, and yet knowledge be not given, it sinks, in fear and humility, into the will of the pure seed; and *there* somewhat springs up, (unknown to the natural wisdom, and not in the way of man's wisdom,) which at seasons preserves and bears it up in such a state. But this is a great mystery; yet sensibly experienced by the true travellers at this day.

Therefore, retire out of all necessities, according to the apprehension of the reasoning mind; and judge that only necessary, which God, in his eternal wisdom and love, proportions out unto us. And when thou comest hither, thou wilt come to thy rest; and as thou abidest here, thou wilt abide in thy soul's true rest, and know the preciousness of that lesson, and of whom thou art to learn it, even, *in every state to be content.*

LETTER XII.

Of Faith in the Healing Power of Christ.

FRIEND,—I have had of late some deep and serious thoughts concerning thee, and a sense of thee, as between the Lord and my own soul, yet I have not had any thing to signify or express to thee, till this morning. But somewhat this morning sprang up in my heart, sweetly and freshly, which I had pure drawings to impart to thee.

There was a quick sense of thee upon my heart, and in

that sense this cry was in me: — Oh! that thou wert acquainted with the pure, eternal power of the Lord, and mightst feel his outstretched arm revealed in thee, and witness the faith which stands in that power; and, in that faith, believe and wait for what God is doing, and willing to do, in and for his children. "If ye had faith," said Christ, "but as a grain of mustard seed, ye should say to this mountain, be thou cast into the midst of the sea, and it should be so." Indeed, the true faith, the pure faith, the living faith, which stands in the power, doth remove all the mountains that are in the way, and makes the crooked ways straight, and the rough ways plain. If thou had lived in the days of Christ's flesh, and wanted outward healing, and had been willing to come to him for healing, but withal had not come with faith that he was able and willing to heal perfectly; mightest not thou have missed of that cleansing and outward health and salvation, which others met with? For, did not he say, "Be it unto thee according to thy faith?" And is not he the Physician of the soul? and is not his skill to be trusted and believed in? He that hopeth, and believeth, and waiteth, and prayeth, and fighteth the good fight of faith, which gives victory over sin, Satan, and the world — he may possibly overcome; yea, he that warreth lawfully, (that is, with the spiritual weapon, which is mighty through God,) he that warreth with this only, and with this constantly, shall be sure to overcome. For, greater is He that is in the true believer, than he that is in the world.

O that thou mightest have experience of these things, and witness the banner of Christ's love and power displayed in thee, and the victories and conquests that are thereby, and the safety and peace which is under it! For, of a truth, we do not speak boastingly, but are witnesses of the majesty of God's love and power, which we testify of. The Lord so enlighten and guide thee, that thou mayest obtain the desires of thy heart; for, I really believe thy desire is after holiness and after communion with the Father and the Son, and with the saints in light: O that thou mayest be led into the true pure light of life, that there thou mayest enjoy what in this kind thou desirest!

This is from one, who singly, as in the Lord's sight, wisheth well unto thee. I. P.

Reading Gaol,
27th of Eighth Month, 1670.

LETTER XIII.

Advice to one Respecting the Dark Suggestions of the Enemy.

Dear Friend, — Thou hast had the path of salvation faithfully testified of to thee, and hast come to a sense of the thing: even to the feeling of *that*, whereby the Father begets life, and manifesteth his love and peace in and to the soul. Now, what remains? but that thou look up to the Lord, to guide thy feet in this path, and to preserve from that which darkens and leads out of the way; that thou mayest pass on thy journey safely, and come to the inheritance and enjoyment of that, which thy soul longeth after.

There is life, there is peace, there is joy, there is righteousness, there is health, there is salvation, there is power of redemption — in the seed: yea, there is so. But thy soul wants, and doth not enjoy these things. Well, but how mayest thou come to enjoy them? There is no way, but union with the seed; knowing the seed, hearing the voice of the seed, learning of, and becoming subject to, the seed. "Learn of me, take my yoke upon you," saith Christ, "and ye shall find rest to your souls." Wouldst thou feel thy soul's rest in Christ? Thou must know the seed's voice, hear it, learn daily of him, become his disciple; take up, from *his* nature, what is contrary to *thy* nature. And then, as thy nature is worn out, and his nature comes up in thee, thou wilt find all easy; all that is of life easy, and transgression hard — unbelief hard: yea, thou wilt find it very hard and unnatural, when the nature of the seed is grown up in thee, either to distrust the Lord or hearken to his enemy. And then thou wilt change that dwelling-place (into which Satan brings dark thoughts, suggestions, and reasonings,) for the dwelling-place which is from above, which is the habitation of the righteous; wherein there is light, life, peace, satisfaction, health, salvation, and rejoicing of soul from and before the Lord.

Now, do not say, Who shall do thus for me? but know, the arm of the Lord is mighty, and brings mighty things to pass; and that arm hath been revealed in thee, and is at work for thee. O that thou couldst trust it! (why canst thou not! hath it not sown a seed of faith in thee?) and come in to and abide in the path, wherein its mighty, powerful operations are felt and made manifest! And, O that thou mayest find ability, to watch against that which bows down, and not so let in, as thou hast done exceedingly, to the grievous wounding and distressing of thy soul! For, the enemy's dark suggestions work according to their nature; and, if thou let them lie upon thee, how can they but darken, afflict, and perplex thee?

Therefore, in the evil hour, fly from all things that thus arise in thee; and lie still, feel thy stay, till His light, which "makes manifest," arise in thee, and clear up things to thee. And think not the time of darkness long; but watch, that thy heart be kept empty, and thy mind clear of thoughts and belief of things, till He bring in somewhat, which thou mayest safely receive. Therefore, say to thy thoughts and to thy belief of things, (according to the representation of the dark power, in the time of thy darkness,) "Get thee hence!" And, if that will not do, look up to the Lord to speak to them; and to keep them out, if they be not already entered, or to thrust them out if they be already got in. And, if he do not so presently, or for a long time, yet do not murmur or think much, but wait till he do. Yea, though they violently thrust themselves upon thee, and seem to have entered thy mind, yet let them be as strangers to thee; receive them not, believe them not, know them not, own them not; and thy bosom will, notwithstanding, be chaste in the eye of the Lord, though they may seem to thee to have defiled thee.

Look up to the Father, that thou mayest learn this of him: and, becoming faithful to him therein, thou wilt find thy darkness abate, and its strength more and more broken in thee; and thou wilt not only feel and taste a little, now and then, but also come to possess and inherit, and rejoice before the Lord in thy portion.

Thy Friend in the Truth, which changeth not, but is pure, and preserveth pure forever. I. P.

From Aylesbury Gaol,
28th of Seventh Month, 1667.

LETTER XIV.

On Obedience, Spiritual Growth, Establishment, and Victory in and through our Lord Jesus Christ.

Dear Friend,—Some Scriptures did spring up and open in my heart towards thee this morning.

One was, that of 2 Cor. x. 4, 5, and 6. That which was chiefly on my heart therefrom, was about the fufilling of obedience. First, there is a knowing the will of God; a waiting to know and understand from God, what is his holy, good, perfect, and acceptable will. Then, as God gives the knowledge, he requires obedience; which is to be learned of God in the new spirit and life. For, in the old nature, mind and spirit, there is nothing but darkness and disobedience; in the new creation is the new obedience. So that, there is first a beginning of knowledge in the Spirit, a beginning of faith in the renewing power, and a beginning of obedience (in the same) to him that calls. Then, there is an increase of knowledge, of true, pure, living knowledge, an increase of faith, and a growing more and more obedient under the exercises, judgments, and chastisements of the Father's Spirit: even till, at length, the soul comes to witness a full readiness, skill, and strength (in and through Christ, in and through the measure of the gift of grace received from him,) to obey in all things. When the new birth is thus grown up into strength and dominion, into the stature of a man in Christ; then the senses, which have been long exercised in discerning between good and evil, grow strong: and there is a quick discerning in the fear of the Lord, and an authority, in his name and power, over the enemy and his temptations: so that every stronghold is broken down, every imagination and false reasoning concerning the Truth, is subjected and broken by the evidence and power of Truth, every thought brought under, into captivity, even to the obedience of Christ; with a readiness to reject all unbelief and disobedience, that will so much as offer to rise up. Now, is not this the Christian state, which God would have his children aim and arrive at? and are not they blessed who witness it? and doth not the true ministration of the gospel light, Spirit, and power lead to it? and should any be at rest in their spirits, in an easeful, formal, dry, dead profession without it?

Another Scripture was 1 Pet. ii. 2, 3, 4, and 5. It is precious to witness the state of a new-born babe, to be begotten to God by the word of life and power, even by the word which God ingrafts into the heart. O what living desires, then, are there, after that which nourisheth the birth of life, which God breathes from his own Spirit, and begets the soul into! Now, as the birth is pure, so the nourishment is pure: — pure milk from the pure word,— sincere, unmixed milk from the word of life,— from the breast of life. Who is it that begets to God? It is the Spirit, the Word, the second Adam, he whose name is the Word of God. Who is the mother of these children? It is the heavenly wisdom, the Jerusalem which is above. ("Jerusalem which is above is free, which is the mother of us all." "Wisdom is justified of her children.") Now, who feeds these children? who nourisheth, who brings them up? Why, the mother which bare them, she holds forth the breast of life to them, she yields to them the pure milk of the word. The new-born babes, they long for it, they cry for their food, they earnestly desire after it; and the tender mother gives it forth to them, even the milk of the breast of life from the pure word of life; and by this they grow. But, how came the babes to desire after such pure, sincere, unmixed food? Oh! they have "tasted that the Lord is gracious." They have had the heavenly taste, they have tasted that which was living and pure from God, from his tender mercy and grace, wherein he ministers life and salvation. O the remembrance and sense of the sweetness of this, is upon their palates! O how precious and living is it, when it comes new and fresh from him! the words which he speaks, they are still spirit and life to the soul. How can they but desire, that from the breast of life, from the heavenly wisdom and divine knowledge of his Father, he would minister unto them of the pure food, that they may know and feed on the Truth as it is in Jesus? Here, they come to him as unto a living fountain, and a living stone, disallowed indeed, and rejected of the builders after the flesh, in all ages and generations; but chosen of God, and precious to all that have the true sense and understanding. They come thus to him daily, and so are built up into a living house, or spiritual temple and dwelling-place for God. He, the foundation stone, the corner stone, the top stone, the hope and crown of their glory; they, living stones in him quickened and kept alive in and by him, and shining in his light and glory.

A third Scripture was Eph. vi. 10, 11, 12, and 13. Is not this a precious state, to be "strong in the Lord and in the power of his might?" to know "the whole armour of God," and to put it on and stand armed against the strength of the enemy, and to overcome him? was there ever such a state witnessed? Yea; John writeth to the young men in his time, because they had "overcome the wicked one." (Compare 1 John, ii. 14, with Eph. vi. 10.) May not such a thing be again witnessed, even now, in these our days? Were not he a messenger of good tidings to thee, who from God could tell thee, how thou mightst come to know, to put on, to fight in this holy armour, and thereby overcome all the adversaries of thy soul? Doth not the apostle say, "The weapons of our warfare are mighty through God?" Wouldst not thou be willing to witness them so in thee? Mind then — in the measure of life, in the measure of grace and truth which is from Christ, all the knowledge, strength, and use of the armour lies. Thus, the Truth as it is in Jesus is the girdle of the loins; and from and through him, in his pure measure of life, righteousness springs up as a breastplate. There likewise, the feet are shod with the preparation of the gospel of peace; for there, the gospel, the life, the redeeming power and virtue is always in readiness, whenever the Lord seeth service for it. And then the shield of faith is known, which quencheth the fire of the enemy's temptations. There also, is the helmet of salvation, the true hope; for in it, Christ, the hope of glory, is revealed, and felt to be near. And then, the sword of the Spirit is witnessed, which is the living Word, the Spirit which quickens and gives life; which Word is quick, piercing, and exceeding powerful, able to smite and wound death. (See Rev. i. 16, Isa. xxvii. 1, and xi, 4, and 2 Thes. ii. 8.) And here, is pure praying in the Spirit of the Lord Jesus, and watching thereunto with perseverance, both for itself in particular, and the whole body of the faithful in general; but for those more especially, on whom lies the weight of the service in and towards the body: so that, here, is prayer in its due season, weight, and order offered up to God, in true life and understanding: which prayer God always heareth.

O mind this thing diligently, for it is of great concernment to thee! In the grace of the gospel, in the measure of truth and life from the quickening Word, thou meetest with the whole armour of God. Thou mayest there know it, thou mayest there put it on, stand armed with it, and fight with success against thy soul's enemies. Out of this, thou mayest get apprehensions in thy mind about it, but canst never truly know it, canst never come at it, or be covered and armed with it, to stand and fight successfully and victoriously against the enemies of thy soul.

Ah! little dost thou know the loving kindness of the Lord in visiting thee with his Truth, in giving thee a sense beyond others, in so tenderly drawing and inviting thy heart; or what this will come to, if thou faithfully give up to hearken to and follow him. I. P.

20th of Tenth Month, 1671.

LETTER XV.

The least Messenger of the Gospel is not to be despised. A Change of Heart is to be sought, rather than a Sign.

WHAT is Paul? what is Apollos? or what is Cephas? It is one and the same pure life and word of power, which springs in all the holy brethren, whom God hath sanctified and prepared to give forth the sound of his holy trumpet. (It is the Lord himself, who gives forth the true and certain sound; great is the company of those, whom he hath chosen and sent forth to publish it; none of whom can be despised in their message, without despising him that sent them; for, he sends forth the least and weakest, as well as the greatest.)

O! take heed of that nature and spirit in thee, which desires or seeks after a sign. It is the evil and adulterous generation which seeks after a sign. But wait to meet with that inwardly, which changeth the heart, and renews the mind to God: which teacheth to love the Lord God with all the heart, soul, mind, and spirit, that so true life from and in him may be witnessed. — And as for *being as one of us*, thou must be formed so by the Lord, by being inwardly changed and renewed by the Spirit and power of the Lord, ere thou canst witness true unity with us. If thou feel the principle of Truth in thy own heart, and in *that* know and own us, and so come among us, and join to us in the Truth, and keep faithful to the principle, thou wilt never be in danger of leaving us, as they that depart from the principle in their own hearts, may soon and easily do.

LETTER XVI.

Advice on Reading the Scriptures.

Friend,—Hearken to a word of advice, which is in my heart to thee; it may be of great use to thee, if the Lord open thy spirit, and cause it to sink in. It is this.

Wait on the Lord, that thou mayest, from him, feel the right limit to thy mind, in reading the Scriptures. For, the mind of man is busy and active, willing to be running beyond its bounds, guessing at the meaning of God's Spirit, and imagining of itself, unless the Lord limit it. Therefore, read in fear; and wait understandingly to distinguish, between God's opening to thee words, concerning the kingdom and the things of the kingdom, and thy own apprehensions about them; that the one may be always cast by, and the other always embraced by thee. And, always wait God's season: do not presume to understand a thing, before he *give* thee the understanding of it: and know also, that he alone is able to preserve the true sense and knowledge in thee; that thou mayest live dependently upon him for thy knowledge, and never "lean to thy own understanding." Little dost thou know, what it hath cost us, to have our own understanding and wisdom broken down; and how demonstratively by this Spirit the Lord opens Scriptures to us, (yea, and the things themselves, which the Scriptures speak of,) ever since he hath taught us to deny our own understanding, and to lean upon his Spirit and wisdom.

The Lord guide thee by his certain, infallible Spirit, into the certain, infallible, everlasting way of life, that by the shinings of his light, Spirit, and power in thee, thou mayest see light and enjoy life. For, if thou didst certainly and infallibly understand all the words, descriptions, and testimonies concerning the thing in the Scriptures; yet, it is one thing to understand words, testimonies, and descriptions; and it is another matter to understand, know, enjoy, possess, and live in *that* which the words relate to, describe, and bear witness of.

And, Friend, if thou wilt be an inward Jew, and know and understand the laws of life, the laws of the new covenant, thou must read them in those tables, where God writes them in and by the new covenant. Indeed, by reading in the letter, thou mayest read testimonies concerning the Spirit and his ministration; but thou must read in the Spirit, if ever thou come rightly to understand the letter. And, the end of words is to bring men to the knowledge of things, beyond what words can utter. So, learn of the Lord to make a right use of the Scriptures; which is, by esteeming them in their place, and prizing *that* above them, which is above them. The "eternal life," the Spirit, the power, the fountain of living waters, the everlasting pure well is above the words concerning it. This, the believer is to witness in himself, and to draw water with joy out of it. I. P.

LETTER XVII.

On the Righteousness which is of Christ, on the Manhood and Godhead of Christ.

To the Friend of Francis Fines.

Friend,—After some deep exercise of spirit concerning thee, under great grief of heart for thee, I felt a constraint of love, forcing these following considerations from me, to lay before thee.

As for William Penn, thou didst not make mention of him to me in thy former letter. And as to thy charge upon him, that he denies the "Trinity," redemption by Christ's blood, and imputed righteousness, thou mayest read his apology touching those things, which it is just thou shouldst seriously weigh, as in God's sight: and then, perhaps thou wilt not so resolutely charge him as now thou dost.

Christ is made unto us righteousness, by faith in his blood, and by faith in his Spirit: and he that doth not believe in his Spirit, and receives not instruction and help from his Spirit to believe, cannot believe aright in his blood. All that is of Christ is righteous; all that is of Christ, the righteous and holy root, is righteous and holy, wherever it is found. And, by Christ, that which is truly holy and righteous is brought up in us, and we forgiven and washed from our sins and iniquities for his name's sake. And the receiving of the pardon of sins is precious, and the bringing forth in the new life is precious also.

I am satisfied in God's Spirit, that that which I have written in the last I sent to thee, is the sum and substance of true religion; the sum and substance whereof, doth not stand in getting a notion of Christ's righteousness, but in feeling the power of the endless life, receiving the power, and being changed by the power. And where Christ is, *there* is his righteousness. He that hath the Son, hath life and righteousness; but he that hath not the Son, hath not life nor righteousness. And where Christ is not, *there* is not his righteousness; but only a notion thereof, from apprehensions formed out of the Scriptures by man's wisdom, which should be destroyed. I would not have thy knowledge here, nor thy standing here, nor thy faith here; but in the truth and life itself.

Christ was anointed and sent of God, a Saviour, to destroy the works of the devil, to break down all rule and authority contrary to God in man; for, his work is in the heart. There he quickens, there he raiseth, there he brings into death that which is to die, raising the seed immortal, and bringing the creature into subjection to it. Now, to feel the power that doth this, and to feel this wrought by the power, this is far beyond all talk about justification and righteousness. Hither would I have thee come, out of the talk, out of the outwardness of knowledge, into the thing itself, and into the trueness of the new and living knowledge, which is witnessed here.

There is a power in Christ, to mortify and overcome sin in the very root; it is not however overcome, but in the revealing of this power; nor is the soul justified, but in and by the working of this power. So that, justification is not the first thing, but the power of life, in and through which (revealed in Christ) the soul is both justified and sanctified, through the working of the faith, which is from the power. And here, salvation is felt nigh indeed, to those that truly fear the Lord; and glory dwells in the land which he hath redeemed. There, mercy and truth do indeed meet together, and righteousness and peace kiss each other. Yea, truth, there, springs out of the earth, and righteousness looks down from heaven, &c. And here, the heavenly place in Christ is sat down in, towards which, is the travel of the disciple. For, saith Christ to his disciples, "I go to prepare a place," and "I will come again," and translate you thither. But, the disciples do not come to this place before their travel, or before any works of righteousness which God hath wrought in them.

Therefore, he that will be justified by Him, must abide in the faith, where the justification is. The Father justifies what is of his own life in the Son, and the Son in his life; and the Son justifies what is of the Father in us, (what is of the Father's nature, the Father's spirit, the Father's life,) and justifies us from that, by his blood, from which we cannot otherwise be justified. O how precious it is, to see and feel this in the true light, where the blood of Christ cleanseth from all sin! Here, is no covenant for us of ourselves to perform; but the true self-denial is witnessed, wherein the covenant is performed; and Christ, the life, Christ, the power, Christ, the righteousness and wisdom of God, working all in us; and we, gathered into him, and living and working in him, by the faith which is of him. And here, is *free-will* indeed, even of the will which was bound and captivated before. And here, is the *election* known, which obtains; and *the obedience and sufferings of Christ,* not looked upon as superfluous, but highly prized, and looked upon as of inestimable value.

Do we cry up works against the workman? man's grace and righteousness against God's? conformity to Christ, against Christ? or make a Christ, a righteousness, a Saviour of our conformity? Oh! how wilt thou do, when God shall plead with thee for these things? — Also, that charge of thine on us, that we deny the person of Christ, and make him nothing but a light or notion, a principle in the heart of man, is very unjust and untrue; for, we own that appearance of him in his body of flesh, his sufferings and death, and his sitting at the Father's right hand in glory: but then, we affirm, that there is no true knowledge of him, or union with him, but in the seed or principle of his life in the heart; and that *therein* he appears, subdues sin, and reigns over it, in those that understand and submit to the teaching and government of his Spirit.

But, we cannot set the manhood above the life, and make *that* the main or chief in the work of redemption, and the life and Spirit of his Godhead, but supporting, enabling, and carrying him up in that great undertaking.

Consider, I pray thee, if what thou sayest be not contrary to the Scriptures? Was the work laid by the Father upon the *manhood,* or upon the *Son,* who, in the life and by the life, was "mighty to save"? *Who* took up the *manhood?* Was it not the *Son?* "Lo! I come," saith he, "a *body* hast thou prepared *me*." And was it not *he*, that laid down his glory, and made himself of no reputation, but came in the form of a servant, (took upon him man's nature,) did not *he* do the work in man's nature? Did not the eternal Spirit sanctify the body in the womb? Did not the eternal Power act in him all along? Yea, did not the eternal Spirit offer the body to God as a sacrifice? For, the manhood would fain have avoided the cup, ("Father, if it be possible, let this cup pass from me!") but, the Spirit taught him to be subject to the will of the Father herein. So that, his giving up to death, was rather to be attributed to his eternal Spirit, than to his manhood: for *that* was the chief in the work, and not merely assistant to him. And doth not Christ confess as much to his Father, when he saith, "I have glorified thee on the earth, I have finished the work which thou gavest me to do; and now, O Father! glorify thou me with thy own self, with the glory which I had with thee before the world was." Though we are willing to honour the manhood of Christ, with the honour which the Father hath honoured it with; yet we cannot honour it in the first place, and attribute redemption to it in the first place, making the Spirit and life of God, but supporting, assisting, and carrying on therein. For, "God was in Christ," and it was his power, life, and virtue, did all in him, as it is a measure of the same life which doth all in us; in which measure, we partake of his death, and not only so, but also of his life and resurrection. For, he is "the resurrection and the life," (which we cannot deny,) and if by his death we be reconciled to God, "much more shall we be saved by his life." And, if righteousness be revealed in us, imputed to us, and we partake of it, as we come into his death; much more shall we partake of it, as we come into his life.

It is precious, indeed, to hear of Christ without; but it is more precious to feel him within; where the wisdom of our Solomon, his love, his riches, his treasures of life, and the glory of his kingdom, and order of his family, and food of his children and of his servants, are witnessed and revealed on his holy mountain ; where he makes the feast of fat things to his, where the bread and wine of the kingdom is ate and drunk abundantly, and the streams of the river of his own pleasures, water his garden and refresh his heritage.

I have looked over all the Scriptures quoted by thee, and find not one of them proving the thing thou assertest; that is, attributing redemption properly to the manhood, and consequently improperly, in the second place, only as an assistant, to the Spirit and life of the Godhead. But, if thou wouldst rightly distinguish, it were more proper to make the Word, (or Life, which was in the beginning,) the agent, which did all; and that body, which the Father prepared and sanctified — the form of a servant or garment, in and through which the life, being clothed with it, did act. Now, the Jews did disdain Christ, as a man, in that his low appearance: therefore is the glory still given to "the man Christ Jesus;" but, not to take the honour from the Son, who was God, and who saved by his Godhead, by the life, virtue, and power thereof. "I, even I, am the Lord," saith Jehovah, "and besides me there is no Saviour." The Word eternal, which made all, redeemeth all that are redeemed: that body of flesh was that wherein he appeared. And so, what he did in it was attributed to his manhood, (and the man Christ Jesus did all that is attributed to him in the Scriptures,) but not in the first place.— Thus I speak for thy sake, and sometimes, upon necessity, to help to scatter the darkness which is seated in men's minds in this particular, which is very gross; many men having heaped unto themselves dark mountains, from their own imaginings and conceivings, upon which they stumble: and so, reading the Scriptures out of the pure life, wherein they were written, they gather not the true food, but food of their own imagining and inventing therefrom; and so, their table becomes their snare.

And whereas, thou chargest us with making Christ only a pattern, not a Saviour — indeed, it is not so in God's sight: for, we own Christ to be a Saviour; but we lay the main stress upon the life, which took upon it the manhood. And that life, wherever it appears, is of a saving nature, and doth save; the least measure of it, is of the nature of the rock, and he proves a rock to them that feel him, and whose minds are stayed upon him: yet none, in the measure of this life, can deny the appearance of the fulness of life in that body of flesh, and what he did therein towards the redemption and salvation of mankind.

Oh! pure, spotless Lamb of God, how precious was thy sacrifice in the eye of the Father! how acceptable a ransom for all mankind! For, in the free, full, and universal love of the Father, "he tasted death for every man."

I. P.

LETTER XVIII.

On the Religious Care of Children.

To a Parent.

Dear Friend, — I have not much freedom to write at present, being retired in spirit and mourning to my God, for the powerful bringing forth of his pure life, yet more perfectly, both in myself and others; yet, the spirit of thy letter doth so strongly draw, that I cannot be wholly silent.

This, therefore, in the uprightness, fear, and tenderness of my heart, I say to thee.

There is a pure principle of life in the heart, from whence all good springs. This, thou art to mind in thyself; and this, thou art to wait on the Lord, to be taught and enabled by him to reach to, in thy children; that thou mayest be an instrument in his hand, to bring them into that fear of him, which is acceptable to him, and will be profitable to them. Mind, therefore, its leadings in thy heart, and wait to be acquainted with its voice there. And, when thy children ask thee any questions of this nature,—What God is? where he dwells? or whether he sees them in the dark?—do not reject it; but, wait to feel somewhat of God raised in thee, which is able to judge, whether the question be put forth in sensibility or in vanity; and which can give thee an advantage of stirring the good, and reaching to that, which is to be raised both in young and old, to live to the praise of him who raiseth it. And, take heed of a judgment after the flesh; for so, thou mayest judge us, our principles and practices, and approve or disapprove, &c. But, wait to feel that raised in thee, which judges righteous judgment in every particular; and wait the time of its judgment, and be still and silent, further than manifestly thou knowest that it, and not thou, judgeth.

And, as to thy children, daily feel the need of instruction from the Almighty, to govern and direct them, and wait daily to receive it from him; and what thou receivest, give forth in fear, and wait for his carrying it home and working it upon their hearts. For he is a Father, and hath tenderness, and gives true wisdom to every condition of his people, that wait upon him; so as *he* may be known to be all daily, and *they* able to be nothing without him.

Breathe unto the Lord, that thy heart may be single, thy judgment set straight by his principle of life in thee, and thy children guided to, and brought up in the sense of the same principle. As for praying, they will not need to be taught that outwardly; but, if a true sense be kindled in them, though ever so young, from that sense will arise breathings to Him that begat it, suitable to their state; which will cause growth and increase of that sense and life in them.

Thus, in the plainness of my heart, have I answered thee, according to the drawings and freedom which I found there, which I dare not exceed; who am thy unfeigned Friend, though outwardly unknown, I. P.

20th of Third Month, 1665.

LETTER XIX.

A Day of Calamity.

TO A FRIEND IN LONDON; SUPPOSED TO BE WRITTEN ON OCCASION OF THE PLAGUE.

AH FRIEND,— Dreadful is the Lord: it is now known and felt, beyond what can be spoken. Doth thy heart fear before him? art thou willing to be subject to him? dost thou desire strength from him, to trust thyself and thy family with him? O that thou mayest be helped daily to cry unto him, that he may have mercy upon thee, who is tender-hearted and able to preserve, when his arrows fly round about!

Retire, deeply retire, and wait to feel his life; that thy soul may be gathered out of the reasonings and thoughts of thy mind, into that which stays from them, and fixes beneath them; where the Lord is known and worshipped, in that which is of himself, of his own begetting, of his own forming, of his own preserving, of his own shutting and opening at his pleasure. And, living in the sense and pure fear of the Lord, (not meddling to judge others or justify thyself, but waiting for his appearance in thee, who is the justifier and justification,) thou wilt be enabled by the Lord, in his seasons, to bring thy children and family into the same sense; that thou and they together may enjoy the same preservation from him, so far as he sees meet, whose will is not to be limited, but to be subjected to.

And, if thy heart be right before the Lord, and thy soul awakened and preserved in his fear, thou wilt find somewhat to travel out of, and somewhat to travel into, and the Lord drawing and leading thee. And this stroke, which is so dreadful to others, nor altogether without dread to thee, will prove of great advantage in thy behalf: in drawing thee more into a sense and acquaintance of the infinite One, and in drawing thee from thy earthly thoughts and knowledge which will not now stand thee instead. Thy Friend, I. P.

8th of Seventh Month, 1665.

LETTER XX.

The Spiritual Life is to be Cherished.

To Friends of Truth in and about the two Chalfonts.

Dear Friends,—I am separated, as to bodily presence, from you; but, I cannot forget you, because ye are written on my heart, and I cannot but desire your peace and welfare, as of my own soul.

And this is my present cry for you. O that ye might feel the breath of life, that life which at first quickened you, and which still quickeneth! and that breath of life has power over death; and, being felt by you, will bow down death in you, and ye will feel the seed, lifting up its head over that which oppresseth it. Why should the royal birth be a captive in any of you? Why should any of you travail and not bring forth? Why should sin have dominion in any of you, and not rather grace reign in its life and power in you all? O that ye may receive quickenings! O that ye may receive help! O that ye may be led into the true subjection, which brings forth the true dominion! Indeed, I cry for my own soul, and I cry for yours also, that in one virtue and power of life, we may be knit together, and serve the Lord our God in perfect unity of spirit.

My Friends, what shall I say unto you? Oh! the Lord keep you living and sensible, and let your walking and converse be with him, both in private and in your assemblings; be serious in your spirits, that ye may feel the weight of his seed springing up in you, and resting upon you, to poise your hearts towards him. And let the earthly thoughts, desires, and concerns, which eat like a canker, be kept out by the power of that life, which is yours, as ye abide in covenant with him that hath gathered you, by his pure light shining in you. O that ye may all dwell there! and not draw back into the earthly nature, where the enemy lies lurking to entangle and to catch your minds, and bring you to a loss.

Feel my love and tender care of you in the quickening life of God; and the Lord God watch over you for good, to perfect his work in you, and draw your hearts nearer and nearer to himself, until they be quite swallowed up of him; that ye may at last find your hearts fitted for, and welcomed into, the bosom of your Beloved, and there may sit down in the rest and joy of his fulness for evermore; which is the blessed end of the Lord's love to you, and all the faithful travails which have been for you.

Your Friend and brother in the Truth, I. P.

From my place of confinement in Aylesbury,
20th of Fourth Month, 1666.

Even when ye were sitting together, waiting on the Lord (some of you, I doubt not,) did these things spring up in my heart towards you; and if ye taste any sweetness or refreshment in them, bow to the Fountain, and be sensible of his praise springing in the midst of you.

LETTER XXI.

On True Judgment, and on Prejudices; also on the variety of Gifts and Stations in the Church.

To Friends of Truth in and about the two Chalfonts.*

As a father watcheth over his children, so do I wait and desire to feel the Lord watching over my soul continually. And in his love, care, wise and tender counsel, is my safety, life, and peace; and I never yet repented either waiting for him or hearkening to him. But if I have hearkened at any time to any thing else, and mistook his voice, and entertained the enemy's deceitful appearance, instead of his pure Truth, (which it is very easy to do,) that grievous mistake hath proved matter of loss and sorrow to my soul.

Now, O! my Friends, that ye might know and hear the voice of the Preserver! so shall ye be preserved, and kept from the voice of the stranger, which draweth aside from the pure principle of life, and the true feeling sense. There is that near you which watcheth to betray: O! the God of my life, joy, peace, and hope, watch over your souls, and deliver you from the advantages which, at any time, it hath against any of you. The seed which God

* I. P. and his wife appear to have been instrumental in gathering the Friends of that neighbourhood to the knowledge of the Truth, as held by the Society.

hath sown in you, is pure and precious. O that it may be found living in you and ye abiding in it! O that no other seed may, at any time, usurp authority over it! but that ye may know the authority and pure Truth which is of God, and therein stand, in the pure dominion, over all that is against him. For, in the principle of life, which ye have known and received in measure, is dominion; and ye, therein preserved, are in the dominion over the impure and deceitful one; and that judging in you hath power to judge all impurity and deceivableness, as the light thereof pleaseth to make it manifest to you; but, out of that, ye will easily become a prey, and set up darkness for light, and account light darkness; and then, a wrong wisdom, confidence, and conceitedness, will get up in you, and lead you far out of the way and spirit of Truth. O my dear Friends! that that may be kept down in you, which is forward to judge, to approve or disapprove; and may the weighty judgment of the seed be waited for. And, O! do not judge, do not judge, before the light of the day shine in you, and give forth the judgment; but stand and walk in fear and humility, and tenderness of spirit, and silence of flesh, that the Lord be not provoked against any of you, to give you up to a wrong sense and judgment, to the hurt of your souls. And mind your own states, and the feeling of life in your own vessels; which will keep you pure, precious, and chaste in the eye of the Lord. And, O! do not meddle with talking about others, which eats out the inward life, and may exalt your spirits out of your place, and above your proper growth: be as the weaned child, simple, naked, meek, humble, tender; easily led by, and subjected to the Father: so will ye grow in that which is of God, and be preserved out of that, which hunteth after the pure life to betray and destroy it. I have an interest in you, my cries are to the Lord for you, and I exceedingly thirst after your preservation and growth in that which is pure; and in that breathing, longing spirit towards you, was it in my heart at this time to write unto you.

The Lord God of my mercies, hope and life, watch over you for good, and keep your hearts in the pure and single watch; that the enemy, by any subtle device of his, break not in upon you; nor ye, by any temptation, be allured or drawn from the Lord; but, may know the pure, eternal, everlasting habitation, and may dwell and abide therein, to the joy of your own souls, and the rejoicing of the hearts of all that have travailed for you in the Spirit of the Lord.

From your brother and companion in the faith, patience, and afflictions of the seed. I. P.

AYLESBURY PRISON,
25th of Eleventh Month, 1666.

POSTSCRIPT.

Thus, feel after that which hath gathered you to the Lord; and then also, in that, ye will feel the life, freshness, and glory in the Lord, of those, who have been made instrumental to gather you, and are still serviceable in his hand and leadings, to build you up; and then, that which is ready to hearken to and receive prejudices, will be kept down, and the pure life will live over it, which he that feels has joy, and peace, and rest in God.

And, Friends, you that are weak, bless God for the strong; you that have need of a pillar to lean upon, bless God, that hath provided pillars in his house; and, in fear and the guidance of his Spirit, make use of these pillars; who are faithful, and have ability from God, in his power and glorious presence with them, to help to sustain his building, even as they had ability from the Lord to gather unto him. He that despiseth him that is sent, despiseth

Him that sent him; and he that undervalues any gift, office, or work, that God hath bestowed upon any person, despiseth the wisdom and disposal of the Giver. Are all fathers? have all overcome the enemy? are all grown up in the life? are all stars in the firmament of God's power? hath God made all equal? are there not different states, different degrees, different growths, different places, &c.? Then, if God hath made a difference, and given degrees of life, and gifts different, according to his pleasure; what wisdom and spirit is that, which doth not acknowledge this, but would make all equal? O my Friends! fear before the Lord; honour the Lord in his appearances, and in the differences which he hath made among the children of men, and among his people. He gave prophets of old, and the rest of the people were not equal with them. He gave evangelists, apostles, pastors, teachers, &c., and the other members of the churches were not equal with them. He hath given fathers and elders now, and the babes and young men are not equal with them. Thus it is, in truth, from the Lord; and that which is of God in you, will so acknowledge it.

Therefore, watch, every one, to feel and know his own place and service in the body, and to be sensible of the gifts, places, and services of others; that the Lord may be honoured in all, and every one owned and honoured in the Lord, and no otherwise. I. P.

26th of Eleventh Month, 1666.

LETTER XXII.

To a Couple about to Marry.

Dear Friends, — It is a great and weighty thing that ye are about; and ye have need of the Lord's leading and counsel therein, that it may be done in the unity of his life; that so Friends in truth may feel it to be of God, and find satisfaction therein.

Friends, the affectionate part will be forward in things of this nature, unless it be yoked down; and it will persuade the mind to judge such things to be right and of the Lord, when indeed they are not so. Now, if it be not of the Lord, but the affectionate part, Friends cannot have unity with it, nor will it prove a blessing to you; but you will find it an hurt to your conditions, and a load upon your spirits afterwards, and the fruits and effects of it will not be good, but evil; and then, perhaps, ye will wish that ye had waited more singly and earnestly upon the Lord, in relation to the thing; and that ye had taken more time, and consulted more with Friends, before there had been any engagement of affections. The Lord, by his providence, hath given you a little time of respite. O retire unto him, and abase yourselves before him, and pray him to counsel you, by his good Spirit, for your good! that, if it be not of the Lord, the power, being waited upon by you, may loosen your affections in this respect. But, if it be of the Lord, and be orderly brought before Friends, and their counsel and advice sought in the fear of the Lord, they will have unity with it, and with gladness express their unity; which may be a strength unto you, against the tempter afterwards.

This is in true love to you, and in singleness of heart, the Lord knoweth. From your Friend in the Truth,

I. P.

4th of Third Month, 1668.

LETTER XXIII.

The day of God's Power and Love.

To John Mannock.

Friend, — Hath the Lord drawn thy heart to hear the sound of Truth, and given thee some sense and savour thereof; though, perhaps, not as yet full satisfaction in all things that are truly and faithfully testified concerning it? O prize this love of God to thee! and watch and pray, and come into the pure fear; that thou mayest walk worthy of it, and mayst discern in spirit what it is that gives thee the savour; and so, receive the leaven of the kingdom and feel its leavening virtue upon thy heart day by day. For, after the Lord hath been at work, the enemy will be at work also; and thou mayest both meet with him without, and within too, in reasonings and questionings against the demonstrations of God's Spirit to thy heart and conscience. Now, if thou wilt hearken to these, they will eat out the sense and belief of what God's Spirit begat in thee. Oh! how many wise men, and how many knowing men, that have tasted of some true experiences, have not the sense and discerning of the Spirit and power of the Lord, as it is now made manifest; but speak hard words, and think hard thoughts of his truth and its precious appearances.

Ah! what are we, any of us, on whom the Lord hath shown his mercy, and whose hearts he toucheth, and maketh sensible of his drawings; yea, and not only so, but also gives us to partake of the eternal life and virtue, which he hath hid in his Son from the eyes of all living. We sought it up and down, in the deeps and heights; but the deep said, It is not in me, and the highest mountain and hill that ever we met with, could not bring salvation to us. But, at length, we found the fear of the Lord to be the true wisdom, and that which taught us to depart from evil, gave us the true understanding. Now, if any among us are not thus taught, but only own the doctrines of Truth published among us, being thereunto overcome by the demonstration of God's Spirit; yet, for all this, they are not felt by us in the life and unity of the Spirit of the Lord with us; and such, the Lord will manifestly prune off, in his own due time, and graft in others in their stead. Yea, such as do indeed give up to Truth, and in measure feel the power of it, and are made by the power of the Lord subject to it — yet, if in anything they let in the spirit of the world, and act according thereto, so far, they are not of the Truth, nor owned by it.

Now, dear Friend, (for, so far as thy heart is touched by God's Spirit, and answereth thereto, thou art dear unto me,) mind thy condition, and wait on the Lord in humility of heart, and in subjection to what he inwardly, by his Spirit, daily makes manifest; that thou mayest come into the obedience of the Truth daily; that thou mayest daily feel the change, which is wrought in the heart and conscience, by the holy, eternal, ever-living power; that so thou mayest witness, according to the Scriptures, "that which is born of the Spirit, is spirit." And then thou wilt feel, that this birth of the Spirit cannot fulfil the lusts of the flesh, but will be warring and fighting the good fight of faith, in the power of life, against them; and thus, in faithfulness to the Truth, and waiting upon the Lord, thou shalt witness an overcoming in his due time. For, indeed, the true faith overcomes, the true shield beats down the most fiery darts, and, in the power of the Lord, the enemy is so resisted, that he fleeth; and the name of the Lord is, indeed, a strong tower to his children, to which his seed know how to retire and feel safety.

O the conquering faith, the overcoming life and power of the Spirit! We cannot but speak of those things; and cry up the perfect gift, and the power of Him, who is not only able to perfect his work in the heart, but delights so to do; and even to tread down Satan under the feet of those, that wait in patience for the perfect conquest; for, nothing else will fully satisfy. The rest, the peace, the liberty, the life, the virtue of the gospel, is not fully known and enjoyed, while there remains any sin to sting and trouble. And this I can faithfully witness; that when the power is revealed, when the blood washeth, the soul is clean and as white as snow; and the enemy hath not power to break in, but life triumphs over him. And why may there not be a continuance of such a state? Yea, I verily believe, many can witness a continuance of such a state; which the Spirit of the Lord doth not call less in them than a perfect state, a sound state; wherein Christ, the heavenly Physician, hath healed them perfectly, and made them witnesses of true soundness of soul and spirit in the sight of God. O that all knew and enjoyed it, who truly desire and long after it!

But as for thee, this is in my heart to thee. Thou hast found the pearl; the Lord, in mercy to thee, hath discovered to thee the true pearl. Now, this remains; that thou be a wise merchant, selling all to purchase it. Thou must keep back nothing. Christ, the living Truth, the holy power of righteousness, must be dearer to thee than all. If father, mother, livelihood, liberty, friendship, outward advantages, &c., or anything else, be dearer to thee than him, he will look upon thee as unworthy of him; and cannot but turn from thee, and suffer hardness and darkness to come again upon thee. Therefore, prize the day of thy visitation from the holy God, from the God of mercy and salvation; and be faithful in the little, in the day of small things, if ever thou desire to enjoy and be ruler over much.

The Lord may exercise thee in, and require of thee, little things; as he hath done the rest of the flock, whose footsteps thou art to follow to the Shepherd's tents; and the enemy will be endeavouring to stop thee, and perplex thee, in every little thing that the Lord requires of thee. But, be thou simple, like a child, not taking care what to answer wise professors, nor what to answer the reasoning of thy own mind; but, seeing thou hast felt the demonstration of Truth from God's Holy Spirit, O! breathe unto the Lord, to preserve thee in the innocency and simplicity thereof, that the Lord may still be with thee; and thereby bring thee through the day of Jacob's trouble, to taste of Jacob's deliverance and salvation out of trouble: for, thou must meet with trials as well as others have done, and the enemy's endeavour will be, to make thee stumble and start back in the day of trial. But, if thine eye be towards the Lord, he will uphold and strengthen thee, and bring thee through all that stands in thy way; manifesting to thee, daily more and more, the path of holiness, in which the ransomed of the Lord walk, and enabling *thee* also to walk therein.

Therefore, watch the thoughts and reasonings which rise in thee, and retire from them, waiting to feel the pure seed, and to hear its voice in stillness; whose voice is otherwise, than after the noises of the questionings and reasonings, which the enemy raiseth in the mind, to fill it with doubts and troubles; and to weaken the faith and sense which God wrought in the heart, when he reached forth his Truth, in the power and demonstration of his Spirit, unto it. This was God's love, this was the day of his power; which loosens the mind from its lovers, and the ways of its own choosing, and begets a willingness to be joined to the Lord and his pure Truth.

O take heed of hearkening to the enemy, to the subtle reasoner, the entangler of the soul! take heed of consulting there, where he lays his baits to entangle the mind, and undo the work of God's power in the heart; and so, to make unwilling again, after the Lord had made willing. The steps which the soul takes in the power, even the inclining of the mind towards the Lord and his pure Truth, tend to salvation; but, if any let in unbelief of those things, concerning which God had wrought faith in them, they draw back to perdition; they hearken to that which tempts from the Lord, and to him whose end is to destroy them.

This is in true love to thee, and from an upright desire, that thou mayest feel the Lord's preservation of thy soul, in that which is of him, and his separating thee from all that is not of him.

From a Friend to all that breathe after the Lord, and desire to know and partake of the power and life of Truth as it is in Jesus, the alone Redeemer and Saviour of the soul.

I. P.

3d or 4th of Tenth Month, 1668.

LETTER XXIV.

On Simplicity of Faith and Dedication.

To John Mannock.

Friend, — It is a wonderful thing, to witness the power of God reaching to the heart, and demonstrating to the soul the pure way to life, as in his sight and presence. Surely, he that partakes of this, is therein favoured by the Lord, and ought diligently to wait, for the giving up to the leadings of his Holy Spirit in every thing; that so, he may travel through all that is contrary to the Lord, into that nature and spirit which is of Him. It is a wonderful thing, also, to witness God's preservation from backsliding, and from being entangled by the subtlety of the enemy; who hath many ways and taking devices to ensnare the simple mind, and draw it from the sense of Truth, into some notions and belief of things; wherein the soul may be lulled asleep with hopes and persuasions, but hath not the feeling or enjoyment of the true life and power.

O Friend! hast thou a sense of the way to the Father? then, be careful that thy spirit daily bow before him, and wait for breathings to him from his pure Spirit, that he would continue his mercy to thee; keeping thee in the true sense, and making thy way more and more clear before thee every day; — yea, and bearing thee up in all the exercises and trials which may befall thee, in every kind; that, by his secret working in thy spirit, and helping thee with a little help from time to time, thou mayest still be advancing nearer and nearer towards the kingdom; until thou find the Lord God administer an entrance unto thee thereinto, and give thee an inheritance of life, joy, righteousness, and peace therein; — which is strength unto the soul against sin and death, and against the sorrow and trouble which ariseth in the mind, for want of God's presence and holy power revealed there.

And, be not careful after the flesh, but trust the Lord. What though thou art weak, and little; though thou meet with those that are wise and knowing; and almost every way able to reason thee down; what though thou hast not wherewith to answer; yet, thou knowest and hast the feeling of God's pure Truth in spirit, with a desire to have the life of it brought forth in thee, and so, to witness the change and renewings which are by his power. O dear heart! herein thou art accepted of the Lord, and here his tender love and care will be over thee, and his mercy will daily reach to thee; and thou shalt have true satisfaction in thy heart, and hold the Truth there, where all the reasonings of men, and all the devices of the enemy of thy soul, shall not be able to reach;—yea, thou shalt so feel the Lord to help his babe against the strength of the mighty, in the seasons of his good pleasure, as shall exceedingly turn to his praise; and so, thou shalt experience, that whom God preserves, all the gates of hell shall not be able to prevail against. Therefore, look not out at men, or at the words and wisdom of men; but, keep where thou hast felt the Lord visit thee, that he may visit thee yet again and again, every day, and be teaching thee further and further the way to his dwelling-place, and be drawing thee thither, where is righteousness, life, rest, and peace, forever!

This arose in my heart this morning, in tender love towards thee. Look up to the Lord, who can make it useful to thee, to warm, quicken, and strengthen thy heart and mind towards the Lord, and his pure Truth, wherewith he has visited thee. And if thou feel any thing therein, suitable to the state and condition of thy soul, O bow before the Lord! that in the true humility thou mayest confess, and give the glory to him of what belongs to him.

From thy Friend in the Truth, which cleanseth the heart from iniquity, as it is embraced and dwelt in.

I. P.

23d of Tenth month, 1668.

LETTER XXV.

The Blessedness of Suffering for Christ's Sake.

To Elizabeth Walmsley.

Dear Friend,—Who art lovely to me in that precious life, wherewith the Lord hath visited thee, and wherein he hath brought thee forth for his service, and to his praise.

Our Father is wise and powerful, who hath begun a work which he is able to carry on; and all the briars and thorns of the wilderness, are not able to stop his course, who is "a consuming fire."

I find the spirits of Friends here much raised, who dwell in the fear and dread of the Lord God Almighty, where the fear and dread of man is removed far away. The Lord preserve us near unto himself, out of that which separates from him and weakens; and nothing shall be able to interrupt our joy in the Lord, nor our delight and pleasure in his will. Lo! I come, saith the child, to do thy will, O God! to drink the cup thou hast prepared; although there is a nature which cannot but say, If it be possible, let it pass away; but, *that* nature is bowed down and subjected under its proper yoke, and, in submission, is kept out of sinning against the Lord; and is accepted by him who bows it, and makes it willing to follow the Lamb in the day of his power.

Truly, the Lord hath done great things for us! he hath given us the sight and knowledge of himself in his Son, which is life eternal: he hath given us of the nature and spirit of his Son; he hath given us of the true faith, whereby the just lives, and obtains victory over sin, death, and the grave; he hath given us of the hope which purifies the heart, and stays the mind in all storms; he hath given us of the Lamb's patience and meekness, &c. And now, if he will brighten these by afflictions, and try them, and cause them to shine to his glory; yea, and take advantage to increase them, and add further virtue to them, what cause have any of us to complain? Israel, of old, after the flesh, murmured upon every trial; but Israel, after the new creation, doth not so, but blesseth the Lord, and repineth not at the instruments which he permitteth to afflict them; but they love the Lord and love his Truth, and are faithful in their testimony thereto, whatever befalls them. Yea, they rejoice that they are counted worthy to suffer in any kind for his name's sake, and are like lambs before the shearers, not opening their mouths in a way of murmuring or reviling; but instead thereof, pitying them, praying for them, and blessing; because God hath made them children of love, children of peace, children of blessing; which nature they retain, in the midst of all their trials and afflictions, and show forth the virtues of Him that hath called them.

So that, men shall not put out our life, nor put out our light, nor sever us from the love and power of God; but, the more need we find of our God, and of his help and strength, the nearer shall we be driven to him, and dwell more closely in union with him, and in holy and humble dependence upon him. And, in this temper, shall we draw and receive more from him: and the more we draw from him, the better will it be with us, and the more like him shall we be.

The Lord keep open that heavenly eye in his children and servants, which looks over this world, with the affairs and concerns thereof, to that which is immortal and invisible; where our life is hid from others, though made manifest in and felt by us, from the living spring which quickens, nourisheth, and refresheth. And as afflictions abound from men, so shall consolations, life, and strength abound from the Lord, unto all, and upon all, who look not out, but abide and await there, where it springs and flows.

My dear love is to Friends in these parts, (particularly M. O.); the Lord preserve them and keep them near to himself, that they may receive counsel and strength from him, according to their need. I am sensible of thy great love to us, expressed in thy care and tenderness of our child, as well as in other things: I hope she is no burden to thee. O that she might feel and be guided by that, which keeps in order all that are subject to it!

I remain thy Friend and brother, in the life and love which never dies nor changes, I. P.

18th of Second month, 1670.

LETTER XXVI.

Exhortation, chiefly, on Revelations, xiv. 7, "Fear God, give Glory to Him," &c.

To Widow Hemmings.

Dear Friend,—Since I last saw thee, there have been many deep and serious thoughts on my heart concerning thee; and a sense of thy state as before the Lord, and breathings of heart for thee. I am sensible, that the Spirit of the Lord is striving with thee, and in some measure opening thy heart towards him and his Truth; and I am sensible withal, that there is much striving against him; and many strong holds of wisdom and reasonings in thee, which must be broken down, before Truth can spring up in thy heart, and exercise its power in thee, and have full command in thee.

Now, this morning, when I awoke, there were three things sprang up in me, which my heart did singly and earnestly desire for thee. One was, that thou mightst be led by God's Holy Spirit into the new and living covenant, where Christ is revealed, and the soul united to him as its Lord and King, in a bond of indissoluble union. Another was, that thou mightst daily be taught of God, and learn of him, in this holy, new, pure, and everlasting covenant. The third was, that thou mightst be true and faithful to God, to obey and follow him in whatever he teaches and requires of thee.

If thou wert but in this state, thou wouldst find sweetness and rest, peace and power, the righteousness of our Lord Jesus Christ, and life eternal, revealed in thy own heart; and with joy draw water out of the wells of salvation.

Now, if thou come to witness Christ's appearance in spirit, and wilt become a disciple unto him, there are three things thou must apply thy heart to learn of him; which indeed are the sum of the gospel, or of what is taught in and by the gospel. The first is, to *fear God*. This is the beginning of true heavenly wisdom, and this is the perfection and the end of wisdom also; for, true wisdom not only brings into the fear, but it builds up in the fear, yea, and perfects in the fear also; according as the apostle saith, "Perfecting holiness in the fear of the Lord." Now, this is not such a fear, as man can attain by all he can do; but is the fear of the new covenant, which God puts into the hearts of his children, as he quickens them and brings them up in the new covenant. This is such a fear, as that those in whom it is placed, cannot depart from the Lord; nor, abiding in it, err from the way of life and holiness; for all sin and transgression, all rebellion against the Lord, and grieving and quenching his Spirit, is out of this fear. O that thou mightst receive this fear from the Lord, and grow up unto him daily in it!

The second, which depends upon and flows from the former, is, to *give glory to God*, in discerning his life and power, and the virtue of his Spirit and his grace, working all in thee; and so, still ascribing the glory to him, of all thou art, dost, or canst do: for, in the day of the gospel, no flesh can glory in the presence of our God; but, the Lord alone is exalted in the spirits of his children, in that day. And indeed, as every one comes into the fear of the new covenant, the presence of the Lord is there, dwelling in the midst of the heart; and he is found working all therein, and bringing forth the seed of life, and working down sin, and death, and corruption. And they that are here, feel their own poverty and nothingness, as in themselves; and that their way to become strong in Christ, is first to become weak in themselves: and so, when they are strong in him, he who is their strength is glorified and admired, and self is of no reputation or value forever and ever; for, that is cleaved to, which brought down self, and that power and spirit being cleaved to, still keeps it down.

The third is, that thou learn to *worship God* in spirit and truth. O this worship is precious indeed! and this is the only sort of worship which God seeketh and regardeth, among the many various kinds of worshippers which appear at this day. This worship was declared by Christ, and taught his disciples; but it has been in great measure departed from; and though many have sought after it, yet none ever could find it, but as they have learned of the Father to return to the anointing; and so, to be gathered into his Spirit, where Christ's name is known, and where they that meet together, worship in his name: and, of a truth, none know or can worship in Christ's name besides these. There have been great mistakes about worship and gatherings; they having not been in the name and power of our Lord Jesus Christ, but only in a profession thereof, and an imitation of things, without the true life and power; and what is that worship and religion in the sight of the Lord?

Now, that thou mayest come into this state, and learn all these lessons of the Lord in the new covenant, there is one thing indispensably necessary for thee; which is, to know *the hour of God's judgment* in thy own heart, and to lie under the judgment of the Lord, bearing it till he finish it, and bring it forth unto victory. For, this is the way whereby he purges and redeems the soul; to wit, by the spirit of judgment and burning. Thou must therefore wait for, and come to feel, the Spirit of the Lord near thee, discovering sin to thee, and revealing judgment against it, and executing his righteous judgment upon the evil nature in thee; that he may raise up that good and tender plant of righteousness, out of the dry and barren ground, to which his mercy is.

If thou come to know God's Spirit, and to receive it, and feel it work in thee, and its pure light shine from the fountain and spring of life, thou wilt have a quicker sense and discerning therefrom, than can arise either from words written, or from thoughts; that is, the Lord will show thee the way whereof thou doubtest, quicker than a thought can arise in thee; and the Lord will show thee evil, in a pure sense of the new nature, quicker than thou canst think or consider of any thing. And indeed, this is needful; for, sin lodges in the evil nature inwardly, and works, not so much by a known law set up in the mind, as by a secret nature; and, if it be not resisted and withstood by another nature, it can never be overcome. Now, by this judgment set up in the heart, doth God overcome and keep down sin forever; for, the judgment of God is stronger than sin, and will bring it down, where his judgment is received and abode in; and that which brought it down, being kept to, will keep it down; and, it being kept down, life and righteousness, even the righteous life, Spirit, and power of the Lord Jesus inwardly revealed, will be uppermost, and reign over it.

Perhaps these words, at present, may be hard unto thee: but, if thou come to wait on God's Holy Spirit, and to the feeling of his appearance in thy heart, and learn of him to know what is good and what is evil in thy words, ways, worship, yea, and in thy very heart and thoughts, and also to choose the good and refuse the evil; they will grow easier and easier, and plainer and plainer, daily, as thou comest into the sense and experience of the things they mention. And thou wilt find Christ, inwardly revealed in spirit, to be very properly called the Word of God, even the ingrafted word which is able to save the soul; for he is quick and powerful, and sharper than any two-edged sword, able to cut down all that shall appear or rise up in the heart, to resist or oppose his work.

The Lord so guide thee, manifest himself to thee, help thee, and lead thee by his Holy Spirit and power, as that thou mayest come undeniably to experience, and to be satisfied by him about these things. And mind not so much to *know*, as to be obedient and subjected to the Lord, both in thy heart and in thy conversation also, in the least thing that he makes manifest. If the Lord would show thee but this one thing,—that, to use "thee" and "thou" to a particular person, is proper language, and Scripture language; and that, to say "you," is improper, and arose from pride, and nourisheth pride, and so is of the world, and not of the Father; and thou should bow thy spirit to him in this one thing, thou little thinkest what a work it would make within thee, and how strongly the spirit of darkness would fight against thy subjection thereto. The Lord lead thee as he seeth good, and give thee faithfully to follow; for else, if the Lord should lead in anything, and thou not follow in that thing, his Spirit would be grieved and vexed thereby, and thy heart in danger of being hardened by the deceitfulness of sin.

The Lord give thee the sense and savour of these things; that thou mayest thereby be kindled to wait on the Lord, to be led into the light of the living; that thou mayest live and walk with him therein, who is, and dwells, and walks with his, in the light. O house of Jacob! come ye, let us walk in the light of the Lord, and let us come up to Zion, the holy hill of God, and to the gospel Jerusalem, that there he may teach us of his ways, and we may there learn of him to walk in his paths; for there, is the place of wisdom and true understanding, which none know but those that are taught of God.

This is in true friendship and tender love to thy soul, from its Friend in truth and sincerity, I. P.

26th of Eighth Month, 1670.

LETTER XXVII.

Advice and Sympathy under Trial.

TO ELIZABETH WALMSLEY.

MY VERY DEAR FRIEND,—Many are the trials, afflictions, and temptations, which the Lord seeth good to exercise us with, for the purifying and making us white, that he may honour his name in us and through us: but this promise stands sure in the seed, "I will never leave thee, nor forsake thee." And, if our God be with us and for us, what can prevail against the work and design of his love and power towards us?

I am deeply sensible of thy condition, feeling it, even in the tender and melting love of my heart towards thee; and this word sprang in me to thee, Look not out, but trust in the Lord, who can make things easier than they seem likely to be; and will certainly carry *his* through the hardest things, which he suffers to befall them.

O! the Lord keep all in his pure innocency; out of the earthly contriving wisdom, which saith, Save thyself, avoid this dreadful brunt, this stroke of the cross; which it is easy to hearken to, if the mind be not kept to that eye and that wisdom, which discovers the tempter, and instructeth the bird to escape his snare.

My dear love is to thee, and to all faithful Friends. The Lord keep you from hearkening to the enemy, and make you faithful to him, in the pure innocency and heavenly wisdom which is of him; for, Truth triumphs over deceit, and the life of the Lamb on the cross, reigns and triumphs over death: glory to Him, who hath overcome in his person, and who teacheth us to overcome, through faith in his power,—and from the overflowings of the conquering life in our hearts, which first brings down that which is contrary to Truth, and then reigns in the Truth.

Thy Friend in the love which never dies, and in the Truth which changes not, I. P.

CATSGROVE,
14th of Tenth Month, 1670.

LETTER XXVIII.

Of Obedience in Confessing Christ; also on the Light of Christ.

TO ELIZABETH STONAR.

DEAR FRIEND,—I am sensible that the Lord hath visited thee with his power, reaching to thy heart in the demonstration of his own Spirit, and that thy heart hath answered, and said in the inward of thy soul, It is God's Truth indeed. Now, so far as God hath reached to thee, so far it behooves thee to confess him, his Truth, and people before men, and to give up in obedience and subjection of Spirit to the Lord. And, if thou say, in the simplicity of thy heart, to any that have any tenderness, Thus it is with me; I believe from my heart this or this is of God; what shall I do? shall I give up in obedience thereto, or shall I disobey the Lord, grieve his Spirit, and wound my own soul? This will reach that which is of

God in any; and this will wound and trouble that which is not of God.

The Lord guide thee, and pity thee, and help thee in thy straits, and doubts, and fears, and troubles, both in reference to thyself and mother. God is my witness, whom I serve in my spirit, in the gospel of his Son, that I have not sought myself, but your good; and that, not of myself neither, but in the leadings and drawings of his Holy Spirit. And I gave thy husband a warning, in true and tender love; though I knew well enough, how hard it would be to his spirit in his present state, and what a bitter enemy he might become to me, for telling him the truth. I did it not unadvisedly, but in the weight of my spirit before the Lord; and I heartily wish, that he were not deceived in heart concerning his own state, but truly knew it, as it is.

Thy soul's true and sincere-hearted Friend, I. P.

POSTSCRIPT.

There is light, which enlightens the soul, or it remains in darkness: "Ye were darkness," said the apostle, "but now are ye light in the Lord." Now, no man can become light in the Lord, unless his nature and spirit be renewed, and changed out of darkness into light. Now, the question is, what this light is, and where is it to be met with. Are the Scriptures, then, this light? or do they testify of this light? If they testify of this light, then, the light is to be come to, and the soul to be enlightened by it. And, he that comes to this light, and is enlightened by it, and walks in the pure shinings thereof, he becomes a child of light; but, he that is not enlightened and changed by it, is yet a child of darkness, notwithstanding whatsoever he learns, professeth, or practiseth, by imitation from the Scriptures. This is a weighty matter.

O come! be not wedded to your own ways, nor prejudiced against what God hath taught others; but let things be fairly scanned, that all things may be proved, and that which is good held fast; for, Truth will not lose ground by being tried; but, darkness is afraid of the light, because it has a secret sense, that it cannot stand before it. I. P.

16th of Twelfth Month, 1670.

LETTER XXIX.

On the Life, inward Sense, and Power of the Spirit; also Respecting the Scriptures, and the Church, &c.

To Nathaniel Stonar.

Dear Friend,—There is somewhat on my heart, to express to thee, in love and great good-will, which is as followeth.

Would it not be sad, if thou should perish from the Lord forever? If thou err in heart from the living way, it may be so: indeed, if thy mind be not turned from darkness, inward darkness, to the inward light of God's Spirit, it cannot be otherwise. Now, if thou feel the inward light, the power of the pure light, and art changed thereby, thou canst not speak against that light.

There was no true religion in the apostles' days, without turning to the inward light, and to *that* the true ministry was sent to turn men; nor is there any true religion now, without being inwardly turned to, and walking in the same light; nor canst thou try any truth, or understand any Scripture aright, but in the light of God's Spirit. No man can understand the things of God, but the Spirit of God. The Scriptures are holy words, and treat of the things of God, which no man can understand, but in a light of the same nature from which they came; and, when once a man comes to the true understanding, he soon finds that the understanding which he had of the same before, was but after the flesh, even short of the nature of the true understanding. And, Friend, consider, if thy knowledge, which thou hast hitherto had, hath changed, or doth change the nature of thy understanding and will? or, is thy old understanding and will yet remaining, notwithstanding all thy knowledge and practices in religion? O do not dally in things of so great concernment, lest thou repent too late! for, I do not tell thee what I see concerning thee, in the light of God's eternal Spirit; but, I would fain have thine own eye, or rather the right eye in thee, opened and brought to see.

And, consider one Scripture seriously concerning the church of Laodicea: had it not the true knowledge outwardly, and a true church state, and right ordinances? Did it not believe in Christ, and look up to him for justification, &c. Nay, what did it want, as to the outwardness of its state? But, it wanted sense, life, warmth, inwardly. So that, if ye had all ordinances and truths of the gospel light outwardly; yet, if ye wanted the inward power, ye could not but want the *tried gold,* the *white raiment,* and *eye-salve:* and so, though ye might think yourselves rich, &c. yet, *the shame of your nakedness* would *appear;* yea, indeed, the nakedness of such as are not clothed with God's Spirit, doth appear to the Lord, and to the eyes and spirits of his children, which he openeth in his own light, and who see with this eye; — I say, the shame of their nakedness doth appear, notwithstanding all the religious covers they can put upon themselves. O that thou hadst desires, living desires, after the nature of Truth! and wert acquainted with the new nature, which can be satisfied with nothing but the virtue, life, and power of Truth.

Come, Friend, wait on the Lord, to have the old nature, the old spirit, mind, wisdom, understanding and will, broken, — the old garment torn to pieces; that thou mayest come to experience that which is new, pure, and living; and find the new vessel filled with that which is new; and know the virgin state of spirit, and the savour of the true ointment. For, life savours life, and death savours death, and living words are but the savour of death, to them that are out of the life; and, the living Stone, which is the foundation of life to us, and very precious, is but a stone of stumbling, and rock of offence, to them that are out of the life; and who judge of things by their apprehensions of the letter, without the spirit of life and power. As the Scribes and Pharisees formerly did, and so condemned Christ in his appearance in the flesh; those who judge after that manner now, cannot but condemn his spiritual appearance in the hearts of his children. The letter killeth, the Spirit gives life. If thou wilt have life, thou must come to that which gives life. If thou wilt come into the ministration of the new testament, thou must come into the Spirit and power; and know the letter of the Scriptures, in the spirit and power which wrote them, if ever thou know them aright. Yea, if thou wilt become a son of God, thou must receive power from Christ so to do; and, if thou wilt believe aright, thou must feel faith wrought in thy heart, by that very power, which raised our Lord Jesus Christ from the dead; all other faith falls short of the nature of true faith.

If thou receive from the Lord the true sense of these things, thou wilt bless his name, for engaging my heart to write them to thee; but, if thou read them, out of that which gives the true understanding, they cannot be of advantage to thee. But, whatever entertainment they have with thee, yet, my judgment is with the Lord, and my work and labour of love with my God, who is my strength and joy; in whom my soul rests in peace, in the bosom of my Beloved. And, O! that thou also mightest feel quickenings of life and true leadings; and thus be acquainted with that faithful travel, which leads thither.

Thy Friend, in the heartiness of true love, so far as the Lord pleaseth to make use of me towards thee, I. P.

7th of the Fourth Month, 1671.

POSTSCRIPT.

The apostle speaks of the state of the Gentiles, before they were turned from darkness to light, and from the power of Satan to God; that their understanding was darkened, being alienated from the life of God, through the ignorance that was in them, because of the hardness of their heart; not that that which might be known of God, was not manifest in them; but their ignorance was, because of their hardness, in not minding it, not turning to it, and so, they became alienated from the life, and their understanding not opened by it.

Now, in this state, men are without God, without Christ, strangers to the covenant of promise, and without any true hope of salvation; and this state, they are as really in, who get a form of godliness without the power, as the very natural heathen. For, nothing makes a true Christian, but the life and power: and he, that doth not hear the voice of Christ's Spirit in his heart, is no better than a heathen and a publican. Yea, any church, built up out of the life and power, (nay, a church, though built by the power, yet, if not preserved in the same,) is not better than a synagogue of Satan. They that say, they are Jews, but are not so; ministers of Christ, but are not, and do lie; alas! what are they? O how precious is life! how precious is the power of God, in which the churches of old stood, and the true churches at this day stand in!

It is precious, to know the Spirit of the living God, to be begotten by him in the life, which is true and pure, to be separated from death and the power thereof, and to be married to life and the power thereof, — to be married to the conquering Lamb, who triumphed over sin and death in his body of flesh, and, by his Spirit and power, delivers his spouse from the strength and dominion of them. And, it is precious, to walk with the Lamb, and to follow the Lamb whithersoever he goes; who always leads out of sin and unrighteousness, into ways of purity and righteousness, into the path which is prepared for the ransomed, where there is no danger of erring, — no, not so much as to the wayfaring ones, though fools, Isai. xxxv. 8.

Oh! is it not precious, experimentally to read that Scripture, and to be able in true understanding to say, The way of life is easy, the yoke easy, the burden easy, the commandment not grievous; *that* being brought down, and subdued in me, yea, removed and cast out, to which it was hard. Alas! men building in the flesh, and after their carnal apprehensions of things, — how loathsome is it! but, God's building, raised in the light and life of his pure Spirit, how glorious, how beautiful, how lovely is it, even in the eye of God himself! "Thou art all fair, my love, there is no spot in thee." Sol. Song, iv. 7.—Into thy holy building, O God! into thy heavenly building, into the spiritual Jerusalem, which thou rearest and buildest up in the Spirit, no unclean or defiled thing can enter; nor is there any room there, for that which loves and makes a lie!—Without, indeed, are swine and dogs, vulturous eyes and crooked serpents, who make a show of what they are not, and lay claim to that which belongs not to them; but, within, are the children, within is the heavenly birth, even the new creation of God in Christ Jesus. For, God doth not strip his people naked, and gather them out of the spirit of this world, that they should be empty and desolate forever; but, he gathers them into, and fills them with his own Spirit, fills them with light, fills them with life, fills them with holiness, fills them with righteousness, fills them with peace and joy, in believing and obeying the gospel! And, in this Spirit, is the kingdom known, which is not of this world, — the inward kingdom, the spiritual kingdom, the everlasting kingdom! — where the everlasting throne is near, and the everlasting power revealed! and the Lord God Omnipotent reigns in the hearts of his! and other lords do not reign, but their horns are broken — and the horn of God's Anointed exalted, who sits ruling as King on his holy hill of Zion! — and they that have suffered with him, and gone through great tribulation, do reign with him; blessed be his name forever! I. P.

10th of Fourth Month.

LETTER XXX.

Of Truth in the Inward Parts.

To Widow Hemmings.

Dear Friend, — I think it long since I heard from thee. I remember the sweet and precious savour that was upon thy spirit, the last time I was with thee, with my dear Friend, J. C. It hath been my hope and desire, that the Lord might preserve thee therein.

The Truth in the inward parts, is of God; that is the thing which all are to mind; and in which, acceptance with God is witnessed. Out of the Truth in the inward parts, there is no acceptance with God, let men profess what they will or can. In the Truth, there is always acceptance; for God never disowned it, nor any that are in it. Here, the flesh and blood, which give life, are fed on;

here, the bread which comes down from heaven, and the water of life, are known; but, out of this, they are not, nor can they be known.

O my Friend! that thou mightest feel more and more the Truth in the inward parts, and be more and more established therein. What is the feeding outward, or supper outward? It is but a shadow. The feeding inward, or the supper inward, is the substance. And, as the day dawns, and the day-star arises in thy heart, the shadows will flee away, and the substance be discovered, owned, and delighted in by thee. The shadows reach but to the outward part, but the ministration of life, the ministration of the substance, reaches to the seed: and, thou must be more and more transplanted into the seed, that Christ may be formed in thee, and thou formed in him; and so grow up into his heavenly nature and image,— out of the earthly, out of the natural. Oh! the Lord God prosper his own seed and holy plantation in thy heart; and keep thee in the meek, lowly, humble, poor, and tender spirit, unto which is his mercy and blessing.

I expected to have heard from thee, or at least from thy daughter S., before this time, supposing I had a promise thereof from her. The Lord uphold, preserve, and bless her. Let her not look out, but only look within, what the will of the Lord is; and mind nothing else; and it will be well with her.

My dear love is both to thee and her, who am thy sincere Friend, I. P.

4th of Ninth Month, 1673.

LETTER XXXI.

Deliverance from Spiritual Enemies by Christ, &c.; also of Offences.

Dear Friend, — For, in those true desires, which I observe in thy heart towards the Lord, thou art, and canst not but be dear unto me — I had a desire to have stayed a little while with thee, the last time I passed through Uxbridge, but was prevented.

The occasion of my writing to thee, was, somewhat which was on my heart towards thee.

Wouldst thou know the Lord in the gospel covenant, and wouldst thou walk with him therein? I know thou wouldst. Wouldst thou have sin destroyed in thee, and Christ reign in thy heart? Wouldst thou so fight against thy enemies, as to overcome, and so run the race, as certainly to obtain the everlasting prize, and eternal weight of glory? O! then, mind Truth in the inward parts, even the grace and truth, which are by Jesus Christ; to whom God hath given power, and who gives power to his, by the grace of his Holy Spirit, over sin and corruption in the inward parts. Did not God conquer the enemies of the outward Jews in Egypt, in the wilderness, and in the good land also? And shall he not do so inwardly, for the inward Jews? There are enemies in Egypt; in the land that is, as I may say, wholly dark, and under the oppression of spiritual Pharaoh. There are enemies in that heart, which is as a wilderness and solitary place; and there are enemies in that heart, which is in some measure renewed, and made good and honest. Now, all the spiritual enemies, all the enemies of a man's own house, are to be destroyed by the power of the Lord Jesus Christ, working by his grace in the heart; which, being received, subjected to, dwelt in, and obeyed, brings deliverance and salvation from them all. And, when salvation is brought home to the heart, and wrought out there by the Lord, it is to be enjoyed and abode in, and the soul is not to return back again into captivity; but, being delivered out of the hands of its inward and spiritual enemies, by the holy, inward, and spiritual covenant, is to serve God in the dominion of his Son's life, in holiness and righteousness all its days here upon the earth.

O my Friend! mind this precious Truth inwardly, this precious grace inwardly, the precious life inwardly, the precious light inwardly, the precious power inwardly, the inward word of life, the inward voice of the Shepherd in the heart, the inward seed, the inward salt, the inward leaven, the inward pearl, &c. whereby Christ effects this. Distinguish between words *without* concerning the thing, and the thing itself *within;* and wait and labour, then, to know, understand, and be guided by, the motives, leadings, drawings, teachings, quickenings, &c. of the thing itself within. And, take heed of being offended, because of any thing, either within or without; for, offences will come, but blessed was he, that was not offended at Christ outwardly in the days of his flesh; and blessed is he, that is not offended at his inward Truth, and inward way of appearance in the day of his Spirit. Moses, that precious servant of the Lord, spake unadvisedly with his lips; how easy is it, then, for those, who come not near Moses' state, so to do; but, wait on God, that thou mayest distinguish between what Truth speaks in any of us, and what any of us may unadvisedly speak, out of the Truth,—if we stand not upon the watch, and our words be not seasoned with God's light and his grace. For, praying to God, as God's Spirit leads and gives ability, and watching unto prayer, and seeking opportunities both alone and in our families, that God may open our hearts, and breathe upon us, and for frequent and diligent reading of the Holy Scriptures,—none can testify from the Truth against these things; though, against men's dead and formal performing of these things, there is a living testimony. Now, take heed of mistaking the testimony in any; or of being stumbled, if any go beyond their due bounds in their testimony.

O my Friend! how precious is the thing, beyond all words or testimonies! O that thou mayest come to know *that* in thyself, and to be sensible of God's ministering by it to thee, and increasing it in thee! that thou mayest experimentally feel the seed in thee, and find it grow more and more, till it come to be a tree; and then, sit under its shadow, and be delighted with its defence, and partake of its sap and fruit. O that, every day, thou mightest have a sense of the life itself, the Truth itself, the power itself, the wisdom itself, the righteousness itself! and, that thou mightest find the Lord Jesus Christ both unclothing and clothing thee, inwardly, sensibly, and experimentally;—that thou mightest find him taking away thy sin, thy iniquities, thy unrighteousness, both within and without also, and filling thee, and clothing thee with his righteousness;—that so in God's sight, and by his putting on thee, and forming in thee, thou mightest find thy heart filled and covered with the nature, image and Spirit of his dear Son;—that thou mightest, indeed, put off the old man with his nature and deeds, and put on the new man, and know the renewing and new creating in Christ Jesus, in the spirit of thy mind;—and so, have a certain understanding of the Truth, as it is in Jesus, and as he manifests it, gives power to it, and causes it to work in thy heart. This is the desire of my soul for thee: the Lord guide thee to it, and remove all lets and hindrances out of thy way.

My dear and true love is to thy husband. The Lord manifest his pure, and living Truth in both your hearts, and gather both your minds thereunto, and make you one therein.

Thy Friend in Truth, who heartily wisheth well to thy soul, I. P.

GROVE PLACE,
17th of Ninth Month, 1673.

LETTER XXXII.

Encouragement to Faithfulness under Apprehension of Sufferings.

TO WIDOW HEMMINGS.

MY DEAR FRIEND,—I have not forgotten thee: but have often inquired after thee, and many times breathed for thee.

O my Friend look not *out* at what stands in the way; what if it look dreadfully as a lion, is not the Lord stronger than the mountains of prey? but look *in*, where the law of life is written, and the will of the Lord revealed, that thou mayest know what is the Lord's will concerning thee; and then show thyself a faithful daughter of Abraham, and be like Sarah, not terrified with any amazement. So soon as I had read thy letter, this arose in my heart to thee, as God's counsel, proper to thy state. Have no fellowship with the unfruitful works of darkness, but rather reprove them. Be not straitened in thy spirit, as fearing what thou shalt suffer for Christ's sake; or, as if God would not stand by thee, or carry thee through. Be thy sufferings as great as possible, yet he is faithful, who hath promised thee an hundred-fold in this life.

O! what can hurt thee, if thy God stand by thee? Be faithful to his testimony in thy place, and he will stand by thee. Take heed of joining with dead worships, which the seed of God in thee disowns, and cannot relish; but meekly and in fear, testify against, and abstain from, what thou feelest not to be of the Lord.

This was what was in my heart to thee at present in true and tender love, and in melting desires for thee, that the Lord may guide and preserve thee, and give thee of the Lamb's courage and strength, who by meekness and sufferings is now to conquer. What if the wicked nature, which is as a sea casting out mire and dirt, rage against thee? There is a river, a sweet, still, flowing river, the streams whereof will make glad thy heart. And, learn but in quietness and stillness to retire to the Lord, and wait upon him; in whom thou shalt feel peace and joy, in the midst of thy trouble from the cruel and vexatious spirit of this world. So, wait to know thy work and service to the Lord every day, in thy place and station; and the Lord make thee faithful therein, and thou wilt want neither help, support, nor comfort.

Thy Friend, in the truest, sincerest, and most constant love, I. P.

LONDON,
1st of Ninth Month, 1675.

LETTER XXXIII.

Exhortation Relative to the Christian Life and Travel.

TO DULCIBELLA LAITON.

DEAR FRIEND, — Concerning whom I feel a travail,— this is the sense of my heart in relation to thee.

There is a pure seed of life, which God hath sown in thee; O that it might come through, and come over all that is above it, and contrary to it! And for that end wait daily to feel it, and to feel thy mind subdued by it, and joined to it. Take heed of looking out, in the reasonings of thy mind, but dwell in the feeling sense of life; and then, that will arise in thee more and more, which maketh truly wise, and gives power, and brings into the holy authority and dominion of life. Many that have been long travelling, are now entering into their possessions and inheritance, which the Lord is daily enlarging in them, and to them. O that thy lot may be among them, inwardly witnessed and possessed by thee! Prize inward exercises, griefs, and troubles; and let faith and patience have their perfect work in them. O desire to be good, upright, and perfect in God's sight! and wait to feel the life, the Spirit, and power, which makes so. Come out of the knowledge and comprehension about things, into the feeling life; and let *that* be thy knowledge and wisdom, which thou receivest and retainest in the feeling life; and that will lead thee into the footsteps of the flock, without reasoning, consulting, or disputing.

O! wait to be taught and enabled by God to fetch right steps in thy travels; and to take up the cross and despise the shame in everything, wherein that wisdom, will, and mind, which is to be crucified, would be judge; for, it will judge amiss, and lead aside, if it be hearkened to by thee. The Lord show thee the snares and dangers to which thou art liable, and lead thee out of them; that whatever hindereth may be discovered to thee, and thy mind singly joined to that which discovereth, that so it may be removed out of the way; and all crooked things be made straight in thee, and the rough plain, and the high low, and the low high, and the weak and foolish strong and wise, and the wise and strong weak and foolish. O! wait to feel and understand my words, that thy conversation may be ordered aright by the power and wisdom of God;

and that thou mayest inwardly come to witness the glorious coming of Him, who is the salvation of God, and in whom thou shalt not fail to see the salvation of God.

Thou must be very low, weak, and foolish, that the seed may arise in thee to exalt thee, and become thy strength and wisdom; and thou must die exceedingly, again and again, more and more, inwardly and deeply! that thy life may spring up from the holy root and stock; and thou mayest be more and more gathered into it, spring up into it, and live alone in the life, virtue, and power thereof. The travel is long, the exercises many, the snares, temptations, and dangers many; and yet the mercy, relief, and help, is great also.

O! that thou mayest feel thy calling and election, thy sinking down, springing up, and establishment, in the pure seed, in the light and righteousness thereof over all; that thou mayest sing songs of degrees to the Redeemer of Israel, and mayest daily more and more partake of and rejoice in him, who is our joy, and the crown thereof.

Thy Friend, in the most sincere, tender love, I. P.

11th of Fifth Month, 1677.

LETTER XXXIV.

On Decay of "First Love," and a Hardened State through the Deceitfulness of Sin.

To George Winkfield.

Dear Friend,—Two things stick upon my heart, since our last short discourse at the window at King's, through my desire that it may go well with thee, and that thou mayest be right in God's sight.

One is, that saying of thine about thy love to Truth

and Friends, as if it were as great as ever it was. Now, I entreat thee to weigh this thing, and to wait on God to know, whether it be really so or no; which thou mayest understand by this: if thou be as really desirous, and waitest, as singly, to know and obey the commands of truth as ever, then, thy love to it is as great as formerly in its first heat and zeal; otherwise, not. "He that hath my commandments and keepeth them," saith Christ, "he it is that loveth me." John, xiv. 21. And hereby, we know that our knowledge of him is true and living; because it leads, quickens, and enables us to the keeping of his commandments. 1 John, ii. 3.

The other is, that thou saidst, thy heart is not hardened. O! consider this seriously; for, if thy heart be hardened, and thou not sensible of it, thy estate is exceeding dangerous. Now, if the Lord by his power hath preserved thee out of that which hardens the heart; then, without doubt, thy heart is not hardened: but, if the enemy hath tempted thee to let in reasonings into thy mind, against anything that is indeed of God; and thou hast run into any practices contrary to Truth, and justifiest them in thy heart, from any reasonings and thoughts the enemy hath suggested to and strengthened thy mind in; then, without doubt, thy heart is so far hardened. It is impossible for thee, or any one else, to let in that which hardens, and not be hardened.

O! mind that precious advice of the Apostle, Heb. iii. 13. Mark, sin deceives, lust deceives, desire after anything that pleaseth the flesh, and is desirable to the worldly nature, deceives. And, whoever is deceived by it, and lets it in, (mind, he doth not let it in as an evil thing, but is deceived by it,) his heart is hardened against that, which would show him the evil of it, and draw his mind from it, if he did in truth hearken to it, and were not lulled asleep in the deceit. And, there must be a daily watching against that which deceives and hardens, as the apostle there adviseth them to exhort one another unto, lest the enemy at any time catch any of them in the snare of sin, and so harden them.

Now, he that would not provoke the Lord to give him up to full hardness, must take heed of the degrees thereof; and happy is he who so doth. O, G. W.! consider, as before the Lord, whether thy walking be answerable to truth, so far as thou knowest truth; and whether thou art willingly ignorant of anything, which the good God is willing and ready to give thee the knowledge of, that thou mayest take more liberty to the flesh in that, which the life of Truth, if felt, would soon condemn and draw from.

This is in most sincere love to thee, from him who hath always been thy Friend. I. P.

11th of Twelfth Month, 1677.

LETTER XXXV.

Propositions Relating to the Truth and Substance of Religion.

To Sir William Drake (so styled).

First. There is a God, a holy, righteous, living, powerful God, who made heaven and earth, and all things therein; and, at last, made man in his own image, and set him over the works of his hands, to have dominion, and to rule in his wisdom and power over them; and to guide, order, and make use of them, to the glory of Him that made them. Now, in this state, God was pleased and took delight in the works of his hands, and in man above all.

Secondly. Man, sinning against his Maker, lost this image, which was his glory, and became brutish in understanding, and an enemy to God in his mind, and liable to the wrath of God's holy and righteous nature.

Thirdly. There is no reconciliation to be had between God and man any more, but by the change of this nature in man: for, God is unchangeable, he is light, he is life, he is holiness unchangeable; and will never be reconciled to, or have fellowship with darkness, with that which is dead and unholy,—which man in his fallen estate is, until he be begotten again to God, changed and renewed from his evil and sinful nature, into a good and holy nature, and till he be turned from evil works, and know what it is to be the workmanship of God, created anew unto good works.

Fourthly. Nothing can produce this change in man, but the spirit and power of Christ, but the grace and truth which is by Jesus Christ. Therefore, a man had need be sure that he receive this Spirit and power, and that he feel the operative, changing virtue of it, and be really changed thereby, being created anew, begotten anew to God, in the holiness and righteousness of Truth, a son and servant to the living God; — or he can never know what belongs to true reconciliation with God, and to fellowship with Him in the light and life of his Son.

Fifthly. All the religions and professions upon the face of the earth, which fall short of this Spirit, life, and power, and wherein this new creation in Christ Jesus is not witnessed, nor power received to abstain from what is evil, and become sons to God, — are not the pure, powerful, gospel religion, wherein the divine virtue and power of life operates; but, that which men in the earthly wisdom have formed without life. And, all religions that have but a form of godliness, and not the power, are to be turned away from, and witnessed against, by such as are called forth to be witnesses to the true, gospel religion and way of worship, which stands in Spirit, life, and power.

Sixthly. This religion and worship, which stands in Spirit, life, and power, is the religion and worship, which Christ set up about sixteen hundred years ago. John iv. 23, 24. 1 Cor. iv. 20. Rom. vi. 4. And, this is the religion which God hath revived and set up again, as they that receive the gospel now preach it; and, believing in the power, which is both outwardly testified of, and also inwardly revealed, they have the witness of it in their own hearts. Rev. xiv. 6, 7. 1 John, v. 10, 11, 12. Isai. liii. 1. O how sweet are these Scriptures, when they are rightly read and rightly understood, the Lord giving the right understanding, and leading into the true experience of them!

FRIEND,—Thou expressed to one of my youngest sons, as he related to me, that thou hadst a desire I should visit thee, that thou mightst have some discourse with me about religion. That is the most profitable kind of discourse that can be, if it be ordered in the fear of the Lord, and in a weighty sense and dread of him. I am very serious in reference to religion, and would not therein mistake or miscarry, by any means; and, if I might be helpful to thee, or to any man, as to the truth and power of religion, it would be matter of gladness to my heart, and of praising and blessing the Lord, in the sense of his stretching forth his hand towards the saving of any. Now, that our meeting and discourse may be the more solemn and advantageous, I have sent thee a few plain propositions to consider of; which I do not only find signified of in the Scriptures, but the Lord hath also written them on my heart; and, if they be plain to thee, and thou be also in the serious sense of them, it may tend towards the making of our discourse the more easy and profitable.

These are the main things; and he that is rightly grounded, I mean, in the true and sensible experience of them in his heart, cannot miss of God's guidance to make a safe and happy progress therein; he daily waiting upon the Lord, to be taught and led by Him, further and further, into the life, Spirit, and power of Truth; so that, he shall be taught of God to know his Son Jesus, and the freedom which is by the Truth as it is in Jesus, daily more and more; which it is my soul's sincere and single desire, that thou, thy wife, and family, may be experiencers and happy partakers of.

O what a glorious state was man once in, before his transgressing the holy law of God! but, when he sinned, how did he fall short of the glory of God! Yet, as he hears His voice and follows Him, that leads out of sin into the image of God, into the holiness and righteousness of Truth; how is he brought back by the Lord, and how doth he return, in the blessed leadings of God's blessed Spirit, into the glory of God again! Read 2 Cor. iii. 18; and, O that thou mayest livingly and sensibly know what it means!

I remain an acknowledger of thy kindness, and a desirer for thee, that thou mayest obtain from God the knowledge of himself and his Son, which is experienced, by them that receive it, to be, indeed, life eternal.

I. P.

This was written in true love and good-will, and in the fear of the Lord, and in the springings and openings of his life in my heart.

19th of Fifth Month, 1678.

LETTER XXXVI.

Concerning the Seed of the Kingdom.

To S. W.

DEAR FRIEND, — I ever had a love to thee, and a deep sense of the serious work of God upon thy heart, and the upright desires of thy soul after Him. And, that the Lord should yet preserve thee alive, in the midst of so great and languishing weakness, is wonderful in my eye, and, I hope, hath a tendency of some honour to his name, and good to thee. I have often inquired of late concerning thee, and was glad to understand what I inquired after, by a letter from thy own hand; upon reading whereof, in the retired sense of my heart, I felt love arise to thee, and breathings to the Lord for thee; and, O! that thou mayest fully feel, and be joined to the seed of life, the seed of the kingdom, which our Lord Jesus Christ, in the days of his flesh, did not disdain to be a preacher of.

O my dear Friend! let not any part of thy life lie in notions above the seed, but let it all lie in the seed itself, in thy waiting upon the Lord for its arisings in thee, and in thy feeling its arisings. O what becomes of flesh, and self, and self-righteousness, when this lives in the heart! My religion, which I now daily bless my God for, began in this seed; which, when I first felt, and discerningly knew from the Lord, my cry to him was, O this is it I have longed after and waited for! O unite my soul to thee in this forever! this is thy Son's gift from thee, thy Son's grace, thy Son's Truth, thy Son's life, thy Son's Spirit! I desire no more, than to be made nothing in myself, that this may be all in me: and, what I meet with and witness here, what I feel the Lord Jesus Christ to be made to me here, none knows, or possibly can know, but they that have felt the pure power of the Spirit of life, and have been led by it into the same holy and blessed experience.

Ah! sin hath no share here, in this blessed seed; but is excluded, by the life and power which is stronger than it. Here, Christ is formed in the soul, of a truth; here, the black garments of unrighteousness, yea, of man's righteousness too, are put off, and the white raiment put on; here, the holy image is brought forth in the heart, even the image of the dear Son, which partakes of the divine nature of the Father; here, the soul is new created in Christ Jesus; here, is no deceit in any kind met with, but only truth from God, even the true life, light, virtue, power, of the Lord Jesus Christ, as livingly felt in the heart, and as effectually operating there, as ever the power of sin did. O! that thou mightst daily discern this, and feel this to grow up in thee more and more, and die to all notions, even of the heavenly things themselves, out of this; that thy soul may fully live in the life, Spirit, and power of the Lord Jesus Christ; and nothing but his life, Spirit, and power, may live in thee; to the glory of God the Father, and to the great joy and gladdening of thy heart in his presence! Amen.

Thy Friend, in the true, sincere love of the heavenly, everlasting seed. I. P.

13th of Twelfth Month, 1678.

LETTER XXXVII.

Comfort and Counsel under Affliction.

To the Lady Conway.

Dear Friend,— In tender love, and in a sense of thy sore afflictions and exercises, I do most dearly salute thee; desiring for thee, that the work of the Lord in thy heart may not be interrupted by any devices of the enemy; but, that it may go on and prosper in thee, in the springing up of the pure seed of life in thy heart, and in the powerful overturning, by the mighty arm of the Lord, of all that is contrary thereto in thee. O that thou mayest daily feel that holy birth of life, which is begotten by the Father, and lives by faith in him! — I say, O that thou mayest daily feel it living in thee, when temptations and trials on every hand increase — feel the birth of life, which will cry to the Father, "Lord, increase my faith!"

Though sorrows, heaviness, and faintings of heart ever so much increase; yet, if thy faith increase also, it will bear thee up in the midst of them. I would fain have it go well with thee, and that thou mightst not want the Reprover, in any thing that is to be reproved in thee; nor the Comforter, in any respect wherein thy soul wants comfort; nor the holy Counsellor and Adviser, in any strait or difficulty which the wise and tender God orders to befall thee.

Ah! that thou mightst come to feel the daily wasting of sin and death, and the daily springing of life and holiness in thy heart. The pearl is worth thousands of worlds, with the greatest earthly glory and pleasure imaginable. O that thou mayest be taught of God to discern it more and more, and to buy it, and to come into the enjoyment and possession of it! The Lord manifest Zion more and more to thee, and show thee the glory of it, and set thy feet towards it; and put into thy heart to seek of him the way to it, renewing thee more and more in the spirit of thy mind, whereby the way comes clearly to be discerned, and faithfully walked in; that thou mayest witness, daily, the everlasting covenant of life and peace, even the sure mercies of David.

The desire of my soul is, that thy afflictions, which how grievous soever, yet are but momentary, may fit thee for, and work out an eternal weight of glory, for thy soul to inherit in another world, forever.

I remain a sympathizer with thee in thy sufferings; who desires all the advantage and blessings from the God of my life, may come to thee, which hardships, temptations, and trials, prepare the heart and make way for. I. P.

14th of Twelfth Month, 1678.

POSTSCRIPT.

My dear Friend,—Some time after writing the foregoing, this arose in me to thee. If the Lord, in thy waiting upon him, to search and try thy heart and ways, shall please to show thee any thing amiss therein; mind this counsel on my heart to thee. Be not looking at it too much, on the one hand, or excusing it, on the other hand; but sink down beneath thyself, retiring thither, where thou mayest receive from the Lord true judgment concerning it, and also strength against it. And know this, in the holy experience; that thou must be weakened by the Lord, and be contented in or with thy weak and distressed estate, if thou wouldst receive mercy and strength from him. And the more thou art weakened and distressed, the more thou art fitted for, and the more abundantly shalt thou partake of, his mercy and strength; waiting upon him in the meek, quiet, patient, and resigned spirit, which he will not fail to work thy mind into; that, in the issue of all, thou mayest reap the quiet fruits of righteousness and heavenly peace from his hand. Amen, so be it from the Lord to thy soul!

LETTER XXXVIII.

On the Benefit of Chastening by Afflictions.

To the Lady Conway.

Dear Friend,— As I was lately retired in spirit and waiting upon the Lord, having a sense on me of thy long, sore, and deep affliction and distress; there arose a Scripture in my heart to lay before thee, namely, Heb. xii. 5, 6, 7, which, I entreat thee, to call for a Bible, and hear read, before thou proceedest to what follows.

O my Friend! after it hath pleased the Lord in tender mercy to visit us, and turn our minds from the world and ourselves towards him, and to beget and nourish that which is pure and living, of himself, in us; yet, notwithstanding this, there remains somewhat at first, yea, and perhaps for a long time, which is to be searched out by the light of the Lord, and brought down and subdued by his afflicting hand. When there is, indeed, somewhat of an holy will formed in the day of God's power; and the soul, in some measure, begotten and brought forth to live to God, in the heavenly wisdom; yet, all the earthly will and wisdom is not thereby presently removed: but, there are hidden things, of the old nature and spirit, still remaining; which, perhaps, appear not, but sink inward into their root, that they may save their life; which, man cannot possibly find out in his own heart, but as the Lord reveals them to him. But, how doth the Lord find them out? O consider! his "fire is in Zion, and his furnace in Jerusalem." By his casting into the furnace of affliction, the fire searcheth. The deep, sore, distressing affliction, which rends and tears the very inwards, finds out both the seed and the chaff, purifying the pure gold and consuming the dross; and then, at length, the quiet state is witnessed, and the quiet fruit of righteousness brought forth, by the searching and consuming nature and operation of the fire. O that thy soul may be tried unto victory over all that is not of the pure life in thee! and, that thou mayest wait to feel the pure seed, or measure of life in thee and die into the seed, feeling death unto all that is not of the seed in thee! and, that thou mayest feel life, healing, refreshment, support, and comfort from the God of thy life, in the seed; — and nowhere else, nor at any time, but as the Lord pleaseth to administer it to thee there. Oh! the Lord guide thee daily, and keep thy mind to him; at least, looking towards the holy place of the springing of his life and power in thy heart. Look unto him. Help, pity, salvation, will arise in his due time; but, it will not arise from any thing thou canst do or think; and faith will spring and patience be given, and hope in the tender Father of mercy, and a meek and quiet spirit will be witnessed; and the Lamb's nature springing up and opening in thee, from his precious seed, which will excel in nature, kind, degree, and virtue, all the faith, patience, hope, meekness, &c., which thou, or any else, otherwise can attain unto. O! look not at thy pain or sorrow, how great soever; but look from them, look off them, look beyond them, to the Deliverer! whose power is over them, and whose loving, wise, and tender Spirit is able to do thee good by them. And, if the *outward* afflictions work out an exceeding weight of glory, O what shall the *inward* do for those, who are humbly, brokenly, and faithfully exercised before the Lord by them! O! wait to feel the seed, and the cry of thy soul in the breathing life of the seed, to its Father, with its sweet, kindly, and natural subjection to him. And wait for the risings of the power in thy heart, in the Father's seasons, and for faith in the power; that thou mayest feel inward healing, of all the inward wounds which the Lord makes in thy soul, through his love to thee for thy good.

If thou wilt receive the kingdom that cannot be shaken, thou must wait to have that discovered in thee, which may be shaken; and the Lord arising terribly to shake the earth, and it removed out of its place as a cottage, and the heavens also rolled up like a scroll. And, while the Lord is doing this, he will be hiding thee in the hollow of his hand, (thy mind still retiring to the seed,) and will, in these troublesome and dismal times, inwardly be forming the new heavens and the new earth, wherein, when they are brought forth and established, dwells righteousness. The Lord lead thee, day by day, in the right way, and keep thy mind stayed upon him, in whatever befalls thee; that the belief of his love and hope in his mercy, when thou art at the lowest ebb, may keep up thy head above the billows; and that thou mayest go on in the disciple's state, learning righteousness and holiness of Him, who teacheth to deny and put off unholiness and unrighteousness, and to know, embrace, and put on newness of life, and the holiness and righteousness thereof.

The Lord God of my life be with thee, preserving and ordering thy heart for the great day of his love and mercy; which will come in the appointed season, when the heart is fully exercised and fitted by the Lord for it, and will not tarry.

I. P.

LETTER XXXIX.

On being Ingrafted into Christ, being Preserved Alive in Him, and Growing up in Him in all Things.

To S. W.

Dear S. W.,—I have ever had a love to thee, and have many times been filled with earnest desires for thee; that thou mayest know the Lord in his own pure teachings, and travel into, and dwell in, the fulness of the kingdom of his dear Son; and that thou mayest be blessed with spiritual blessings in heavenly places in Christ.

In order to arrive here, thou must wait to know God and Christ, in the mystery of their Spirit, life, and power; and, by that Spirit, life, and power, find the secrets of the mystery of darkness searched and purged out, and the mystery of godliness opened and established in thy heart, in the room thereof;—Christ formed inwardly; the soul formed, yea, and created inwardly anew in him; a real transplanting into his death, and a real feeling of his springing and rising life; and an experience of the sweetness, safety, and virtue of his rising life;—and daily to be sensible, what it is to lie down in the holy, quickening power, and to rise again in the risings of the life and power; and so, be only what thou art made and preserved to be, in the light, grace, life, virtue, and power of the Lord Jesus Christ; and to feel him remove any thing that is unrighteous, and clothing thee with his pure life, Spirit, and righteousness.

Oh! this is indeed the pure, precious, living knowledge of the Lord Jesus Christ; which all the outward knowledge tends to lead to, and is comprehended and ended in.

This is the excellency of the knowledge of Jesus Christ our Lord, which Paul was so ravished with, and counted all things but dross and dung for. Now, that thou mayest obtain this, mind the inward appearance, the root, the fountain, the rock within, the living stone within, — its openings, its springings, its administering life to thee; and take heed of running into the outwardness of openings, concerning the heavenly things; but keep, O learn to keep, O mind to keep in the inwardness of life within! This is the everlasting habitation of the birth, which is begotten and brought forth, bred up and kept alive, alone by the presence, power, and operation of the living Spirit; — and the Lord Jesus is that Spirit, as really as he was man, even the holy, heavenly, immaculate, spotless Lamb of God. And, in this state, life reigns in the heart, and the horn of the Holy One is exalted, the head of the serpent crushed, yea, Satan trod under foot, by the God of peace; who would have his children dwell in the sweetness and fulness of the gospel, — in the peace, life, righteousness, and joy of his blessed Spirit and power.

Oh! who would not desire after, and wait for, and walk with the Lord, towards the obtaining and possessing of these things? All the promises, in Christ, are yea and amen. Inward victory is promised; the inward presence of God is promised; God's dwelling and walking in the soul is promised; Christ supping with the soul, and the soul with him, is promised; putting the law in the heart, and writing it there; putting the pure, living fear into it; yea, also putting the holy, powerful Spirit into it, which can cause it to walk in God's ways, and to keep his righteous judgments and do them: and He is able to do this work in the heart; for, what cannot the spirit of judgment and burning consume and burn up within? Yea, all these things are promised. He can cause the soul to rejoice in the Lord, and work righteousness, and to remember the

Lord in his ways, as some were taught and enabled to do in former times, Isai. lxiv. 5; yea, he can bring into the way of holiness, the King of glory's highway, into which no unclean thing can enter, and [can] keep undefiled therein; and, they that are kept undefiled therein, taste the sweetness, blessedness, purity, and holy pleasure thereof.

I would fain have my own soul and thine, and all the real, serious, faithful people of God experience, and be able to say with David, that which, after his many trials, afflictions, troubles, temptations, and grievous fall, he was able to say, in relation to his walking with the Lord, "For I have kept the ways of the Lord, and have not wickedly departed from my God. For all his judgments were before me, and I did not put away his statutes from me. I was also upright before him, and I kept myself from iniquity." Psal. xviii. 21, 22, 23. Oh! this is precious, when a man comes to know his iniquity, wherein the enemy's strength lies as to him, and whereby the enemy hath most advantage to tempt and gain ground on him, brought down and subdued. Certainly, when one gains strength from God, to overcome the enemy here, and to keep out of this, he comes very near to the keeping of himself, in and by virtue of the Holy Spirit and power, so as the wicked one cannot touch him, nor draw him to touch any unclean thing. If that be indeed put off, wherein the enemy's power lies; and that indeed put on, wherein the strength of the Lord Jesus is revealed; and the soul be really in the possession of, and abide in this state; how can it but be strong in the Lord, and in the power of his might; and witness the good pleasure of the goodness of the Lord fulfilling, and the work of faith going on with power, daily, more and more; a little measure whereof, kept to, removes the mountains inwardly, and gives strength over the enemy. How, then, doth it increase and grow up in life and virtue, and in a sensible understanding and experience of the name of the Lord Jesus! Is there not, in this state, a feeling of remission of sins, a feeling of redemption, a feeling of reconciliation, a feeling of oneness with God in Christ, a feeling of God being the salvation, strength, and song, and a trusting in him, and not being afraid? Isai. xii. 2. Is there not a being careful in nothing, but in every thing making the requests to God, by prayer and supplication, with thanksgiving, in that Spirit and holy breath of life, which the Father cannot deny; and so, the peace of God, which passeth all understanding, keeping the heart and mind through Christ Jesus?

O my Friend! there is an ingrafting into Christ, a being formed and new created in Christ, a living and abiding in him, and a growing and bringing forth fruit through him unto perfection. O mayest thou experience all these things! and, that thou mayest so do, wait to know life, the springings of life, the separations of life inwardly, from all that evil which hangs about it, and would be springing up and mixing with it, under an appearance of good; that life may come to live fully in thee, and nothing else. And so, sink very low, and become very little, and know little; yea, know no power to believe, act, or suffer any thing for God, but as it is given thee, by the springing grace, virtue, and life of the Lord Jesus. For, grace is a spiritual, inward thing and holy seed, sown by God, springing up in the heart. People have got a notion of grace, but know not the thing. Do not thou matter the notion, but feel the thing; and know thy heart more and more ploughed up by the Lord, that his seed's grace may grow up in thee more and more, and thou mayest daily feel thy heart as a garden, more and more enclosed, watered, dressed, and delighted in by him.

This is a salutation of love from thy Friend in the Truth, which lives and changes not. I. P.

27th of Twelfth Month, 1678.

LETTER XL.

Counsel to One Tossed as with Tempests.

Dear Friend, — Thy condition cannot but be weak and dark, until the light of life arise in thee, and the power of the Lord overcome and subdue the power of darkness, which strives to keep the seed of life in the grave and bonds of death.

It is the Lord's mercy, to give thee breathings after life, and cries unto him against that which oppresseth thee; and happy wilt thou be, when he shall fill thy soul with that, which he hath given thee to breathe after. Only, let thy heart wait for strength to trust him with the season; for, his long tarrying is thy salvation, and the destruction of those enemies, which, while any strength remains in them, will never suffer thee and thy God to dwell uninterruptedly together. Therefore, they must needs die, and He who hath the power to kill them, knows the way; which, to the appearing of thy sense, will be as if he meant to kill the life of *thy soul,* and not of *them.* But, lie still under his hand, and be content to be unable to judge concerning his ways and workings in thy heart; and thou shalt at times feel an inward leaven of life from his Holy Spirit, whereby he will change and transform thy spirit into his likeness, in some measure, for the present. And, though it be quickly gone again, and the whole land so overspread with enemies, that there is no sight of redemption or the Redeemer left, but the soul in a worse condition than before; yet, be not troubled: for, if troubles abound, and there be tossing, and storms, and tempests, and no peace, nor any thing visible left to support; yet, lie still, and sink beneath, till a secret hope stir, which will stay the heart in the midst of all these: until the Lord administer comfort, who knows how and what relief to give to the weary traveller, that knows not where it is, nor which way to look, nor where to expect a path.

How shall I speak to thee, how shall I mourn over thee? O that thou mayest be upheld to the day of God's mercy to thy soul! and be gathered, out of all such knowledge, as thou canst comprehend or contain in what is natural, into the feeling of life; that thou mayest know the difference, between living upon somewhat received from God, and, having God live with thee, and administer life to thee at his pleasure; thou being kept in the nothingness, emptiness, poverty, and perfect resignation of spirit.

This counsel is to thee, through a poor, weak vessel,

I. P.

LETTER XLI.

Encouragement under Trials incident to bearing the Cross of Christ.

WHO is able to undergo the crosses and afflictions, either inward or outward, which befall those, whom God draws out of the spirit of this world and path of destruction, into the way of eternal rest and peace? Yet, the Lord is able to uphold that which feels its weakness, and daily waits on him for support, under the heaviness of the cross.

I know, dear heart, thy outward trials cannot but be sharp and bitter; and I know also, that the Lord is able to sustain thee under them, and cause thee to stand thy ground; that thou give not advantage to that spirit, which hereby would draw from the Lord, and from the way of life and happiness. O that thou couldst dwell in the knowledge and sense of this! even, that the Lord beholds thy sufferings with an eye of pity; and is able, not only to uphold thee under them, but also to do thee good by them; and to bring forth that life and wisdom in thee by means thereof, to which he will give dominion over that spirit which grieves and afflicts thee, in his due season. Therefore, grieve not at thy lot, be not discontented, look not out at the hardness of thy condition; but, when the storm and matters of vexation are sharp, look up to Him who can give meekness and patience, can lift up thy head over all, and cause thy life to grow, and be a gainer by all. If the Lord God did not help us by his mighty arm, how often should we fall and perish! and if the Lord God help thee proportionably to thy condition of affliction and distress, thou wilt have no cause to complain, but to bless his name. He is exceedingly good, and gracious, and tender-hearted, and doth not despise the afflictions of the afflicted, for his name's sake, in any kind.

This is in tender love towards thee, with breathings to my Father, that his pleasant plant may not be crushed in thee, by the foot of pride and violence; but may overgrow it, and flourish the more because of it.

From thy truly loving Friend in the Truth, and for the Truth's sake, I. P.

LETTER XLII.

On being Offended with those who fall into Temptation.

It is of the infinite mercy and compassion of the Lord, that his pure love visiteth any of us; and, it is by the preservation thereof alone, that we stand. If He leave us at any time, but one moment, what are we? and who is there that provoketh Him not to depart? Let *him* throw the first stone at him that falls.

In the Truth itself, in the living power and virtue, there is no offence; but, that part which is not perfectly redeemed, hath still matter for the temptation to work upon, and may be taken in the snare. Let him that stands, take heed lest he fall; and, in the bowels of pity, mourn over and wait for the restoring of him that is fallen. That which is so apt to be offended, is the same with that which falls. O! do not reason in the high-mindedness, against any that turn aside from the pure Guide; but fear, lest the unbelieving and fleshly wise part get up in thee also. O know the weakness of the creature in the withdrawings of the life! and the strength of the enemy in that hour! and the free grace and mercy which alone can preserve! and thou wilt rather wonder that *any* stand, than that *some* fall.

When the pure springs of life open in the heart, immediately the enemy watcheth his opportunity to get entrance; and many times finds entrance soon after — the soul little fearing or suspecting him, having lately felt such mighty, unconquerable strength; and yet, how often then doth he get in, and smite the life down to the ground! and, what may he not do with the creature, unless the Lord graciously help!

Oh! great is the mystery of godliness, the way of life narrow, the travel to the land of rest long, hard, and sharp; it is easy miscarrying, it is easy stepping aside, at any time; it is easy losing the Lord's glorious presence; unless the defence about it, by his Almighty arm, be kept up. There is a time for the Lord's taking down the fence from his own vineyard, because of transgression, and then, the wild boar may easily break in. Ah! who tastes not of this, in some measure? and what hinders, that he taste not of it in a greater measure?

Ah! turn in from the fleshly wisdom and reasonings, unto the pure river of life itself; and wait there, to have that judged which hath taken offence; lest, if it grow stronger in thee, it draw thee from the life, which alone is able to preserve thee; and so, thou also fall!

This is in dear love to thee: retire from that part which looketh out, and feel the inward virtue of that which can restore and preserve thee. I. P.

LETTER XLIII.

The Mind may be stayed in Peace amidst the Enemy's Accusations.

To Widow Hemmings.

My dear Friend, — Whom I have always truly and faithfully loved as in the sight of the Lord, and to whom my love in the Lord still continues.

Since I heard of thy illness and weakness, by M. S., whom I desired to visit thee, I have had an earnest desire to see thee; and have been considering how to effect it, but cannot with any convenience at present, as my Friend T. E., the bearer hereof, can further inform thee. But, the desires of my heart to the God of my life, are, that he would give thee a visit in his tender pity, and guide and help thee to stay thy mind upon himself, in his most precious Truth; of which he hath not only given thee a taste, but, many times, a full sense and experience.

O my dear Friend! that nothing might come between thy soul and God's Truth; that thy comfort, peace, and joy, might be full, and that thou mightst lay down thy head quietly in the bosom of Him, who loves thee, and accepts the sincere desires of thy heart towards him; as I have always told thee, and as is still true concerning thee. Mind not temptations nor accusations, nor the many noises the enemy will make in thee and against thee, to the Lord; but, wait to feel Truth and life springing in thy heart from the holy well, and to hear the still voice of the Spirit of the Lord; and he will testify his love to thee, and speak peace.

Oh! the tender bowels of my heavenly Father relieve thee; and gather thee inwardly in thither, and preserve thee there, where the enemy cannot break in upon thee. Look not upon thy sins, even since thou hast known the Truth, wherein thou mightst have met with strength against, and preservation from sin, and have been in some measure blessed by the Lord; but, wait to feel somewhat inwardly, wherein God appears and breathes, and gathers, and receives — and eases of the loads, fears, doubts, troubles, temptations, and accusations, &c.; and the Lord God of my life and tender mercies, which he hath made sure to my soul in the everlasting covenant, give thee solid peace and consolation in the Son of his love, through the measure of his grace and Truth springing in thy heart, and staying thy mind upon him.

O! feel the seed, and the faith which springs from the seed, which gives victory over the enemy, and all his mysterious workings in the heart.

Thy Friend, in the truest and most sincere love, I. P.

LETTER XLIV.

On Resisting, and on Receiving God's Spirit; also on Redemption by Christ Jesus.

To Nathaniel Stonar.

It is a dangerous thing to resist God's Spirit; and yet very easy for a man so to do, who hath not received a true understanding from the Lord, nor is acquainted with the leadings and outgoings of Him, who is pure. He that is tender and truly sensible, may discern when he resisteth, when he quencheth, or when he grieveth the Spirit of the Lord; but, he that is not truly enlightened, nor in the true sense, cannot do so. The Scribes and Pharisees, who were interpreters of the law, and very strict in outward observations and ordinances, &c., who blamed their fathers for killing the prophets, and said, if they had been in the days of the prophets, they would not have dealt so with them as their fathers did; yet, concerning these, said Stephen, "Ye stiff-necked, and uncircumcised in heart and ears, ye do also resist the Holy Ghost; as your fathers did, so do ye." For, till the stiff will and stiff wisdom be brought down in a man, he cannot but resist God's Spirit, and fight for his notions and practices, according to his apprehensions of the letter, against the testimony of God's Spirit and power.

Paul, who walked, according to the letter of the law, blameless, yet resisted the Spirit which gave forth the law. He must know the Spirit, receive the Spirit, live in the Spirit, walk in the Spirit, and not fulfil the lusts of the flesh, who would be found not resisting God's Spirit. He who is indeed turned to the redeeming arm, to Christ the power of God, and gathered into the power, and dwelleth in the Spirit and power of the Lord Jesus, and is taught and led by Him from path to path, and from pasture to pasture, as the Lamb, the Shepherd, goes before and guides him; — he is preserved from grieving the Holy Spirit, which moves and draws, instructs and quickens, all that are born of God. But he that is only in the letter, and in the form of godliness, out of the inward life and power, he is of that birth, mind, nature, and spirit, which cannot but resist God's Spirit. He knoweth not, he heedeth not, His drawings, His movings, His light, His life — the way thereof, — either in his own heart, or in the hearts of others; and so, walks in a way of rebelling against and resisting Him, who is the only Saviour and Redeemer of the soul. See Job, xxix. 3, 4, and xxiv. 13. O that thou mightst learn to wait aright to learn these things! and come into the true sense and discerning of the Spirit and power of the Lord, that thou mightst not any more resist it, neither in thyself, nor in others.

The Lord open thy heart, and lay thy spirit low before him; that thou mayest come into a right sense and judgment, concerning the state of thine own soul; and mayest experience the Lord manifesting things to thee, as indeed they are. I. P.

15th of Fifth Month, 1671.

POSTSCRIPT.

O Friend! — Wait to receive an understanding from the Lord, that thou mayest come truly to know, whether thou hast resisted God's Spirit, or no; that thou lose not the advantage of making peace with thy adversary, while thou art in the way with him.

I would not have thee deceived about that virtue, life, and power which redeems the soul. For, there is no other Redeemer besides the Lord Jesus Christ, and he redeems by the grace of his Spirit, and by faith in his blood, which cleanseth from sin; which blood is sprinkled on the consciences of those that believe, — and that, not in the darkness, but in the light; as is said in 1 John, i. 7 "If we walk in the light, as He is in the light, we have fellowship one with another, and the blood of Jesus Christ, his Son, cleanseth us from all sin." Under the law, the blood of bulls and goats was sprinkled outwardly, on the outward things, which sanctified to the purifying of the outward things; but, under the gospel, the blood of the Lamb is sprinkled inwardly, upon inward and heavenly things. See Heb. ix. 13, 14, and 22, 23, and ch. x. 22, and xii. 24. O that thou didst truly and understandingly know the difference, between *thy own* applying Christ's blood to thyself, *and the Lamb's sprinkling it upon thee, and washing thy soul therein!* Rev. i. 5, and also, between *thy own* believing, according to thy own apprehension of things, and *his giving thee to believe* in the light of his Spirit! and, between *thy own* praying in thy own spirit, and *his giving thee to pray* in his Spirit!

Ah! the truth of our God is precious! the knowledge of his Christ precious! It is a precious thing, to have the Son revealed by the Father to the renewed mind. God himself is the teacher, in the new covenant, of all the true disciples of our Lord Jesus Christ, and, O how do the teachings of his Spirit differ, from all the knowledge and learning men can attain unto of themselves! The Lord give thee the true understanding; and to know what it is to begin thy religion in his Spirit; and batter down and bring to nought the understanding in thee, which is not true; that thou mayest not find thy soul deeply deceived at last, as to the true knowledge of Christ and mysteries of God's kingdom, — and so, perish forever!

This, in very dear, true, and tender love, from him, who most sincerely and heartily wisheth well to thee, I. P.

17th of Fifth Month, 1671.

LETTER XLV.

Respecting some Snares of the Adversary to Distress the Soul.

To Bridget Atley.

Dear Friend,— I am sensible of thy sore travail and deep distress, and how hard it is for thee to meet with that which is comfortable and refreshing, and how easily again it is lost; and — whence it ariseth,— even, from the working of the enemy in a mystery of deceit in thy heart; wherein thou dost not perceive nor suspect him, but swallowest down his baits, and so he smites thee with his hook, and thereby draws thee back into the region of darkness; and then, entereth that part in thee which is in nature one with him, filling it with his wickedness; and then, laying loads of accusations upon thee, as if they were true. These are not strange things to the travellers after the Lord, but such as are usually met with in the like cases: but, if thy eye were made single and opened by the Lord, thou wouldst see those baits, and turn from that, which thou now so readily swallowest down; and so, avoid the stroke, and keep thy station, in the light and mercy of the Lord. Thou must not look so much at the evil that is nigh, but rather at that, which stands ready to pity and help,— and which hath pitied and helped thy distressed soul, and will pity and help it again. Why is there a mercy-seat, but for the sinner to look towards in time of need?

Neither must thou hearken to the questionings of the insnaring questioner: but, cleave to that which shuts them out, keeping to the sense of the love and mercy, when the Lord is kind and tender to thee. When the enemy entered thy habitation again, and broke thy rest, peace, and enjoyment of the Lord: again, an earnest desire after cleansing arose in thee; not from the life, but in the evil; this was also a means to rob thee of that, which, in its abiding and powerful operation, cleanseth the heart; and here, thou wouldst be limiting the Lord in his dealings, who worketh according to the counsel of his own will, and visiteth when and where he pleaseth. And thus the enemy having caught thee with his mysterious workings, he then draws thee into the pit of darkness, where the remembrance of life, and the sense of mercy and love, vanisheth; and there is no help for thee, by any thing thou canst do or think. But, be patient, till the Lord's tender mercy and love visit thee again; and then, look up to him against this and such like snares, which would come between thee and the appearance of the Lord's love; that thou mayest feel more of his abidings with thee, and of the sweet effects thereof. For, these things are not to destroy thee, but, to teach thee wisdom; which the Lord is able, through many exercises and sore trials, to bestow upon thee; which my soul will exceedingly rejoice to hear the tidings of; that thy heart may be rid of all that burdeneth, and filled with all it rightly desires after, in the proper season and goodness of the Lord: to whose wise ordering and tender mercy I commit thee, remaining, Thy faithful Friend,

I. P.

LETTER XLVI.

Weighty Counsel.

To Sir William Armorer (so styled).

Friend,—The weighty sense of an eternal condition after this life, hath been upon my heart from my childhood; and it is often with me, that I must give an account to God, when I pass out of this transitory world, of all things done in the body; and shall enter into eternal rest and blessedness, or eternal woe or misery.

This causeth me to call upon the Lord daily, for grace and wisdom from him; that my conscience, being cleansed through the blood of his Son, may be kept void of offence, both towards him and men. And truly, (I speak not boastingly, but in the fear of the Lord, and in the sense of his goodness and tender mercy to me,) my heart is preserved in love and innocency towards those, who most injuriously, and without provocation on my part, have taken away my liberty, for aught I know, for my whole lifetime. What thou further intendest towards me, the Lord knows, to whom I have committed my cause: but this is on my heart to express to thee, because, when I was with thee thou spakest words to this purpose, that *we wished thee hanged, or would be glad if thou wert hanged.* God, who knows my heart, is witness, that I wish thee no evil, neither to thee nor thy family; but wish, thou mayest avoid all such things, as may bring his wrath and curse upon thee, either in this world or the world to come.

And, friend, do not provoke the Lord by afflicting those that fear him; but, cease to do evil, learn to do well; and this will please the Lord, and is more acceptable to him, than all the worship that can be offered up to him, without this.

I have sent thee a little book, as a token of my love, desiring thee to peruse it seriously. O! do not endeavour to bring me into such a condition, as is there related. I have had greater light, in the way into which the Lord hath led me, than this man had; and, in that light, I have seen, that I ought not to swear, but to give the "Yea" and "Nay" of truth, which comes from the Christian nature, and is of far more certainty and assurance than swearing. For, the man that swears may easily break his oath, but he that keeps to the truth cannot alter his yea and nay, but it stands in the truth; and this our Lord and Master hath set above, and on the top of, and instead of swearing; which, if we should vary from and deny, we should deny him who hath taught us not to swear. Indeed, if we had not learnt it of the Lord, and if it was not by him required of us, we should rather swear than otherwise; for, we would very willingly give men satisfaction, in those particulars which they require us to swear about.

Friend, God hath given thee an immortal soul, and doth require of thee righteousness towards thy fellow-creatures, and temperance and moderation of spirit, and sensibleness of the judgment to come after this life. Thou art stricken in years, and thou hast but a little moment left remaining of thy time; and then, it will be determined concerning thy soul, what or how it shall be forever! Let the words of love, truth, and innocency from me, prevail upon thee to be serious, and to let in the sense and fear of God upon thy heart. Thou hast spent much time in serving man; O spend a little in serving and fearing God! There is somewhat, which is pure, of God, appointed by him to exercise the conscience towards him. Thou hast such a thing near thee. O that thou mightst know it, and be joined to it! for, till then, thou canst never truly serve nor fear the Lord; but, mayest spend thy time here in a vain show, and at last be judged and condemned by the Lord, and lie down in eternal sorrow; which, it is the desire of my heart, may not be thy portion from the hand of the Lord.

This is from a sufferer by thee, who never gave thee the least cause or provocation so to deal with me. I. P.

LETTER XLVII.

On an Unfaithful Profession of the Truth.

To Abraham Grimsden.

Friend, — Thou hast made some profession of Truth, and at times come amongst us; but, whether thou hast been changed thereby, and been faithful to the Lord in what has been made manifest to thee, belongs unto thee diligently to inquire. There is no safe dallying with Truth. He that puts his hand to the plough, must not look back at any thing of this world; but, take up the cross and follow Christ, in the single-hearted obedience, hating father, mother, goods, lands, wife, yea, all for His sake; or he is not worthy of Him. The good hand of the Lord is with his people, and he blesseth them both inwardly and outwardly; and, they that seek the kingdom of heaven, and the righteousness thereof, in the first place, have other things also added: but, they that neglect the kingdom, and are unfaithful to Truth, seeking the world before it, the hand of the Lord goes forth against them, and they, many times, miss of that also of the world, which they seek and labour for.

Truth is honourable. O! take heed of bringing a reproach upon it, by pretending to it, and yet, not being of it, in the pure sense and obedience, which it begets and brings forth in the hearts and lives of the faithful. But, if any be careless and unfaithful to what they are convinced of, and so, for the present, bring a reproach upon God's Truth, which is altogether innocent thereof; the Lord, in his due time, will wipe off that reproach from his Truth and people; but, the sorrow and burden will light upon themselves, which will be very bitter and heavy to them, in the day that the Lord shall visit them with his righteous judgments.

O consider rightly and truly! It had been better for thee, thou hadst never known Truth, nor been directed to the principle and path of righteousness; than, after direction thereto, to turn from the holy commandments, and deny obedience to the righteous One. The Lord give thee true sense and repentance, if it be his holy pleasure, and raise thee out of this world's spirit, to live to him in his own pure Spirit. It is easy to profess and make a show of Truth, but hard to come into it. It is very hard to the earthly mind, to part with that which must be parted with for it, before the soul can come to possess and enjoy it. Profession of truth, without the life and power, is but a slippery place, which men may easily slide from; nay, indeed, if men be not in the life and power, they can hardly be kept from that, which will stain their profession. The Lord, who searcheth the heart, knows how it is with thee: O consider thy ways, and fear before him, and take heed of taking his name in vain, for he will not hold such guiltless!

I am, in this, faithful and friendly to thy soul, desiring its eternal welfare, and that it may not forever perish from the presence and power of the Lord. I. P.

LETTER XLVIII.

Christ the Resurrection and the Life. On His Appearance in the Flesh, &c.

Friend, — God breathed into man the breath of life, and man thereby became a living soul to God, to whom by transgression he died. But Christ (who was before

Abraham, and, in due time, took up that body prepared by the Father,) is the resurrection and the life, who, from the Father, breathes life into man again, and so he comes to live again. And, man, being quickened by Christ, is to rise up from the dead, and travel with Christ into the land of the living. And, Christ is all to the believers, in whom dwells all fulness; the circumcision is in him, the baptism in him, and the righteousness, rest, and peace also; yea, in him are all the treasures of wisdom and knowledge; and, he is made of God, unto them that believe in him, wisdom, righteousness, sanctification, and redemption. Now, it is very precious to feel this; but, of little value to imagine or comprehend apprehensions about this. For, the end of words is to bring men to the thing; but, the Scribes and Pharisees, by their apprehensions upon the words given forth by the Spirit, missed of the thing: (though, they thought they missed not, but were blessed in the knowledge of the law, and they that knew not the law were cursed;) and the same spirit is alive in many that profess Truth now, who, by their understanding of Scripture words, are kept from the thing which the Scriptures testify of. What did Christ come in the flesh and suffer for, but to unite and reconcile to God? and, what is the antichristian way of erring from the Truth, but to cry up the appearance of Christ in the flesh, his sufferings, resurrection, ascension, &c., in that spirit, wherein the true union and reconciliation is not witnessed? If we receive the light, and walk in the light, as God is in the light, then have we a share in his Son's death and atonement, and his blood cleanseth from unrighteousness; but not otherwise.

O that all who truly desire salvation, might know the way hither, and receive that from God, which cleanseth and keepeth clean. Amen. I. P.

LETTER XLIX.

To one who sent a Paper of Richard Baxter's.

Dear Friend, — Whom I often remember with love and meltings of heart; desiring of God, that thou mayest enjoy, in this world, what of his presence and pure life he judgeth fit for thee, and that thy soul may, after this life, sit down in rest and peace with him forever.

I received from thee a paper of Richard Baxter's, sent, I believe, in love; and, in love, am I pressed to return unto thee my sense thereof. It seems to me very useful and weighty so far as it goes; but, indeed, there is a great defect in it, in not directing sinners to that principle of life and power, wherein and whereby they may do that, which he exhorteth them to do. For, how can they come to a true sensibility or repentance, or join in covenant with God through Christ, until they know and receive somewhat from God, wherein it may be done? O my dear Friend! that he, and thou, and all who in any measure turn from this world, and do indeed desire life eternal, might know the instruction of life, and feel that from God wherein he is known, loved, and joined with in covenant; that so, there might be a pure beginning, a pure growth and going on unto perfection, and not notions concerning things set up in the earthly understanding, which easily putrefy and defile; but, pure life, felt and enjoyed in the heart, which is undefiled, and never saw nor shall see corruption. I have not freedom to write many words; but, my love breathes for thee, and my life desires fellowship with thee, (if it may seem good unto my God,) in that which is pure of him, and will remain so forever.

And, whatever men may say or think of me, I have no other religion now, than I had from the beginning; only, a clearer leading into and guidance by that principle of life, in and through which, it pleased the Lord then to quicken me. And this is it, which I have daily experience of in my heart; that it is no less than the light of the everlasting day, in which the renewed man is to walk, and no less than the life of the Son, (whom God gave a ransom for sinners,) which can quicken man so to do; and, none but Christ, none but Christ, by his life revealed in the soul, and blood shed there to wash it, can save the poor sinner from sin, wrath, and misery; and, my hope is not in what I have done, do, or can do; but, in what he hath done *without me*, and also doth *in me*.

This is the account of my love unto thee, drawn forth at this time by the outward expression of thine in sending that paper, who remain, and, from my first acquaintance, have ever been, a Friend and lover of thee. I. P.

PETER'S CHALFONTE,
19th of Sixth Month, 1665.

LETTER L.

Of the Gospel state in general, and of the state of Believers in particular.

FRIEND,—The Lord God on whom I wait, and whom I worship in spirit and truth, and whom it is my delight to serve and obey, hath divers times engaged my mind to write to thee in true and tender love. There is somewhat, also, on my heart at this time to thee, concerning the state of the gospel, in general, and, in particular, concerning the state and condition of those, who truly know and serve the Lord Jesus Christ, the King of saints.

The state of the gospel in general, is a state of redemption and deliverance from the soul's enemies; of which redemption every soul partakes, according to its faith in and obedience to the Truth, and according to its growth in Him who is true. The babes in Christ and little children, their sins are forgiven them for His name's sake. The young men have fought valiantly, and have overcome the wicked one. The old men, or elders in the Truth, they are experienced in the heavenly wisdom and knowledge of Him, who is from the beginning.

Now, there are some things which belong to all in general, or which are common to all, and somewhat which is peculiar to each member in particular. These things, which belong to all in general, are very many; but, it is only on my heart to mention to thee at this time those few, which the apostle recites together in Eph. iv. 4, 5, 6, which indeed comprehend much; and, he that knoweth and partaketh of them, hath also a share in, and benefit by, all the rest. First, he saith, "There is one body." There is one head; and this one head hath one body, of which all that are truly living are members. Secondly, "There is one Spirit," which quickens, keeps alive, and gives nourishment to, ordereth, comforteth, defendeth this one body. Thirdly, "There is one hope of" their "calling;" for they are all called from the land of darkness, and out of the shadow and dominion of death, to travel towards an inheritance of light, and life everlasting. Fourthly, There is "one Lord," who hath power over, and the rule and dominion of this one body; to whom they are all to give an account daily of what they do, and at the last day, of what hath been done in their body of flesh. Fifthly, There is "one faith," wherewith they all believe in, and draw virtue from the head; which faith is the gift of God, and springs from the root of life in his Son, and is of another nature than that natural ability of believing, which is found in mankind. Sixthly, There is "one baptism," by the one Spirit; whereby, all the true members are baptized into the one living body, and come to partake of the virtue, benefits, and privileges thereof. Lastly, There is "one God and Father of all," who begat them all, and is to be worshipped by them all, as their Lord and God; he being witnessed and experienced by them to be "above all, and through all, and in" them "all." This is the state in general, the gospel state, into which Christ gives his sheep, his Father's children, entrance; and, it is a blessed thing to know and experience this state, that is, to have a real interest in, and really to partake of these things.

The state of every one in particular is thus; "Unto every one" in particular "is given grace, according to the measure of the gift of Christ." Grace and truth come by Jesus Christ; for the fulness is his, yea, he is the fulness; and of his fulness doth he give a measure to each member in particular. Not to all a like proportion, but to every one some; as he pleaseth to distribute and proportion out the gift of his grace to them. For, it is his own, and he may dispense his gifts and heavenly talents as he pleaseth; and, according to the state of each in the body, and according to their work and service, so doth he proportion out his gift of grace to them. Now, this is that which every one is to mind; even, the grace given to them, their own gift from Christ, to grow in that, and to be what they are in that. He that hath none of this grace, he is none of Christ's; and he that hath received the grace, the free gift, he is to keep to the measure of it, in all he is and does.

Now, shall I say to thee, feel my love in these lines? or, shall I not rather say, feel the love of my God, who visits thee yet again, and would not have thee perish, in resisting his Holy Spirit, and slighting the grace and truth which is by Jesus Christ, which is now powerfully revealed in many hearts: — blessed be he, who hath visited his people with the horn of salvation. I. P.

LETTER LI.

On Shunning the Cross.

To Catherine Pordage.

Ah! my poor, distressed, entangled Friend, while thou seekest to avoid the snare, thou deeply runnest into it: for, thou art feeding on the tree of knowledge, in giving way to these thoughts, reasonings, and suggestions, which keep thee from obedience to that, which hath been made manifest to thy understanding. And thou mayest well be feeble in thy mind, while thou art thus separated from Him who is thy strength, and lettest in his enemy. This is not the right feebleness of mind which God pities, nor the right way of waiting to receive strength. Why shouldst not thou act, so far as God gives thee light? and why shouldst thou not appear willing to obey him, even in little things, so far as he hath given thee light? What if I should say, that all this is but the subtlety of the serpent's wisdom to avoid the cross, and is not that simplicity and plainness of heart towards God, which thou takest it to be; and that thou art loath to be so poor, and low, and mean in the eyes of others, as this practice would make thee appear?

Thy Friend in the Truth, and in sincere love, I. P.

Amersham,
25th of Ninth Month, 1675.

LETTER LII.

On Love, Meekness, and Watching over each other.

To Friends in Amersham.

Friends, — Our life is love, and peace, and tenderness; and bearing one with another, and forgiving one another, and not laying accusations one against another; but praying one for another, and helping one another up with a tender hand, if there has been any slip or fall; and waiting till the Lord gives sense and repentance, if sense and repentance in any be wanting. O! wait to feel this spirit, and to be guided to walk in this spirit, that ye may enjoy the Lord in sweetness, and walk sweetly, meekly, tenderly, peaceably, and lovingly one with another. And then, ye will be a praise to the Lord; and any thing that is, or hath been, or may be amiss, ye will come over in the true dominion, even in the Lamb's dominion; and, that which is contrary shall be trampled upon, as life rises and rules in you. So, watch your hearts and ways; and watch one over another, in that which is gentle and tender, and knows it can neither preserve itself, nor help another out of the snare; but the Lord must be waited upon, to do this in and for us all. So, mind Truth, the service, enjoyment, and possession of it in your hearts; and so to walk, as ye may bring no disgrace upon it, but may be a good savour in the places where ye live — the meek, innocent, tender, righteous life reigning in you, governing over you, and shining through you, in the eyes of all with whom ye converse.

Your Friend in the Truth, and a desirer of your welfare and prosperity therein, I. P.

Aylesbury,
4th of Third Month, 1667.

LETTER LIII.

On the Spiritual Appearance of Christ.

O! Friend, — That thou hadst the true sense of the drift of my heart in writing and sending things to thee! — which is and hath been this — that thou mightst be acquainted with that of God in the heart, which quickens to him: and, in the light of that, mightst try thy heart and ways, and so, only justify in thyself what God justifies, and let all else go.

Shall the Lord appear mightily on the earth, and Israel not know him? Shall the professors of this age understand no more his appearance in Spirit, than the Jews did his appearance in flesh? Shall they stumble at the very same stumbling stone? Yes, the same stumbling stone is laid, for that wisdom to stumble at, as in all generations; and, there is no avoiding stumbling, but by coming out of that wisdom into babe-like simplicity, which gives entrance into pure, heavenly wisdom. And this I dare affirm, as in God's presence and in his pure fear, having received the sense thereof from him — that there is none that opposeth this his present appearance, (by the greatest knowledge and wisdom of their comprehensions from the letter,) but would also have opposed and denied his appearance in that body of flesh, had they lived in that day. For, the wisdom which *they* gathered from the letter did not reveal Christ in that day, but the Father; and the same reveals Him in *this* day.

O that thou couldst feel the pure revelation from the Father to thy heart! O wait for a new heart, a new ear, a new eye! even to feel the pure in thee, and thy mind changed by the pure, that all things may become new to thee; the Scriptures new, (they are so, indeed, when God opens them,) duties new, ordinances new, graces new, experiences new; a new church of the Spirit's building, wherein He and thy soul may dwell together; and thou mayest be able to say, in the presence of the Lord, This is a city of God's own building, the foundation whereof is laid with sapphires, whose walls are salvation, and its gates praise! I. P.

12th of Third Month, 1669.

LETTER LIV.

To one under Divine Visitation.

Oh! dear Friend,—The eternal love of my Father is to thee; and, because he loves thee, and would entirely enjoy thee, therefore doth he so grievously batter and break down that which stands in the way. What he is doing towards thee, thou canst not know now, but thou shalt know hereafter. Only be still, and wait for the springing up of hope, in the seasons the Father sees necessary; that thou mayest not faint under his hand, but be supported by his secret power, until his work be finished. The great thing necessary for thee at present to know, is, the drawings of his Spirit; that thou mayest not ignorantly withstand or neglect them, and protract the day of thy redemption.

Oh! look not after great things:—small breathings, small desires after the Lord, if true and pure, are sweet beginnings of life. Take heed of despising "the day of small things," by looking after some great visitation, proportionable to thy distress, according to thy eye. Nay, thou must become a child, thou must lose thy own will quite by degrees. Thou must wait for life to be measured out by the Father, and be content with what proportion, and at what time, he shall please to measure.

Oh! be little, be little; and then, thou wilt be content with little; and if thou feel, now and then, a check or a secret smiting, — in *that* is the Father's love; be not over-wise, nor over-eager, in thy own willing, running, and desiring, and thou mayest feel it so; and by degrees come to the knowledge of thy Guide, who will lead thee, step by step, in the path of life, and teach thee to follow, and, in his own season, powerfully judge that which cannot, nor will not follow. Be still, and wait for light and strength; and desire not to know or comprehend but to be known and comprehended in the love and life, which seeks out, gathers and preserves the lost sheep.

I remain thy dear Friend, and a well-wisher to thy soul, in the love of my Father. I. P.

LETTER LV.

The Kingdom of God within. Of the New Covenant. Professors of the Day. Trial of spirits. Exhortation to wait for, and walk in the Spirit.

Dear Friend,—I received thy letter kindly, and in the tenderness of love, which desires thy enjoyment of the Lord in this world, and the eternal welfare of thy soul with him forever.

It is a great matter, to have the mind rightly guided to that wherein God appears, that the soul may wait at the posts of wisdom to hear wisdom's voice; and he that hears and observes wisdom's voice, what saith wisdom concerning such an one? "I will pour out my spirit unto you, I will make known my words unto you." Prov. i. 23.

Thou hast read in the Scriptures, of the kingdom of God, which, Christ told the Pharisees, was within them. He also, in parables, expressed what it was like; even, like a grain of mustard seed, like a pearl of great price, like a lost groat, or piece of silver, like a treasure hid in a field, like leaven, &c. Now, O that thou mightst come to the discerning of this. Is there any such thing in thee? Surely, there is. Dost thou know it? art thou in union with it? is it grown and enlarged in thee? is there room made for it, and doth it overspread thy heart? O that it were thus with thee!

Whereas thou sayest, The covenant, the new covenant, is contained in the Scriptures; that expression of thine is not clear, and to the nature of the thing. There are, indeed, descriptions of the covenant in the Scriptures; but, the covenant itself is an agreement of life and peace, made with the soul in the Lord Jesus Christ, upon his believing in His power and obeying His voice; according to that Scripture, "Hear, and your soul shall live, and I will make an everlasting covenant with you, even the sure mercies of David." Isaiah, lv. 3. Now, this is it the soul is to wait for; even to feel the power of life breaking the bonds of death, and opening the ear to the voice of God's Spirit, that it may receive the impressions thereof, and feel the new creation inwardly, the new heart, the new mind, the new law of life, written within by the finger of God's Spirit, even the law of the Spirit of life in Christ Jesus. And then, this law is the rule inwardly as the outward law was the rule to the outward Jews.

Thou thinkest me somewhat too sharp and severe, in my sentence concerning the ministers [of the day]. I do not remember that passage. I have received great mercy, and I would not be sharp or severe towards any. If, therefore, any such thing was, be assured it was in faithfulness to the Lord. All sorts of Christians own Christ in words, but all do not distinguish, discern, [nor are] subject to the appearances of his Spirit and power; but resist, gainsay, and oppose, through error and mistakes at first, till at length they come to hardness. These are the builders who refuse the Corner-stone. The builders rejected Christ's appearance in flesh, in the days of his flesh; and the builders again refuse his appearance in spirit, in this day of his Spirit. O that any who are tender among them might be sensible of it, that they might not draw down God's severity and sharpness upon their heads! which, if they do, it is not our joy, but matter of grief to us. And, Friend, the state of profession is not what it was, when thou and I were acquainted; but, a withered state in comparison of that. I can truly say, concerning many professors, O that I could find them to be now, what they were twenty years ago! They have got more head-knowledge; but, that savour of life, which then was in them, is not now to be found among them. Truly, I speak not otherwise concerning them, but as I feel the Spirit of the Lord testifying in me; neither would I have mentioned this at this time, but for thy sake. Whatever is of God in any, my heart cannot but own: but, many take that to be of God, (that fear, that faith, that love, those prayers, those hopes, that peace, that joy, &c.) which is not of him. O how precious is that, which truly and rightly distinguisheth! "My sheep hear my voice." The voice of the Shepherd distinguisheth every deceit and every deceiver.

But, whereas thou sayest, The spirits are to be tried by the Scriptures; I have found it otherwise in my experience. The Scriptures may try words; but, nothing can try spirits, but the Spirit. "I will know," said the apostle, "not the words of them that are puffed up, but the power." Deceivers may come with Scripture words; but they cannot come with the true power. Therefore, the apostle John, who bade the believers try the spirits, told them, they had an unction from the Holy One, and pointed them to the anointing. 1 John, ii. 20 & 27. But, who can judge of this, but he that hath the anointing, and is taught of the Lord to try things by it? he knows how it tries, and what a certain judgment it gives concerning the nature of things, and concerning every voice and every appearance. The Spirit of God searcheth all things, discerns all things, discovers all things,—every snare, every device of the enemy, the net spread ever so secretly; blessed are they, whose eyes are opened and kept open by Him!

There was a time of great darkness befell me, wherein all that I had known and formerly experienced, was hid from me; and I cried out, "I know not the Lord; and yet, I cannot live without him;—O! what shall I do?" &c., but I never denied Christ to be the way of salvation, in my deepest darkness and distress. And now, at length, —blessed be the Lord!—I have lived to see the day, wherein he is made of God, wisdom, righteousness, sanctification, and redemption, to me; and I feel his blood sprinkled and overflowing, which makes whiter than snow; and find him to be the mercy-seat, through whom I have access to God; and live by mercy and the deep compassions of God towards me, which, because they fail not, but are daily renewed upon me, therefore is my soul preserved in life before my God.

O wait to know that wherein the Lord inwardly appears! and take up the cross of our Lord Jesus Christ to every thing that is contrary to God; that, it all may be crucified in thee, that thy soul may live in the abundance of life and peace. God is not straitened to any of the children; O that none of them may be straitened in their own bowels! And, be not discouraged because of any weakness, or because of thy age. What knowest thou, what the Lord will do for thee? Thy weakness is not thy disadvantage, but advantage; for the weaker thou art in thyself, the fitter art thou to have Christ's power revealed and manifested in thee. Only wait to know that wherein God appears in thy heart, even the holy seed, the immortal seed of life; that that may be discerned, distinguished and have scope in thee; that it may spring up in thy heart and live in thee, and gather thee into itself, and leaven thee all over with its nature; that thou mayest be a new lump, and mayest walk before God, not in the oldness of thy own literal knowledge or apprehensions of things, but in the newness of his Spirit.

The Lord appear to thee, in the light and demonstration of his spirit in thy heart and conscience,—touch thee, quicken thee, lead thee,—guide and make thee sensible of every appearance of his; that no motion or drawing of his Spirit may be quenched in thee, nor any motion of the contrary spirit, under any deceivableness, hearkened to; that thou mayest travel faithfully, and come to the end of thy travels with joy and full peace, reaping the sheaves in life everlasting, of all that thou hast sown to the Spirit.

This is the earnest and single desire of my soul for thee, who am thy true and faithful Friend, and an hearty well-wisher to thee and thine. I. P.

LETTER LVI.

Encouragement to look up to the Lord, amidst his Chastenings and the Smitings of the Enemy.

Friend,—Thy advantage in thy travels is great over what it hath been; the Lord having given thee a better sight both of thy enemies, and of that wherein his strength against them is revealed.

Now, what remains? but that thou hope in him, and breathe unto him, and hang upon him; that his virtue may flow into thee, and the mountains and difficulties may pass away, before the presence of the Seed, who is revealed in thee. Look down no more, look out no more; but, dwell with thy Beloved, in the tent that he hath pitched for thee. Let him do what he will, let him appear how he will, wait on him in the daily exercise; stand still in the faith, and see him working out thy salvation, and scattering the bones of them that have besieged thee. Think not hardly of him, by no means; question not his carrying on of his work. He knows what yet he hath to do, and what stratagem the enemy yet hath to surprise and entangle thee. O feel his arm stretched out for thee! and be not so much discouraged, in the sight of what is yet to be done, as comforted in his good-will towards thee. 'T is true, he hath chastened thee with rods and sore afflictions; but, did he ever take away his loving kindness from thee? or did his faithfulness ever fail in the sorest, blackest, thickest, darkest night that ever befell thee? And breathe to him, for the carrying on of his work; that thou mayest feel his presence and life, getting dominion over death daily in thee, more and more. And wait to feel strength of life, that thy growth may be pure, and the holy seed may have dominion and be all in thee. I. P.

8th of the Eighth Month, 1666.

POSTSCRIPT.

The enemy will be laying snares, and forging subtle devices to darken and bow thee down, which, (thou, not being hasty to believe, join with, and let in as true, but waiting on the Lord in singleness, fear, and humility,) his light will spring up in thee, and help thee to discern. And oh! how sweet will it be for thee, who hast so often been ensnared, to escape the gins and nets of the fowler, and to dwell in the rest and peace, which thy soul hath tasted of, and which is the proper place of thy habitation.

Indeed, the Lord's thoughts have not been towards thee, as thou hast apprehended all along. His anger was towards the enemy, towards the oppressor, not towards thee. Nor doth He judge and smite the mind, after that manner that the enemy doth accuse; but, according to his own nature, sweetness, and tender love. And, His judgments and smitings have other effects, than the serpent's accusings and piercings; for, *they* do not drive *from* Him, but, they melt, and tender and prepare the heart for union with Him. O! keep close to the measure of life, wherein thou mayest discern and distinguish these things; and, take heed of letting in one bowing-down thought, (how manifest or demonstrative soever,) but look up to him who hath freely loved, and hath abounded in mercy towards thee; that in the faith, patience, stillness, and meekness of his seed, thou mayest be found always waiting upon him, in the several exercises, wherewith he shall daily see good to exercise thee; till he bring forth his seed in dominion in thee, and thereby give thee thy desired and expected end.

I. P.

9th of the Eighth Month, 1666.

LETTER LVII.

Of the Gospel Dispensation, and of the States of its Professors.

To COLONEL KENRICK.

THE gospel dispensation consists in spirit and power. The kingdom which Christ and his apostles preached, (which the true believers were to receive, and to wait for an entrance to be ministered to them into,) stood not in word, but in power. Now, there are four sorts of professors of the Christian religion in this our day, one sort whereof only, are acquainted with the gospel dispensation.

First, There is one sort, which have been nurtured in a profession of Christianity by education, and have improved it by study, but have never known the power, virtue, and inward life thereof; but, as men, with the man's part, wisdom, understanding, and seriousness of mind, have considered of the truth and weight of things contained in the Scriptures, and so have received somewhat of the holy doctrine into their natural understanding, and given themselves up to the observation and practice thereof, according as they have apprehended and understood things. These have become more serious and excellent men than others, but fall very far short of the nature and state of Christianity; yea, the strictest among these, many times, become the greatest opposers and persecutors of true Christianity.

Secondly, There are some who have had a taste of the true power, and have had living desires and breathings after it, and a sense of the preciousness and excellency of it; who have also felt the quickening Spirit, and began therein; and yet, have afterwards lost that sense, and centered in a literal knowledge and wisdom about those very things, which they had once some living experience of. These are like salt, which hath lost its savour; and it is hard for them ever to be seasoned again; and from among these, do rise the greatest persecutors and bitterest persecution against the life, Truth, and power.

Thirdly, There are some, who, though they never came to the distinct knowledge of the power, yet have had a great sense of their want of it, and have abode in that sense; and, in all the ways and forms of religion they have been or are in, still seek after it; and reckon no form anything, but as the power in some measure appears in it; and the cry of their souls is daily after it, and their waiting is for it. These, wherever they are, are of the true seed; these are the birth of the heavenly Spirit and wisdom; these are sheep of the true Shepherd's fold, though not yet gathered home to the fold to which they properly belong. These are the broken, the bruised, the sick, the wounded, the captives, the distressed, the poor, the naked, &c., to whom the gospel of peace, the gathering, the salvation, and redemption belongs. And, the bleating of these is known; yea, their longing and cry after the redeeming and gathering power of the Shepherd, is felt; however they may be, at present, prejudiced against that very dispensation of Truth, life, and power, whereby the Shepherd gathers.

Fourthly, There are some, whom God hath brought to the distinct sense and knowledge of the power. There are some, whose minds God hath turned to the inward light and power. There are some, whom the Shepherd hath gathered home to the Father's house, where is bread enough, and to the true fold, where is rest and peace enough — some, who have seen an end of all perfection, in the legal comprehendings and creaturely strivings after life, righteousness, and holiness, and are come to the commandment which is exceeding broad, and, wherein is life everlasting. Now, these experience somewhat of the gospel dispensation, and know the difference between being under the law and under grace; and can tell, what the kingdom is, which Christ preached and bade men seek; and what the gospel is, which the poor in spirit receive; and what the healing is, which drops from under the wing of the Saviour and Redeemer. And, they can tell what justification is, and what sanctification, regeneration, and redemption is; and can distinguish between truth as testified in the letter, and as it is in Jesus; between the law of the letter, and the law of the Spirit, which is written in the new heart and mind, by the finger of God's pure and living power. Now, the knowledge of these, the faith of these, the peace, the joy, the justification, and sanctification, and redemption of these, differs greatly from all the former; from the two first sorts in nature and kind, from the latter in degree, clearness, and purity. For, though all the sheep of the true Shepherd have somewhat of the true knowledge, somewhat of the true faith, somewhat of the true justification, somewhat of the true sanctification, and may at times have some taste of true peace and joy, and have true breathings and supplications in their spirits towards their Father that begat them; yet, they are not clear, they are not pure, they are not unmixed; there is a great deal, which is not true, which passeth for true with them; because, they are not come to the anointing, to the eye-salve which opens the eye, nor to the Spirit of judgment and burning, which separates inwardly in the heart, understanding, mind, and judgment, between the precious and the vile. So that, when they speak of the heavenly things, they do but stutter and stammer; and though truth can sometimes own their sense, yet, many times, not their words; there is such a mixture of the dark, earthly comprehension in them, which they are not delivered and redeemed from. But, it is otherwise with those, who are turned to the light and power of our Lord Jesus Christ, and have known it, and been exercised, fanned, and purged by it: for, in them, the blind eye is opened, the deaf ear unstopped; and, to them, the pure understanding and language is given, whereby they know and understand, not only words concerning Him, but Him *himself* who is true, and are in him that is true, even in Him, who is *the very God and life eternal.*

Yet, there are different states among those, who are thus effectually called and gathered home, according to their growth in the Truth, and faithfulness to it. For, if there be not a great care and watchfulness, there may be a neglecting to hear the voice of the Shepherd, and to walk with him: and then, such miss of the pastures of life, and of the pure rest, joy, and peace, which he administers to others; and of the garment or covering of the Spirit, which they, who live and walk in the Spirit, (in everything giving up to the Spirit, and denying all the lusts and fruits of the flesh,) daily find themselves covered with. Nor doth God so "dwell in them and walk in them," as he doth in those, that remain separate from all evil, (from which the Spirit of judgment and burning purifies and separates,) and touch no unclean thing. Yea, they who grieve Christ's Spirit, and do not heed his call and knocks, he doth not so sup with them, nor they with him; nor do such partake so of the river of life and wine of the kingdom, as those whose ear is open to him, and who are always ready to obey and follow him "whithersoever he goeth."

I. P.

19th of Fourth Month, 1673.

LETTER LVIII.

On the Lord's Supper with Believers.

To Widow Hemmings.

My dear Friend, — Whom I truly love, and whose prosperity in the Truth I earnestly desire. Because I find thy mind much engaged about one thing, to wit, receiving bread and wine in remembrance of Christ's death, which I am tender to thee in; yet withal, it is on my heart at this time to say somewhat to thee; perhaps the Lord may open thy mind, and let thee into some sense of the thing.

There is a supper, or supping with Christ, beyond outward bread and wine, which he promised to those that heard his voice, opened the door, and let him in. Rev. iii. 20. Now, it is *that* supper, it is the desire of my heart, thou mayest be acquainted with and partake of. And as thou comest to be acquainted with it and partake of it, thou wilt call it the feast of fat things, and of wines on the lees well refined. Christ said, *Henceforth I will drink no more of this fruit of the vine; till I drink it new with you in my Father's kingdom.* What wine, what fruit of the vine is it which Christ drinks new with his disciples in his Father's kingdom? Is it not that wine, which he and they drink *now* together, when he sups with them? O! the Lord give thee an understanding, that thou mayest come to the substance, feel substance, and inherit substance forever.

"Flee from idolatry, my dearly beloved," said the apostle, 1 Cor. x. 14. What idolatry did he mean? "I speak as to wise men;" said he, "judge ye what I say. The cup of blessing which we bless, is it not the communion of the blood of Christ? The bread which we break, is it not the communion of the body of Christ?" About the outward cup and bread, might they not easily run into idolatry? but they that knew, discerned, and minded the body and blood indeed, they did not run into idolatry. "For we, being many, are one bread and one body; for we are all partakers of that one bread." O deep, deep, indeed! The bread which comes down from heaven, *that* is the bread which gives life to the soul: and, unless we eat the flesh of the Son of man and drink his blood, we have no life in us. And, if we eat his flesh and drink his blood, we become one flesh with him, and bone of his bone; yea, we become of the same bread with him, and so, of the one body of the living bread.

My dear Friend, the Lord give thee an understanding, and open thy heart, and cause thee to grow into union and into sense of his Truth; that by growing up in the Truth, thou mayest come more and more to understand it, and be acquainted with it.

Thy unfeigned Friend in the Truth, which is pure.

I. P.

READING GAOL,
3d of Sixth Month, 1670.

LETTER LIX.

Respecting the Payment of Tithes.

TO JAMES EELES.

FRIEND, — God is my witness, to whom I must give an account of all my actions, that it is my desire to be found in all true love, courtesy, and righteousness, in my dealings towards all men; and that I would by no means deny any man his just due, which he can by any just law or right claim from me.

Now, as touching tithes, the payment or refusing of them is to me a matter of conscience, weighty on my heart before the Lord; and I would do therein as he might justify, and not condemn me. I know, tithes were ordained by God, to be paid to the Levitical priesthood, under the law: but, the same power that ordained them under the law, disannulled them under the gospel. Heb. vii. 12 & 18. Here is God's power and authority for disannulling them. Now, that any man or men have true right, power, and authority to set up or require to be paid, under the gospel, what God's power hath disannulled,— indeed, I do not see; nor can I be subject to any human authority or law in this thing, without sinning against God, and incurring his wrath upon my soul; which I have formerly found very dreadful, and would not, for fear of sufferings in this world, expose myself to the bearing of. Besides, Christ saith, "He that denies me before men, him will I deny before my Father." He is the substance of all the figures under the law; he hath put an end to them; he is King, Priest, and Prophet in the church of God; all power in heaven and earth is given to him, and he sent forth his ministers without tithes. Now, tithes were set up in the dark time of popery, and not by the gospel light; and, they who know the gospel light, dare not be subject to that, which was set up in matters of religion by the dark power of Rome, in the time of darkness.

I was willing to give thee this plain and naked account, that thou mayest see how weighty the thing is with me, and how dangerous it would be to me, to do what thou requirest of me; for, in so doing, I should lose my peace with God, I should be unfaithful to the testimony he hath given me to bear, I should dishonour his name and Truth, and bring his sore wrath and displeasure upon my soul and conscience. Judge, thyself, in this matter; whether I had not better expose myself to any outward sufferings, though evêr so great, (either from thee, or any thou shalt make use of,) than expose my soul to so great inward misery and sufferings, for disobedience to the Lord in this particular. Consider Ralph Trumper,* a just, tender, honest-hearted man,—how much he hath suffered in this respect, to keep his conscience clear in this thing; who, I believe, would rather suffer all his former losses ten times over again, than suffer what he did, (to my knowledge,) for paying tithes, after he was convinced of the evil and unlawfulness of it. I do not contend with thee by the law of the land; but, I must be subject to the law of God, who shows me from what root tithes came; and that they are not the maintenance of the ministry of Christ, or

* See Besse's Sufferings of Friends, Vol. 1st, pages 78, 79.

allowed by Christ; but, the maintenance of the ministry Rome's power set up, both which ministry, and its maintenance, is to be denied and witnessed against, by those, whom he calls forth to testify to his Truth in these things.

So, at present, I say no more; but remain thy Friend, ready to do thee any good, though I should suffer ever so deeply from thee. I. P.

25th of Fourth Month, 1677.

LETTER LX.

On Election, and on Falling away. Of our own Righteousness and of Christ's in us.

To Ruth Palmer.

My dear Friend,—Whose love I am sensible of, and whom I entirely wish well unto, and desire for thee, that thou mayest purchase and possess the pearl of price; and so know and enjoy Christ Jesus, the Lord, as that thou mayest witness him to be eternal life to thy soul.

I received a letter from thee, which occasions this my writing to thee. It is precious, indeed, to have the Spirit of God witness to us, that our sins are pardoned. And they who are truly pardoned, to whom the Spirit so witnesseth, receive the Spirit; indeed, all that are Christians receive the Spirit; for, he that hath not the Spirit of Christ, is none of His. And where the Spirit is, there is He who hath power over sin, who delights to exercise his power in mortifying and subduing sin, and in reigning and triumphing over it. Now, they that have received the Spirit, are to live in the Spirit, and walk in the Spirit; and, doing so, they cannot fulfil the lusts of the flesh, nor love the world, nor the things of the world, nor fashion themselves according to it, but are redeemed out of it, in heart, spirit, life, and conversation, up to God. O my Friend! let no religion satisfy thee, but that which brings thee hither, and which brings forth this fruit in thee. We must needs own Christ to be the spring, and that we can do nothing without him, but only by, and in, and through him; because we daily experience it to be so.

As touching election, we do believe it, according as the Lord hath taught us, and as the Scriptures express it: but, such an election, as shuts out any from the salvation God hath prepared for the sons of men, we cannot own; because the Scriptures expressly testify that God "would have *all* to be saved, and come to the knowledge of the Truth." Yea, also, we know it to be his nature. It is the nature of the destroyer to destroy, — he would have none saved; but, it is the nature of God, the Saviour, to save, — he would have none perish. But, as there is a making the calling and the election sure, so, there is first a coming into the calling and into the election. Now, the election cannot perish, nay, the elect Seed cannot be deceived. And, as we are chosen in him, and come into him, (out of darkness in his marvellous light, out of death into his life,) so, we must abide in him: and the promise is to him, that continues unto the end. And Christ said to the church of Ephesus, "Remember from whence thou art fallen, and repent, and do the first works: or else," &c.: and mind, what a state they fell from, and how far they were fallen, when so severely threatened. It was not wholly; it was but from the first love and first works; and yet, if they repented not, how great was their danger.

As for that place of Rom. xi., it is manifest, that there is an election, and that this election is not of works, but of grace. Yet there must be a hearing of the voice;

"To-day," said the apostle, "if ye will hear his voice;" and so, there must be a coming to Christ, and an abiding in him, and a walking in the strait way; for, it is the way God chooseth. God hath chosen Christ, and the soul in him; and the message is, to invite to come to him, and abide in him to the end. And the condemnation is, upon rejecting him, and the salvation, to them that receive him, which is not of man's self neither, but, men are made willing so to do, in the day of God's power; and the power is not far from, or wanting to any, in the way that the Lord hath appointed; though there are also the *aboundings* of love, mercy, and power according to his pleasure. The falling away is, not because persons were not elected, but because they let in that, which is contrary to the election, and cleave to it. So, there is, a "heart of unbelief," in which men depart from the living God, and make shipwreck of faith and of a good conscience; and the ground of their falling is, their hearkening, not to the Lord, but to the voice and temptations of the enemy. There are called, and faithful, and chosen. These are states, to be come into and abode in. Many may be called, who never come to be faithful, nor chosen. To witness the peculiar choice of God, this is precious: — and then, not to be content with a touch of the calling, or a touch of the election, but to "make" them "sure." There is no choosing, but in the seed. Make sure of that seed, and thou makest both thy "calling and election sure." For indeed, "many are called, but few chosen." And yet, when a man comes thus far, so as to know himself chosen, is he quite out of danger? Did not Paul know his election sure? yet, was he not afterwards careful to keep that under and in subjection, which was to be kept under and in subjection? "lest," saith he, "when I have preached to others, I myself should be a castaway."

Thou sayest, Whom God once loves, he loves to the

end. Did he not once love all men, even the whole world? Did he not manifest it, in sending his Son for them? And they that come into his Son, they come into his love; and they that come into his love, must continue in his love and in his goodness. For, it is not *persons*, ("God is no respecter of persons,") but the seed, God loves. "In thy seed shall all the families of the earth be blessed;" and, in that seed, they are loved, and continuing there, they continue in the love. It is true, God's grace appears, and thereby many are gathered. And when any fall, the grace of God appears again, and thereby many are restored. But, if any be hardened by "the deceitfulness of sin," that they hearken not to the voice of grace, when it comes to restore, are they restored by it? And, God's compassions failed not to Israel of old, nor to Israel now; yet, were none consumed then, who, though they came out of Egypt, yet rebelled, and lusted, and tempted Christ, &c., and so, were destroyed of the destroyer! And so, do none make shipwreck of faith now, whereby the standing is? as the apostle ex presseth, Rom. xi. 19, 20, 21, 22. Read, and consider. And the apostle, in the sense of things, cries, "O the depth!" &c. Love in severity, mercy in severity! If it be stopped one way, it will break forth more abundantly in another way. And, "who hath known the mind of the Lord," or given him counsel, which way he should manage his love and mercy? as in ver. 33, 34, of that 11th chapter. Indeed, all the salvation is to be ascribed to God, and is ascribed to God by all that receive salvation from him; but still, God saves in the way he has appointed, (in coming into the way, in abiding in the way, in walking in the way,) — there alone is safety; but, out of it, death and destruction forever.

All *our* best righteousness is as filthy rags, it is true; but, the gift of God is not as filthy rags, the righteousness of his Son revealed in the heart, is not as filthy rags. The pure offerings and incense, which are offered up to God in the times of the gospel, are not as filthy rags. See Mal. i. 11; and consider whether he that offers up to God the male, offers up a corrupt thing, a filthy rag, or no, ver. 14. O what a state of blindness are many in, that they cannot distinguish between what is of themselves, and what is of God in them; and so, avoid offering up the corrupt thing, and offer up that which is holy and pure, even the holy sacrifice, with the holy fire, upon the altar of God! Consider 3d ch. 3d verse of Malachi; and tell me, if thou knowest, what an offering in righteousness is, whether it be as filthy rags, or no. Consider that place, John, iii. 21. "He that doeth truth cometh to the light, that his deeds may be made manifest, that they are wrought in God." And what are those deeds that are wrought in God? Is not God holy and pure? And is any thing wrought in him, but what is holy and pure? And mind that place, where the prophet speaks, "All our righteousnesses are as filthy rags," &c. Mind ver. 5, and ver. 6, of Isaiah lxiv., and see if they be not two different states? None of those, whose righteousness was as filthy rags, called upon the name of the Lord, ver. 7. Did not the prophet call on the name of the Lord? The prophet there represents the state of backsliding Israel, that did not remember God in his ways, nor, through faith, work righteousness, as some others did, ver. 5; all *their* offerings, all *their* sacrifices out of the faith, was as filthy rags, as the cutting off of a dog's neck, &c.; but the offering of Abel, and the sacrifice of the righteous were not so, in any age or generation. Therefore, we should wait rightly to distinguish things, and not jumble the precious and the vile together, as if they were all one.

As for method of speaking, I have none of my own, but wait for the method and words, which God's wisdom teacheth. Indeed, when I speak of the light, and the life, and the power, I do mean Christ Jesus, who is the light, life, and power; but, it is a great matter, to come to know him so revealed in the heart; for, where he is so revealed, darkness and death, and the power of Satan, is scattered and put to flight by him. Yea, Satan falls like lightning before the power of his kingdom, where it is revealed.

This is a blessed experience; and these know Christ indeed. The Lord grant that thou mayest so do! which is the hearty desire of thy soul's true and faithful Friend,

I. P.

LETTER LXI.

To his brother Arthur, who became a Roman Catholic.

Dear Brother,—I have been a traveller after the Lord from my childhood, and great misery have I undergone for want of him. That which I wanted, was his Spirit, life, virtue, and redeeming power to be revealed in my own heart. O blessed be the Lord! beyond my expectation, he hath directed me, where to wait for this within, and hath revealed it in me; and now I can say in truth of heart, and in the sense of that birth, which God hath begotten in me, "Lo! this is my God, whom I so wanted and waited for;" and, I find him stronger in my heart than the strong man, which possessed it before He cast him out from thence, and made a spoil of his goods. And now, dear Brother, how can I hold my peace, and not testify of the love, mercy, and good-will of the Lord towards me, and invite others to the redeeming power, of which the Lord in his goodness hath made me a partaker? And now, Brother, a few words respecting thy return to what I sent thee; not for contention's sake, (the Lord knows, my dwelling is in that life and peace which shuts them out,) but, in the tender love and care of my heart concerning the eternal welfare of thy soul, which I would not, by any means or device of the enemy, have eternally deceived.

All sides may agree in notions about the regenerating power; but all do not *receive* the regenerating power, nor are truly regenerating in the sight of God; nor come to witness the head of the serpent inwardly crushed, and his works destroyed, and kingdom laid waste inwardly by this power; which must needs be, before a man be translated out of the kingdom of darkness, into the kingdom of the dear Son. There is a kingdom of darkness inwardly, which the unbelieving and disobedient to God's Spirit and power, dwell in; and there is a kingdom of light inwardly, wherein, the children of light dwell with God, and walk in the light as he is in the light.

But, that the work of regeneration is only begun in this life, and not finished till the other life, *that* is a great mistake. For, the Scriptures testify, that salvation is to be wrought out *here*, and not hereafter. Christ had all power in heaven and earth, and he sent forth his Spirit and power to work out the work *here;* and his sanctifying Spirit and power is able to sanctify throughout, in soul, body, and spirit; and the gifts of the ministry are for perfecting the saints, till they all come in the unity of the faith, unto a perfect man, that they may be presented to God perfect in Christ Jesus. The holy leaven is put into the lump *here*, and it is able to leaven the lump *here;* and holiness is not only to be begun, but *perfected in the fear of God*, as the apostle exhorts, who did not exhort to a needless, or impossible thing; and the whole armour of God, is able to defend the whole man from all the assaults of the wicked one; for, greater is He, in the saints, that preserves from sin, than he that tempts to sin. O! how precious it is to war with the enemy in this conquering faith, and to resist him therein; that he may still flee away, for fear of God's power and sword, which will pierce him, and can easily overcome him.

There is a state where the spirit is willing, but the flesh weak: yet, it is not so, where the spirit is become strong in the Lord, and in the power of his might. There is a holy hill of God, a spiritual Zion, a mountain whereupon his house is built, which the wing of the Almighty overshadows; and his sheep that are gathered by the great Shepherd and Bishop of the soul, feed there, and none can make afraid. The flesh *will* be rebelling against the Spirit, until it be destroyed by the cross of our Lord Jesus Christ. But, when a man is really crucified with Christ, and dead to sin, sin hath no more power over him; for, Christ lives in him, and reigns in his heart over sin and the temptations thereof. When the God of peace treads Satan under the feet of the soul, that was once captived by him, there it is known, whose the kingdom, and the power and the victory, and the dominion is.

And, this is true blessedness begun, carried on, and upheld, by the pure, sanctifying power of the word of life in the heart; and the birth which is born of God, knows it to be no delusion, but the truth as it is in Jesus. And such are obedient to the holy church of God, and to the holy ministry, which he hath brought out of the wilderness; and know, of what nature the churches and ministry have been, which have appeared and been set up in the world, since the true church fled into, and was hid in the wilderness, and was fed there by the Lord God of life. The devil hath long transformed himself into the likeness of an angel of light, and cheated and beguiled souls; while the false church hath reigned, antichrist sitting in the temple,—the man-child having been caught up to God, and the true church in the wilderness; and men have generally put darkness for light, and light for darkness. But, blessed be the Lord! the true light which shone in the apostles' days, now shines again; and discovers the mystery of iniquity, and the golden cup of abominations, wherewith the earth hath been made drunk; and Satan falls down like lightning before the power of Him, on whom the true church leaned, when she came out of the wilderness,—and still leans, and will lean upon forever; and the gates of hell shall not be able to prevail against her.

And blessed be the Lord! who hath brought many wanderers and distressed ones to the sight of the true church, and to delightful obedience to her; whose voice is not different to Christ's, but one with it; and such are in fellowship with the Father and Son, and with the saints who dwell in the light. These are clothed with the Lamb's innocency and righteousness, and do not dwell in darkness, nor in sin; having crucified the old man with his affections and lusts, and put off the body of the sins of the flesh by the circumcision of Christ, and put on the new man which is created, in Christ Jesus, in the righteousness and holiness of Truth. They that are here, dwell not in fancies, nor feed on fancies, but on eternal life, in the pure pastures of life, where the Shepherd of the inward and spiritual Israel, feeds his holy flock day by day.

As for the Romish church, or any other church, built up in the apostacy from the spirit and life of the apostles; the Lord hath given me to see through them, to that which was before them, and will be after them. And, O dear Brother! if thou couldst but rightly wait for and meet with the holy, regenerating, purifying power, which in tender love I testified to thee of; it would lead thee to that which is the true church indeed, which hath been persecuted by the dragon and false church, and the blood of her seed made drunk by the bloody dragonish church, for many ages.

The Lord hath made me thy Brother in the line of nature; O that thou wert my Brother in that Truth, which lives and abides forever! O that thou knew the church, of the first-born, which are written in heaven, the Jerusalem which is above, which is free, which is the mother of all who are born of the regenerating virtue and power?

I. P.

20th of Seventh Month, 1676.

LETTER LXII.

Respecting his Brother, a Roman Catholic.

To Joseph Wright.

I entreat thy Son to acquaint my Brother Arthur, that I took very kindly, and was very glad of his affectionate expressions towards me; having been somewhat jealous, that though *my* religion had enlarged my love towards him, yet, *his* religion might have diminished his to me. I bless the Lord on his behalf that he enjoys his health so well: and for myself, though I have been exceedingly weakly formerly, yet, the inward life and comfort, which the Lord daily pleaseth to administer to me, increaseth the health and strength of my natural man, beyond my expectation; blessed be my tender and merciful Father, who hath visited one so distressed, miserable, and helpless as I was, for so many years!

And, whereas he saith, he is like me in speech, but most unlike me in opinion; I pray, tell him from me, that my religion doth not lie in opinion, but in that which puts an end to opinion. I was weary and sick at heart of opinions; and, had not the Lord brought that to my hand which my soul wanted, I had never meddled with religion more. But, as I felt that in my heart, which was evil and not of God, so the Lord God of my life, pointed me to that of him in my heart, which was of another nature, teaching me to wait for and know his appearance there; in subjection whereto, I experience him stronger than the strong man, that was there before; and by his power, he hath separated me from that within, which separated me from him before; and, thus being separated, truly, I feel union with him, and his blessed presence every day,— which, what it is unto me, my tongue cannot utter.

I could be glad, if the Lord saw good, that I might see my Brother before I die; and, if I did see him, I should not be quarrelling with him about his religion, but embrace him in brotherly love, and in the fear of the Lord. As for his being a Papist, or an arch-Papist, that doth not damp my tender affection to him. If he be a Papist, I had rather have him a serious than a loose Papist. If he hath met with any thing of that, which brings forth an holy conversation in him, he hath so far met with *somewhat of my religion*, which teacheth to order the conversation aright, in the light, and by the Spirit and power of the Lord Jesus. My religion is not *a new thing*, though newly revealed more fully than in many foregoing ages; but consists in *that*, which was long before Popery was, and will be when Popery shall be no more. And, he that would rightly know the true church, must know the living stones whereof the true church is built, against which the gates of hell cannot possibly prevail. O the daily joy of my heart, in feeling my living membership in this church! where the true "gold," the "white raiment," the pure "eye-salve" (with which the eye, being anointed, sees aright) is received and enjoyed inwardly, by such as the world knows not, but despiseth: blessed be the name of the Lord!

I desire my sincere, entire affection, as in God's sight, may be remembered to my dear Brother. I. P.

LETTER LXIII.

On Baptism by Water.

To William Rolls.

Friend,—David saw through sacrifices and burnt offerings in his time; and the spiritual eye sees through all shadows to the substance, which have no place in the brightness of the day of God: and outward washing is no more than outward circumcision, (no more of a gospel nature,) nor can avail any more, but is of the nature of the things, that were to be shaken and pass away; that the spiritual kingdom of our Lord Jesus Christ, and the things which cannot be shaken, might remain.

I could say very much to every passage of thy letter; but to what purpose would it be? The Lord give thee a sense, where the true understanding is given, and teach thee aright to wait for it; that thou mayest receive it from him, and thereby discern the nature of that wisdom, from which God hath hid the mystery in all ages and generations, and from which he hides it still; that so thou mayest experimentally know, what it is to become a fool in thyself for Christ's sake, that thou mayest be wise in him; concerning which, it is easy to have many notions in the mind, but, hard to come to the true experience of.

These are the breathings of my heart for thee, in the

flowings of my love; who desire, that thou mayest not seek after the knowledge of the Scriptures in that, which cannot understand them; but, mayest meet with the right key and the right understanding, wherein thy soul will be safe and happy: which is my heart's desire for thee, who am a real Friend, and well-wisher to thy soul in the Lord.

I. P.

LETTER LXIV.

On Unreserved Obedience.

To Bridget Atley.

Dear Friend,—I know thy soul desires to live; and my soul desireth, that thou mightst live. O! why art thou so backward to hearken to the voice which is nigh thee, wherein is life? why dost thou reason? why dost thou consult? why dost thou expect? why dost thou hope? why dost thou believe against thy own soul?

The snares of the subtle one will entangle forever, unless thou wait for, hearken to, and obey the voice of the living God, who leads the single-hearted and obedient out of them. Is there any way of life but one? Is not the Lord leading his children in that way? Must not all that come after, follow in the footsteps of those that go before? Is there any Saviour, but the seed of life and the Father of it? Is it not the same in thee as in others? Hath it not the same voice? O that thou hadst the same ear and the same heart, that thou mightst hear, receive, and live! They wait aright; dost thou wait so? they hope aright; dost thou hope so? If not, what will thy waiting and expecting come to? In *that*, which hath sometimes inclined thy heart, *there* is Truth, *there* were the beginnings of salvation; but in *that*, which draws thee out, to expect some great matters, and dries up thy present sense, and hinders thy present subjection, *therein* is deceit and the destruction of thy soul. Therefore, if thou desire and love the salvation thereof, O hasten, hasten out of it! wait for the reproofs of wisdom; and what it manifests to be of the earthly and worldly nature in thee, (the words, ways, thoughts, customs thereof,) hasten out of. O turn thy back upon the world with speed, and turn thy face towards the heavenly wisdom and light eternal! which will be springing up in thee, if thou turn thy back upon the world, and wait for it.

And, do not look for such great matters to begin with; but, be content to be a child, and let the Father proportion out daily to thee what light, what power, what exercises, what straits, what fears, what troubles, he sees fit for thee; and do thou bow before him continually, in humility of heart, who hath the disposal of thee, whether to life or death forever. Ah! that wisdom, which would be choosing, must be confounded, and the low humble thing raised, which submits, and cries to the Father in every condition. And, in waiting to feel *this*, and, in joining to *this*, thou mayest meet with life; but death, destruction, and separation from God, is the portion of the *other* forever! O! that thou mayest be separated from it, and joined to the seed and birth of God; that, in it, thy soul may spring up to know, serve, and worship the Lord, and to wait daily to be formed by him, until thou become perfectly like him. But, thou must join in with the beginnings of life, and be exercised with the day of small things, before thou meet with the great things, wherein is the clearness and satisfaction of the soul. The rest is at noon-day; but, the travels begin at the breakings of day, wherein are but glimmerings, or little light, wherein the discovery of good and evil are not so manifest and certain; yet *there* must the traveller begin and travel; and in his faithful travels. (in much fear and trembling, lest he should err,) the light will break in upon him more and more.

This have I written in tenderness to thee, that thou mightst not miss of the path of the living, which is appointed of the Father to lead, and alone can lead the soul to life. O! that thou mightst be enlightened and quickened by the Lord to walk therein, and mightst be thankful for, and content with, what he gives thee, and walk therein, from the evil to the good, from the earthly to the heavenly nature daily, and mightst not despise the cross or the shame of the seed. For, I know there is a wisdom in thee, which will despise and turn from it, until the Lord batter and crucify it; and, I can hardly put up a more proper request for thee, than, that the Lord would draw out his sword against it, and deeply perplex and confound it in thee. I. P.

1665.

LETTER LXV.

TO THE POOR AMONG FRIENDS, WHO ARE RELIEVED BY THE CHARITY AND BOWELS OF LOVE, WHICH GOD OPENS IN OTHER FRIENDS TOWARDS THEM.

O FRIENDS,—Ye ought deeply and often to consider of God's visiting you with his precious Truth, whereto being faithful, ye are sure to be happy forever; how hard soever it should go with you, and how strait soever your condition should be, in reference to the things of this world.

But, ye have not only this assurance and benefit by the Truth, but ye are also come to partake of a better provision, as to your necessities outwardly, than other poor meet with. For, God himself takes care of you, in drawing the hearts of his children to consider of your wants, and make supply unto you; so that, many of you are so provided for, as ye had never like to have been while in this world, had it not been for the interest, God gives you in the hearts of others, through and because of his Truth. Surely, this should not be forgotten by you, but daily acknowledged to the Lord, in the use and enjoyment of those things, which ye ought to receive as from his hand, through those who minister to you in his name, and for his sake.

And, take heed of murmuring, if the supply answer not any of your expectations; for, if we wait upon the Lord, to be ordered and guided by him in this matter, and answerably witness his presence with us, and holy wisdom ordering us in these affairs; your murmurings are not against us, but against the Lord. And, if ye watch narrowly over yourselves, ye will find, it is the unsubdued part, which is apt to be repining and murmuring; but, that which is of the Lord and eyes him, is that which is sensible of his goodness, and thankful to him for it. But, if there be judged to be any neglect towards any, or any just cause of complaint; let it, in tenderness, meekness, and the fear of the Lord, be laid before us; and we will wait upon him to give it a due and full consideration, and do therein as the Lord shall open and guide our hearts. For, great exercises of spirit do we meet with in these affairs, and great are our cries of spirit to the Lord, to guide and order us according to his will and holy counsel therein.

And, dear Friends, wait to feel that which stays your minds on the Lord, and keeps your eye towards him; and take heed of judging us in things, wherein we truly desire to act singly towards the Lord, and of which we must give an account to him; and, if ye in anything judge us, wherein our God justifies us, certainly the Lord will therein condemn you. Therefore, be wary and watchful in this matter. I. P.

LETTER LXVI.

Afflictions may work out a Weight of Glory.

To my dear suffering Friends in Scotland.

Dear Friends and Brethren,—Who have partaken of the tender mercies and blessed visitation of the Lord.

O! blessed be the Lord, who pitied and helped us in our low estate, and whose tender love and mercy hath followed us, from his first visiting us to this present day! And indeed, the Lord is with us, (what can we desire more?) preparing us for himself, preserving us in the life of his blessed Truth, building us up more and more, and causing his Spirit of glory and living power to rest upon us, and the virtue thereof to spring up in us day by day.

O! the beauty and glory of the day of our God increaseth upon his heritage, blessed be the name of the Lord! And, to what tend all the workings of the contrary spirit and power, but, to eat out its own interest and kingdom, through the Lord's blessed ordering of things; so that, all things work together for good, and for the advancing of Truth, and the growth of it in the hearts of God's heritage.

So, my dear Friends, none look out, either at outward or inward sufferings; but to the Lord only, whose life, Spirit, and power is above them, and bears up all over them, who are in spirit joined to him, faithfully waiting upon him; which God daily teaches and enables his to do. Thus, my dear Friends, feel the Lord's presence and power among you, who is always near his, but especially in the time of their straits, trials, and sufferings; and wait to feel the life springing, and doing its proper work in each of you day by day; working out what is to be wrought out in any, and working more and more into the glory of the heavenly image; that, through the sufferings, ye may come into the glory, and be crowned with the glory, virtue, holiness, righteousness, and dominion of life over all; and thus the Son may sit upon his throne in you, and wield his holy and righteous sceptre, and give you dominion in and with him over all that would veil life, or keep it under, in any of you. So, my dear Friends, be strong in the Lord, with the strength of the Lord, with which he is clothing those, whom he hath emptied and made weak; for the trials, temptations, and afflictions, prepare for, and (as I may say) lead into the possession of the desired inheritance; where, all that the soul hath breathed and waited for, is bestowed upon it, by the bountiful hand of the Father of mercies, who keeps covenant and mercy forever, and renews covenant and mercy day by day.

So, the tender God of my life, and Father of the blessings and mercies of my once greatly distressed and miserable soul, instruct you, preserve you, watch over you; exercise your spirits most advantageously, daily open you to himself; keep you empty and naked before him of all your own clothing and righteousness, and fill you with that, which flows from the pure living fountain; to the unspeakable joy of your hearts, and the glory of his own name over all forever!

Be of good faith, my dear Friends, look not out at any thing; fear none of those things ye may be exposed to suffer, either outwardly or inwardly; but trust the Lord over all, and your life will spring, and grow, and refresh you, and the love and power will purge out, and keep out, what would hinder its growth; and ye will learn obedience and faithfulness daily more and more, even by your exercises and sufferings; yea, the Lord will teach you the very mystery of faith and obedience; (oh blessed lesson!) and ye shall not be disappointed of your hope or crown, by any thing the enemy can plot or bring about against you, but have the weight of glory increased and enlarged by his temptations, and your many sufferings; the wisdom, power, love, and goodness of the Lord, ordering *every* thing for you, and ordering *your* hearts in every thing,—you having given up to him, and keeping them continually given up to him, in the holy seed of Truth, in which he hath in some measure already joined, and is daily more and more joining you to himself.

This is the salutation and tender visit of the love of your brother in the Truth; whose breathings are to God for you, and his praises unto Him, through the sense of his being with you, and daily showing mercy to you, upholding and preserving you in the midst of your sore trials and afflictions. I. P.

London,
5th of Fifth Month, 1676.

LETTER LXVII.

Against Earthly Reasonings and Expectations.

To Sarah Bond.

Dear Sarah,—I have had many thoughts of thee in this my imprisonment; wherein, I have seen in spirit thy error and miscarriage, and a hope and expectation in thy heart, which will deceive thee.

O how much precious time hast thou lost! wherein thou mightst have been travelling far on thy journey, while thou art disputing in thy mind, and wandering in the deceitful reasonings of thy heart. And indeed, it must not be, it must not be as thou imaginest; but, thou must begin low, and be glad of a little light to travel with out of the earthly nature, and be faithful thereunto; and in faithfulness expect additions of light, and so much power as may help thee to rub on. And, though thou may be long low, and weak, and little, and ready to perish; yet, in the humble and self-denying state, the Father will help thee, and cause his life to shoot up in thee, in the shooting up whereof, will be thy redemption.

But, O hasten! O hasten out of the earthly nature, whilst thou hast time, or any visitations from the Spirit of the Lord! and do not in thy wisdom limit him, but accept what at present comes from him; for the flood is breaking out, and will swallow up and drown all, that are not found in the ark. Oh! therefore, enter, enter apace; mind that which checks in thy heart; mind also that which reasons against those checks, to hold thee still in captivity, and to keep thee from travelling out of the earthly nature, spirit, wisdom, and practices; and come out of the spirit and way of this world, that thou mayest live, and not die. For, none shall live, but those that walk in the way of life, and leave the paths and course of the dead, in which thou art yet entangled. O! that thou mightst be loosed, and travel out thence, with a little light and a little help; and not limit the Holy One of Israel in thy desires or expectations, but thankfully receive the smallest visitation that comes from him to thy soul; for, there is life and peace in it, and death and perplexity in turning from it. And, *this* will not be thy comfort or satisfaction hereafter, to have had a day of visitation and mercy from on high; but to have received the visitation, and to have been turned in it, from the darkness of the earthly mind and nature, into the light of the living and redeemed souls — this will be comfortable, indeed!

And this is my tender counsel to thee: wait for, and *gaspingly* receive the checks of the Most High, and take heed of reasoning against them; but, as that (though in a low, and mean, and despicable way to thy wisdom) draws and leads thee out of any earthly thought, word, custom, or practice, follow diligently; not reasoning against it, but, waiting to have thy reasonings subdued to the smallest motions, and lowest guidance of life in thee. For, I know that life is near thee, even the life that would effectually redeem thee; but, it is bowed down and held captive under the dominion of the earthly wisdom; and so, thy redemption (which is to be wrought out by it) sticks, and will stick, until thy heart be persuaded to join to it and become subject, without reasoning, without consulting, without disputing. For, I certainly know, the light manifests in thee; but, the darkness puts off the present manifestation of the light, and expects another; and, this is in the will of the flesh, which the Father will not answer; and, *in this* will and expectation, thou wilt perish; but, thy help, life, and salvation, is, in being subject to the present manifestation of light, parting with, and departing from, what thou already knowest to be of the earth, and not of God.

And, in thus doing, more will be made manifest in the Lord's season, and power given to become a child, after some belief in the Father, and some entrance into the child-like nature; but, the will and expectation of the flesh in thee, shall never be answered:—it hath been long written in my heart concerning thee, but I dare never utter it to thee — O that it may be now uttered, to the melting and advantage of thy heart! for, indeed, I love thee, and have travailed for thee, and desire the salvation of thy soul, as of my own. O that thou mayest be led out of that wisdom which destroys, into that which saves! and mayest there, in humility of heart, receive instruction daily, according to thy need. But, indeed, of a truth, thou must come into and come under that, which crucifies *thy* nature and wisdom; and there, (in the seasons of God's wisdom, who answers the desires of his own Spirit in the heart, but regards not the flesh,) mayest thou meet with life and power, but no where else.

I am thy Friend, and a dear lover of *that* in thee, which desires the Lord; and, O that *that* might come up in thee, and be severed from *the earth*, that thy soul may live! I. P.

LETTER LXVIII.

An Invitation to Heavenly Substance.

FRIEND, — The vessel, or created nature, poisoned by sin and death, nothing can redeem, but the life and power of God revealed in the vessel. This life, this peace, this power, this righteousness, this salvation, is the Lord Jesus Christ. And he that feels any thing of this, feels somewhat of Christ; and being joined to, and partaking of it, partakes somewhat of his redemption; for, it is not by an outward knowledge, but, by an inward virtue and spiritual life, received from Christ, and held in Christ, that those who are saved, are saved. This is the thing of value with me, for which I have been made willing to part with all, and into this purchased possession am I daily travelling; and in my travels, the Father of life and tender mercy pleaseth to help me.

Now, to have thee gathered into this light, this life, this power, which is of Christ, and in which he is, and appears, is the desire of my soul, in uprightness of heart before the Lord, for thee: and, if he please, I am willing to be instrumental in his hand, towards the bringing forth of this in thee. It is not my desire, to bring forth new notions in thee; but rather, that thou mightst wait on the Lord, for him to bring up his living, powerful Truth in thee, wherein the knowledge of the new and living way, is alone revealed.

I am a worm, I am poor, I am nothing; less than nothing, as in myself; weaker than I can express, or thou imagine; yet, in the midst of all this, the life, power, righteousness, and presence of Christ, is my refreshment, peace, joy, and crown: and that, to which I invite thee, is substance, everlasting substance, which thou shalt know and acknowledge in spirit to be so, as that is created and raised in thee, which can see and acknowledge it in Truth. O! wait on the Lord, fear before him, pray for his fear in the upright breathings, (which are not of thy spirit's forming, but of his pure begetting;) that thou mayest be led by him, out of that wisdom which entangles, into that innocency, simplicity, and precious childishness, in which the Father appears to the soul, to break the bonds and snares of iniquity; for, hereby, the evil spirit not only involveth in iniquity, but also begets a belief, as if there could be no perfect redemption therefrom, till the time of redemption be over.

Thy truly loving Friend, desiring the right guidance and happiness of thy soul, by the Lord Jesus Christ, the alone skilful Shepherd and Guide, even as of my own soul. I. P.

Aylesbury Prison,
20th of Tenth Month, 1666.

LETTER LXIX.

Exhortation to Walk in the Truth.

FOR MY DEAR FRIENDS IN THE TRUTH AT LEWES.

THE God of truth plants his Truth in the hearts of people, that it might grow there, and bring forth fruit to him. O my dear Friends! feel it grow in every one of your hearts, and bringing forth the proper fruits of its growth to the Lord.

Mind what ariseth from the Truth, what Truth brings forth, and wait for and receive your nourishment from the Lord, that it may be brought forth in you. And, that which the Lord hath made barren (in you, who have experienced his righteous judgments,) let it be kept so, by the same power which made it barren, that no more fruit may be brought forth to sin and unrighteousness, by any of you. Then shall ye live the life of Truth, and no life but the life of Truth, and dwell and walk in the Truth, than which, there is no greater joy, delight, or peace to be desired or enjoyed.

O my dear Friends! know, and every day experience Enoch's life, — a being translated out of the kingdom of darkness, into the kingdom of the dear Son, and of walking with the Son in his kingdom; then, ye will walk with the Father also, and know the heavenly paths of life, joy, righteousness, and peace in the pure light of life, which is no less than a paradise to the renewed soul.

I would fain have seen you together, had the Lord made way; but, let me feel you in the hidden life, and meet you at my Father's throne, where, let us beg of our God, what our souls and His whole flock stand in need of, praying for the peace and prosperity of Jerusalem, unto the God and Father of our Lord Jesus Christ, who hears our prayers; that we may daily see and feel the going on of the work of our God, in our hearts and in the kingdoms of the world, (which must become the Lord's and his Christ's,) and may bless and magnify his name, who hath power over all, and orders all for good to his chosen heritage.

This is the salutation of my love to you, which lay so upon me, that I could not pass it by, who am your Friend, in the everlasting unchangeable Truth of our blessed God and Saviour. I. P.

LETTER LXX.

Consolation for a Mother on the death of her Child.

To SARAH ELGAR.

THE child, which the Lord hath taken from thee, was his own. He hath done thee no wrong, in calling it from thee. Take heed of murmuring, take heed of discontent, take heed of any grief, but what Truth allows thee. Thou hast yet one child left. The Lord may call for that too, if he please; or he may continue and bless it to thee. O mind a right frame of spirit towards the Lord, in this thy great affliction! If thou mind God's Truth in thy heart, and wait to feel the seasoning thereof, that will bring thee into, and preserve thee in a right frame of spirit. The Lord will not condemn thy love and tenderness to thy child, or thy tender remembrance of him; but still, in it, be subject to the Lord, and let his will and disposal be bowed unto by thee, and not the will of thy nature set above it. Retire out of the natural, into the spiritual, where thou mayest feel the Lord thy portion; so that now, in the needful time, thou mayest day by day receive and enjoy satisfaction therein. O wait to feel the Lord, making thy heart what he would have it to be, in this thy deep and sore affliction! I. P.

NUNNINGTON,
Sixth Month, 1679.

Now let the world see, how thou prizest Truth, and what Truth can do for thee. Feed on it; do not feed on thy affliction; and the life of Truth will arise in thee, and raise thee up over it, to the honour of the name of the Lord, and to the comfort of thy own soul.

LETTER LXXI.

Advice respecting Church Discipline.

TO THE WOMEN'S MEETING OF FRIENDS IN THE TRUTH, AT JOHN MANNOCK'S.

DEAR FRIENDS, — Dearly beloved and honoured in the Lord, because of his honourable presence and power, which is so preciously manifested and found to be among you in your meetings.

Blessed be the Lord, who hath thus gathered you! and given you hearts to meet together, to feel his precious presence and power, and wait to do his will therein, as he shall please to call, and make your way clear thereto. And, blessed be the Lord! who doth encourage and reward you daily, and make your meetings pleasant and advantageous to your own souls, and towards the seasoning and holy watching over the several respective places, where your lot is fallen.

Oh! what could the Lord do more for his people, than to turn them to that pure seed of life, which will make them all alive, and keep them all in life and purity; and then, to make use of every living member in the living body, as his Spirit shall please to breathe upon it, and his power actuate it! And indeed, there is need of all the life and power to the body, which the Lord sees good to bestow on any member of it; every member of the body having life given it, not only for itself, but likewise for the use and service of the body. Only, dear Friends, here is to be the great care, that every member keep within the limits of life, wherein its capacity and ability for service lies, and, out of which, it can do no real service for God, or to the body. O! therefore, eye life, eye the power, eye the presence of the Lord with your spirits! that he may go along with you, and guide you in every thought ye think, in every word ye speak, in reference to his work and service.

And mind, Friends, what is now upon me to you: it is one thing, to sit waiting to feel the power, and to keep within the limits of the power, thus far; and another, yea, and harder, to feel and keep within the sense and limits of the power, when ye come to act. Then, your reasonings, your wisdom, your apprehensions, have more advantage to get up in you, and to put themselves forth. O! therefore, watch narrowly, and diligently against the forward part; and keep back to the life, which, though it rise more slowly, yet acts more surely and safely for God.

O wait and watch, to feel your Keeper keeping you within the holy bounds and limits, within the pure fear, within the living sense, while ye are acting for your God! that ye may only be his instruments, and feel him acting in you. Therefore, every one wait to feel the Judge risen and up, and the judgment set, in your own hearts; that, what ariseth in you, may be judged and nothing may pass from you publicly, but what hath first passed the pure judgment in your own breasts. And, let the holy rule of the blessed apostle James, be always upon your spirits, "Let every one be swift to hear, slow to speak, slow to wrath." O let not a talkativeness have place in any of you! but, abide in such gravity, modesty, and weightiness of spirit, as becomes the judgment-seat of the Spirit and power of the Lord. Ye can never wait too much for the power, nor can ye ever act too much in the power; but, ye may easily act too much without it.

And as for this troublesome, contentious business, (if the Lord should yet order it to be brought before you,) the Lord teach you to consider of, and manage it in a wise, tender, and healing spirit. Ye must distinguish in judgment, if ye judge aright, between enemies and erring friends. And, take heed of the quickness and strength of reason, or of the natural part, which avails little: but, wait for the evidence and demonstration of God's Spirit, which reaches to the witness and doth the work. Are they in a snare? are they overtaken in a fault? yea, are they in measure blinded and hardened, so that they can neither see nor feel, as to this particular? Retire, sit still awhile, and travail for them. Feel how life will arise in any of you, and how mercy will reach towards them; and how living words, from the tender sense, may be reached forth to their hearts, deeply, by the hand of the Lord, for their good. And, if ye find them, at length, bowing to the Lord, O let tender compassion help them forwards! that what hath been so troublesome and groundedly dissatisfactory in the progress, may, at length, have a sweet issue for their good, and our joy and rejoicing in the Lord.

So, my dear Friends, the Lord be with you, and guide you in this, and in all that he shall further call you to; and multiply his presence, power, and blessings upon you, and make your meetings as serviceable to the honour of his name, as he himself would have them, and as you yourselves can desire them to be.

Your Friend and brother in the tender Truth, and in the pure love and precious life. I. P.

19th of Fifth Month, 1678.

LETTER LXXII.

On Prayer in Families, &c. Also on the state of Professors of the day.

Because my not praying in my family, according to the custom of professors, seemed to be such a great stumbling-block to thee, it sprang up in my heart to render thee this account thereof.

I did formerly apply myself to pray to the Lord, morning and evening, (besides other times,) believing in my heart, that it was the will of the Lord I should so do. And this was my condition then: — sometimes I felt the living spring open, and the true child breathe towards the Father; at other times, I felt a deadness, a dryness, a barrenness, and only a speaking and striving of the natural part, which I, even then, felt was not acceptable to the Lord, nor did profit my soul; but, apprehending it to be a duty, I durst not but apply myself thereto.

Since that time,—since the Lord hath again been pleased to raise up what he had formerly begotten in me, and began to feed it, by the pure giving forth of that breath of life which begat it, (which is the bread that comes down from heaven daily to it, as the Lord pleaseth freely to dispense it,) — the Lord hath shown me, that prayer is his gift to the child which he begets; and that it stands not in the will, or time, or understanding, or affectionate part of the creature, but in his own begetting, which he first breathes upon, and then it breathes again towards him; — and that he worketh this at his own pleasure, and no time can be set him when he shall breathe, or when he shall not breathe; and that when he breathes, then is the time of prayer, then is the time of moving towards him, and following him who draws. So that, all my times, and all my duties, and all my graces, and all my hopes, and all my refreshments, and all my ordinances, are in his hand, who is the spring of my life, and conveys, preserves, and increases life of his own good pleasure.

I freely confess, all my religion stands in waiting on the Lord, for the riches of his Spirit, and in returning back to the Lord, (by his own Spirit, and in the virtue of his own life,) that which he pleaseth to bestow on me. And, I have no faith, no love, no hope, no peace, no joy, no ability to anything, no refreshment in anything, but as I find his living breath beginning, his living breath continuing, his living breath answering, and performing what it calls for. So that, I am become exceeding poor and miserable, save in what the Lord pleaseth to be to me by his own free grace, and for his own name's sake, and in rich mercy. And, if I have tasted anything of the Lord's goodness sweeter than ordinary, my heart is willing, so far as the Lord pleaseth, faithfully to point any others to the same spring; and not discourage or witness against the least simplicity, and true desire after God, in them. But, where they have lost the true living child, and another thing is got up in its stead, (which, though it may bear its image to the eye of flesh, yet is not the same thing in the sight of God;) and, where this nourisheth itself by praying, reading, meditating, or any other such like thing, feeding the carnal part with such a kind of knowledge from Scriptures, as the natural understanding may gather and grow rich by; this, in love and faithfulness to the

Lord and to souls, I cannot but testify against, wherever I find it, as the Lord draweth forth my spirit to bear its testimony.

And this I know, from the Lord, to be the general state of professors at this day. The Spirit of the Lord is departed from them, and they joined to another spirit, as deeply and as generally as ever the Jews were; and that their prayers and reading of the Scriptures, and preaching, and duties, and ordinances, are, as loathsome to the soul of the Lord, as ever the Jews' incense and sacrifices were. And this is the word of the Lord concerning them. Ye must come out of your knowledge, into the feeling of an inward principle of life, if ever ye be restored to the true unity with God, and to the true enjoyment of him again. Ye must come out of the knowledge and wisdom ye have gathered from the Scriptures, into a feeling of the thing there written of, as it pleaseth the Lord to open and reveal them in the hidden man of the heart.

This is it, ye are to wait for from the Lord; and not to boast of your present state, as if ye were not backslidden from him, and had not entered into league with another spirit; which keeps up the image of what the Spirit of the Lord once formed in you, but without the true, pure, fresh life.

From a faithful Friend and lover of souls. I. P.

LETTER LXXIII.

Of Preservation and a Growth in the Heavenly Life; its Power over the Earthly Nature.

TO THE SINGLE, UPRIGHT-HEARTED AND FAITHFUL FRIENDS OF TRUTH, IN AND ABOUT THE TWO CHALFONTS.

DEAR FRIENDS,— Have ye in any measure drunk in the sense of what the Lord hath done for you? and have ye felt meltings of spirit, and bowings before him, with praises to his name therefor? Indeed, my request is to the Lord for you, that he would please to keep you truly sensible of what he already is to you, and of what he hath already done for you; that he would also, of his tender mercy and great goodness, visit you yet further, increase life in you, cause faith to abound, give you to dwell in his power, and always abide in his seed, and feel *that* to be your hope, peace, joy, life, and strength, continually; that ye may more and more give thanks unto him, as ye feel his pure life arising in you, and death and the grave swallowed up thereby.

Ah! my Friends, can we ever forget the lost and miserable estate, wherein the mercy of the Lord and his power from on high visited us? O the blackness of that day, the misery, the deep distress of that day, which some of your souls felt! Did ye not know, what it was to want God, and to lie open to the furious assaults of the enemy; when ye felt no strength, nor knew whither to retire, to keep out any hurt, any temptation, any vain thought and imagination, or to give you any grounded hope in the goodness and mercy of the Lord? How did ye mourn, how did ye cry out, and pine away in your iniquities day and night! and knew not which way to look, nor what to wait for! Are there not among you, who have known this state, and felt somewhat of that which I now relate? Sure I am, there are upon the earth, who can witness it to the full, whose mouths and hearts are now filled with a sense of the Lord's goodness, and of his great salvation, and with deep and high praises to his name.

But, my dear Friends, is there any of you, (I know to whom I speak, even, to the sensible, to the diligent, to the faithful among you,) who cannot in truth witness, as in God's presence, concerning the arm and power of his salvation, which ye have often felt? insomuch, that ye can sing that song, "He hath raised up an horn of salvation for us in the house of his servant David; as he spake by the mouth of his holy prophets." Do ye not know the house of his servant David, with the horn of salvation in it, and that horn raised up to you for your defence and comfort? Yea, do ye not daily feel the Lord, ministering out salvation to you from it? Are not your enemies daily overcome by the faith, which he hath given you in his power. May I not say to you, where is the strength of the tempter? Have ye not felt the seed of the woman to bruise the head of the serpent? so that, in the fear of the Lord, and in the strength, virtue, and dominion of his life manifested in you, ye can say, though as yet somewhat tremblingly, Where are those temptations, those lusts, vain thoughts, and imaginations, which once I was overcome by and overrun with? Surely, I may speak thus; for, I know assuredly, that the power of the Lord God, as it is lifted up in any of you, scatters these, and gives you dominion over them. For, the life and its power is given as a bulwark and weapon of war against iniquity and its power; and, where it is received, it opposeth, warreth, striveth, until it overcome.

And, this is that which gives the victory and overcoming; to wit, faith in the seed. The seed felt, the soul joined to it, faith in it and from it given to the soul.

Then, it becomes the Leader, the mighty undertaker for the soul, and overcomes its snares and enemies for it; and, when it hath overcome them, they are overcome indeed. And then the soul lies down in peace, dwells in peace, feeds on the living nourishment, in the green pastures of life, in peace. Then Jerusalem, the building of life in the heart, becomes a quiet habitation, where God and the soul dwell sweetly together; and there is nothing that hath power in it to disturb, annoy, or make afraid. Why so? Because the Lord God of power is present there, stretcheth out his wings there, is a pillar of cloud by day, and a pillar of fire by night there! He hath raised up his glorious life in that heart, whereof he is very choice; and he hath also spread a defence over his glory, with which the soul is so encompassed and defended, that it feels the walls of this city to be salvation, and its gates praise.

O my soul, travel on! — O dear Friends! do ye also travel on, into the fulness of the glory of this state. There is no other thing to be desired and waited for. This is your portion, both here in this world, and forever. Therefore, wait in the seed of *this* life; wait to feel yet a further gathering into it, and a growing up in it; and give yourselves up to it, that it may overspread and cover you. And, the Lord God of life daily open it, and manifest it more and more in you and to you: that ye may be more found in him, and yet more acceptable and pleasing in the eyes of your God; and may sing praises unto him, not only at the foot of the hill, in some true proportion and measure of his life, but in the very heights of Zion, even in the fulness of the measure of your stature in Christ; which ye are all diligently to press after, till ye arrive at. And then, there is no more to be done, but to spread abroad into, and drink in of, and live in, the full pleasure and safety of life, forever! Then may ye eat freely of the tree of life, which is in the midst of the paradise of God, and draw water with joy out of the wells of salvation!

Therefore feel, O! feel in spirit, the mark of the high calling of God in Christ Jesus; and be daily looking up to that, which quickens to God, and keeps fresh and lively in him; that none of you grow slothful, drowsy, or negligent, and so, unfaithful, in relation to the great talent, which God hath put into your hands; and so, the Lord be provoked against you, and suffer the enemy to tempt and prevail upon you; that a veil come over your hearts again, and the air thicken, and the earthly nature cover the seed; and he that hath power in that earth and over that air, captivate, oppress, entangle, and lead you back from God again. O! cry to the Lord, to keep the eye open, and the heart single, and the soul in the true sense and feeling; that the heavenly voice, which drew you out of the earth, may be daily heard further instructing you, and gathering you more and more up into Him, who is your life. — So, ye that fear the Lord, and love his name, and have tasted of his goodness and powerful salvation, O hate evil! All that his light hath made manifest, and drawn you from, O take heed of ever dallying with again! O never hearken to the tempter! but pray to the Father, that ye may discern his baits, and at no time consult or reason with him; but still wait, in everything, to feel the motion, guidance, quickening, and sweet, pure, heavenly leading of the Spirit of your Father!

Hath the Lord spoken peace to you, peace which passeth man's understanding, and only flows from him? hath he given you any proportion of this precious peace? O! may he watch over you, and preserve you in that wisdom, in those heavenly instructions, in that heavenly life, divine power, and holy conversation, wherein ye met with that peace, and wherein alone ye can enjoy and possess it! and keep you out of all manner of sin, lust, and foolishness of the fleshly mind and spirit; — for, the peace is not there. That is the fruit of the enemy to your peace, and it hath of his nature in it; it always breaks your peace, and sows distance, difference and division, between the Giver and Maker of your peace and you. Do ye not always (ye that are in the true sense, and have received the holy understanding,) feel it thus, and know it to be thus? it is an eternal truth, and the eternal eye, wherever it is opened, witnesseth and sealeth to it. Therefore, this little thing, this light of God in you, to which ye were first directed and turned, which discovers all the darkness of the enemy, and all his deceits and devices, and keeps the minds of those that are stayed by it, — in this wait, to this let your minds be still turned, and in it still abide; and the power and glory of eternal life, will daily more and more appear in you, yea, flow and break in upon you; to the filling of your vessels with its virtue, and the causing of your hearts to abound with joy before the Lord, and with thanksgivings to him.

May the God of tender mercies and everlasting compassions, cause the bowels of his love to be daily yearning towards you; that you may be nursed up with the living food, and that which would overturn and destroy his work, may be opposed; that ye may feel it daily go on, yea, mightily preserved and carried on by him, even till it be finished, and the top stone laid; and your souls, in the true and full sense of life, cry, *Grace, grace,* to Him that laid the foundation, raised up, defended, and carried on the building, and now at length had perfected it. And thus, whatsoever ye have hitherto witnessed in measure, ye shall then witness in fulness; and see, that all the promises of God are of a precious nature, and are, "yea and amen" from God to the seed.

May the life, presence, and power of the Lord be with

you in this seed; in your breathings after it, in your joinings to it, in your abidings and waitings upon him in it; and, the Lord God give you to breathe after it, give you to join to it, give you to abide always, and wait upon him in it, and never to hearken to and go out after a contrary spirit and wisdom; but keep you in the simplicity, lowliness, humility, and tender spirit which is in Christ Jesus, to the praise of his own name, and preservation and joy of your hearts before him forever, amen!

Written, in the tender bowels and motion of the pure life, from the place of my confinement in Aylesbury.

I. P.

1st of Third Month, 1667.

LETTER LXXIV.

The Holy Scriptures not the Primary Rule.

To Nathaniel Stonar.

Dear Friend, — There was somewhat on my heart towards thee this morning, which I am willing in truth and uprightness to express to thee, as the Lord knoweth.

There is a great dispute between us and professors, concerning *the rule;* which they hold forth the Scriptures to be. Now, truly I could wish, from the depth of love in my heart to them, and from my desire of their good, that the Scriptures, rightly understood by them, *were* their rule; and not their own reasonings, conceivings, and apprehendings upon the Scriptures. But yet, if it were so, they must needs assent to me, that the Spirit of life,—that the Truth, which lives in the heart,—that the law, written by the finger of God in the inward parts, — is nearer and more powerful, than the words, or outward relations concerning those things in the Scriptures. There is a measure of life to be received, — there is the Spirit of life to be received, there is a well of life, from which pure life springs up, to be received and enjoyed by them that truly and rightly believe.

The Lord, in the gospel state, hath promised to be present with his people; not as a wayfaring man, for a night, but to *dwell in them and walk in them.* Yea, if they be tempted and in danger of erring, they shall hear a voice behind them, saying, "This is the way, walk in it." Will they not grant this to be a rule, as well as the Scriptures? Nay, is not this a more full direction to the heart, in that state, than it can pick to itself out of the Scriptures? Truly, this ensuing testimony is true, which now springs up in my heart unto thee, which is this: — the Lord hath poured out his spirit upon his sons and daughters, in and by this precious dispensation of Truth, and of the pure seed, which is so despised. And the Spirit, which gave forth the words, is greater than the words; therefore, we cannot but prize Him himself, and set Him higher in our heart and thoughts, than the words which testify of Him, though they also are very sweet and precious to our taste.

There was a measure and rule, whereunto the true minister of Christ and the believing Gentiles had attained, by which they were to walk; as is mentioned in 2 Cor. x. 13, 15, "According to the measure of the rule, which God hath distributed to us"—"according to our rule," &c.; and in Philippians, iii. 16, "Whereto we have already attained, let us walk by the same rule, let us mind the same thing;" as also in Galatians, vi. 15, 16, "For, in Christ Jesus, neither circumcision availeth any thing, nor uncircumcision, but a new creature. And as many as walk according to this rule, peace be on them, and mercy," &c. Now, consider what *that rule* was. O! that thou mayest know it, and walk thereby, as they that had received God's Spirit did. For, I am assured in my heart, that, if thou receive God's Spirit, and live and walk therein, thou canst not fulfil the desires of the flesh; but, thou wilt find thy heart opened thereby into a true sense, understanding, and right use of the Scriptures. For, the Scriptures of the New Testament were written to the saints, and cannot be truly or rightly understood or made use of, but as men come into their spirit and state.*

---

* It will scarcely be supposed I. P. meant, without qualification, that we must be *saints*, or be brought into such a degree of religious experience as that to which the holy penman had arrived, before we can be benefitted by perusing the sacred writings. His meaning appears to be this,—that, in order to receive instruction hereby, we must let into the mind somewhat which can discover to us good and evil, which inclines us to the one, and reproves for the other. These are the earliest operations of the Spirit of God and of Christ, the same Spirit which so eminently ruled in the prophets, apostles, and saints, and now worketh in the children of obedience. Undoubtedly, when any have been reached or impressed in reading the Holy Scriptures, it has been, because divine light beamed (however feebly) upon their souls, whereby they discerned the things that belonged to their peace. For we read, that "the natural man," while in that state, "receiveth not the things of the Spirit of God;" and again, "The things of God knoweth no man," of or by himself, "but the Spirit of God." 1 Cor. ii. 14 and 11.

It seems, therefore, very wholesome and necessary counsel, to direct the minds of people, above all other means, to the light of Christ, to Christ in his inward appearance, as a seed of life, or quickening Spirit; that, receiving him in the way of his coming and operation, all the means of his appointment may be blessed to them; and thus, they may know the things that are freely given them of God. For, it is only in proportion as men become willing by virtue of some degree of faith, *to learn* CHRIST, and to be *taught by* HIM, *as the Truth is in Jesus*, that they can, through patience and comfort of the Scriptures, have hope; those precious testimonies having been given forth by Him, who is indeed the promise of the Father, and was to be sent in the Son's name, to teach us all things, and to guide into all Truth.

These things are of great weight and concernment: the Lord open and guide thy heart into true satisfaction in this and other things also, from the demonstration of his own Spirit; that thou mayest be able truly to say, as in his sight, Now I believe and understand things; not because this or that man hath so said, but because the Lord, who is the Teacher indeed, hath taught and assured my heart concerning the Truth itself, as it is in Jesus; which I feel to be so, by its living virtue and powerful operation in and upon my heart.

This is my desire for thee, who am thy soul's true and sincere Friend, who would by no means have thee deceived about anything that concerns it. I. P.

READING GAOL,
24th of Seventh Month, 1670.

LETTER LXXV.

On True, Living, Heavenly Knowledge.

TO THE LADY CONWAY.

DEAR FRIEND, — I have heard both of thy love to Truth, and of thy great afflictions outwardly; both which, occasion a sense concerning thee, and breathings to the tender Father of my life for thee: that thy heart may know and be joined to the Truth, and thou mayest live and walk in it, reaping the sweet comfort, support, and satisfaction, which God daily ministers in and through it, to his gathered and preserved ones. I am satisfied thou hast need of comforts and support; O! that thou mayest be led thither, and be daily found by the Lord there, where the Comforter doth daily delight to supply the afflicted and suffering ones, whether inwardly or outwardly, with comfort.

And, my dear Friend, take heed of that wisdom and knowledge which is not of the seed, and which can be held in the mind, without the springing life of the seed. The first day I was convinced, I was not only convinced in my understanding concerning the seed, but I felt the seed in my heart, and my heart was enraptured with the sense and feeling of it; and, my great cry to the Lord was, that I might faithfully travel, through all the sufferings and death of the other part, into union with and enjoyment of it; and that that wisdom, which was not of the pure living root and nature, might die in me. Now, how I have been exercised and taught since, is hard for me to utter. What poverty, what weakness, what foolishness I have been led into! how I have learned, in a sense, out of the reach of the comprehending, knowing mind; how tender I have been of every secret shining of light in my heart; how the Lord hath taught and enabled me, to pluck out my right eye, and cut off my right hand, and cast them from me, that I might not see with that eye, nor work with that hand, but be greatly maimed in the sight of men, and in my own sight too.

O Friend! wait daily to feel the seed, to feel the seed live in thee, and the most pleasing part of thy nature die, as it can live out of the seed. O that thou couldst change all old knowledge, for that which is new and living! The seed is the well: receive the seed, then thou receivest the well: let it spring, wait for its springing, wait to know its springing: bear all the trials and judgments, which the Father of life sees necessary, to prepare the heart for its springing. O feel that which limits and subdues thoughts, and brings them into captivity and subjection! Be not exercised in things too high for thee; — David, the man after God's own heart, who was wiser than his teachers, was not; — but, come out of knowledge into feeling, and there thou wilt find the true knowledge given,—arising, springing, and covering thy heart, as the waters cover the sea. And, still wait to be taught of God, to distinguish between the outwardness of knowledge,—the notional part of the thing known, as it can be comprehended in the mind,—and the life of it, as it is felt and abides in the heart.

The Lord God of my life be thy Teacher; point thy mind to the pure seed of the kingdom, and open it in thee;—make thee so little, that thou mayest enter into it, and keep thee so low and poor, that thou mayest abide in it; managing these troublesome times in the outward, for thy advantage in the inward; that the city and temple of the living God may be built in it, and thou mayest know him daily dwelling and walking therein. Thus, mayest thou be married to the Lord, and become one spirit with him; finding that daily removing from thee, [which is to be removed, even] by the mighty arm and pure operation of his Spirit, till all that is contrary be done away; then, may thy soul dwell with its Beloved, in fulness of joy, life, and peace for evermore.

This is from the tender love, and fresh breathings of life, in thy soul's true Friend, and most hearty well-wisher. I. P.

17th of Third Month, 1677.

Note.—Respecting the interesting character addressed in this and two other letters, (see pages 107 and 109,) the editor regrets he has not been able to procure information, beyond what follows. George Fox, in his Journal, about the year 1677, writes, "I had meetings at Pershore and Evesham; then struck to Ragley in Warwickshire, to visit the Lady Conway, who I understood was very desirous to see me, and whom I found tender and loving, and willing to have detained me longer than I had freedom to stay." It is also stated, in an authentic manuscript respecting Robert Barclay, *the Apologist;* that the meeting-house, belonging to Friends at Aberdeen, was "mostly bought with his own money, and some by his means obtained from the Countess of Conway, *one of the same persuasion* in England," &c.

LETTER LXXVI.

On Disputation; and on Hearing Wisdom's Voice. Also Respecting the Puritan State.

To E. Terry.

Friend,—If the Lord hath extended favour to thee and shown thee mercy, I therein rejoice on thy behalf.

Thy desire, that what thou wrotest may be looked upon as nothing, and that no contest may be raised from it, I am content fully to answer thee in; nor do I desire to have any advantage against thee, nor art thou at all disparaged in my thoughts by what thou hast written, but it is in my heart as nothing, and my love flows to thee; for, I take notice of thy seriousness, and what I have unity with in this letter, and overlook the other.

As touching disputes, indeed, I have no love to them: Truth did not enter my heart that way, nor do I expect to propagate it in others that way; yet, sometimes a necessity is laid upon me, for the sake of others. And truly, when I do feel a necessity, I do it in great fear; not trusting in my spear or bow, I mean, in strong arguments or wise considerations, which I (of myself) can gather or comprehend; but, I look up to the Lord for the guidance, help, and demonstration of his Spirit, that way may be made thereby in men's hearts for the pure seed to be reached to, wherein the true conviction, and thorough conversion of the soul to God, is witnessed. I had far rather be feeling Christ's life, Spirit, and power in my own heart, than disputing with others about them.

Christians that truly fear the Lord, have a proportion of the primitive Spirit; and, if they could learn to watch and wait there, where God works the fear, they would daily receive more and more of it, and, in it, understand more and more the true intent and preciousness of the words of the Holy Scriptures. He that will truly live to God, must hear wisdom's voice within, at home, in his own heart; and he that will have her words made known, and her spirit poured out to him, must turn at her reproof. Prov. i. 23. Indeed, I never knew, and am satisfied that none else can know, the preciousness of this lesson, till they are taught it of the Lord.

There is one thing more on my heart to express, occasioned by thy last letter, which is this: — I have more unity in my heart and spirit before the Lord, with the Puritan state, than with the churches and gatherings, which men have built up and run into since. Indeed, men have enlarged their knowledge and comprehension of things; but, that truth of heart, that love, that tenderness, that unity upon Truth's account, which was then amongst them, many have made shipwreck of, and do not now know the state of their own souls, nor Truth in the life and power of it. This principle of life and truth was near me, as well as others; yea, with me in that day; but, I wandered from it into outward knowledge, and, with great seriousness, into a way of congregational worship, and thereby came to a great loss; and at length, for want of the Lord's presence, power, and manifestation of his love, was sick at heart. But now, the Lord, in great love and tender mercy, having brought me back to the same principle, and fixed my spirit therein; I discern the truth and beauty of that former estate, with the several runnings out from it; and find what was true or false therein, discovered to me by the holy anointing, which appears and teaches in that principle. And, Friend, it is not a notion of light, which my heart is engaged to testify to; but, that which enlivens, that which opens, that which gives to see, that wherein the power of life is felt. For truly, in the opening of my heart by the pure power, was I taught to see and own the principle and seed of life, and to know its way of appearance; and so, can faithfully and certainly testify, that that which is divine, spiritual, and heavenly, is nearer man than he is aware, as well as that which is earthly and selfish.

O Friend! if thou canst not yet see and own the principle and seed of Christ's life and Spirit, nor discern his appearance therein; yet take heed of fighting against it; for indeed, if thou dost, thou fightest against no less than the Lord Jesus Christ himself. I. P.

LETTER LXXVII.

Advice as to Self-deceit. On the Unity of the Spirit. The Younger are to submit to the Elder

To Miles Stanclif.

Dear M. S.,— Thou art often in my heart; and indeed, I do many times bow unto the Father of spirits, for the preservation of whatever is good in thee, for the clear discovery to thee of what is not of his pure life, and for the separation of thy mind from it; that the life of Christ may conquer in thee, and thou thereby be fully redeemed to the Lord. I often inquire after thee; and, when I hear of any tenderness or diligence in thee towards the Truth, my heart rejoiceth therein.

Dear Friend, deceit is very deep, and hath much prevailed; but, the Lord is gathering out of it, and preparing such, by the power of his life, against future snares. O dear Friend! take heed of thy own wisdom, thy own sense, thy own judgment, which thou mayest easily, through mistake, call the Lord's: but, to have all that is of self searched out and brought under, and the mind made truly sensible of, and fully subject to the life in every thing,—this is a sore travel; and it is very hard to come hither, through all deceits and entanglements. The Lord entirely join thy mind to that, and preserve thee in that, which gives thee at any time a sense of Truth, and of those who are in the Truth: these are to be known and honoured in the Lord, according to their growth. And, take heed of that which prejudices and disjoins; but feel and cleave to that which uniteth in love, life, and pure power. Know that unity and fellowship, which is in the Spirit; and keep it, keep it in the bond of pure peace: and take heed, O forever take heed of whatever would break the bond! but, that which makes of one mind and one judgment, one heart and one soul, *that* is the living principle, *that* is the living power, which all the members of the body are to inhabit and be one in. And, watch against the reasonings of the mind, and the thoughts of thy heart; watch to the sense, which riseth up in the fear, in the love, in the humility, that thou mayest feel the leadings of God's Spirit, and come through all that stands in thy way; having the help of all whom the Lord hath ordained, and made able to be helpers to thee. For, life is not to be limited, but we are to be limited by that which is of the life; and, in cases of doubt, it is the ordinance of the Lord, for the weak to receive counsel and help from the strong, and for the lesser to be watched over and blessed by the greater,—by such as are more grown in the life, and into the power.

So, the Lord God Almighty lead thee fully into, and preserve thee perfectly in, the way everlasting!

Thy Friend in the true love, I. P.

16th of Third Month, 1668.

LETTER LXXVIII.

The Loving-Kindness of the Lord.

To Elizabeth Walmsley, of Giles Chalfont.

Dear Friend, — The thoughts of thee are pleasant to me; indeed, I am melted with the sense of the Lord's love to thee, as to my own soul.

What were we, that the Lord should stretch forth his arm to us, and gather us? And what are we, that the Lord should daily remember us, in the issuings forth of his loving-kindness and mercies? O his pity, his compassion! — (must I forever say,) — that my soul yet lives, and hath hope before him! And, canst not thou also say the same? O my Friend! we feel mercy and salvation from the Lord. O that he might have pure praise and service from his own in us! and yet, that will be little thanks to us, but rather a new mercy received from him. But, all is his own, and of his own do we give him, — and that, only when he quickens, helps, and enables us to give. Dear Friend, my desire for thee is, that the power and blessings of life may descend upon thee, and that thou mayest feel thy God near, and thy heart still ready to let him in, and shut against all that is of a contrary nature to his; that thou mayest know *that* death passing upon thee, and perfected in thee, which prepares for, and lets into, the fulness of his pure, unspotted life.

Thou mayest commend my dear love to thy sister, and to all Friends, as thou hast opportunity, who breathe after the Lord, and desire in uprightness of heart to walk with him.

I am thy Friend, in the affection which is of the Truth,

I. P.

Aylesbury,
20th of Fourth Month, 1666.

LETTER LXXIX.

On Confessing Christ before Men, &c.

To Elizabeth Stonar.

Dear Friend,—Whose life in the Lord, and prosperity in the Truth, my heart greatly desireth; even, that thou mayest come to the perfect service, and free and full enjoyment of thy soul's Beloved; in which, if I could be in any way helpful to thee, my heart would greatly rejoice and bless the Lord. This morning, when I awoke, my heart was exercised before the Lord concerning thee; and several things did spring up in my mind relating to thee, which I may now signify to thee, as the Lord shall please to bring them again to my mind, and open them in my heart in reference to thee. I would fain have thee rightly understand, and be found doing, what the Lord requires of thee; that it may go well with thee, and that thy heart may be satisfied, and thy soul blessed, in believing and obeying the Truth as it is in Jesus.

The first thing that rose up in my heart concerning thee, this morning, was, about confessing Christ before men. It is a great duty, and I would not have thee mistake about it, or fail in it; but diligently wait on God to know what it is, and faithfully to practise it in thy state and place; which, if thou do, thou wilt find life and blessedness flowing with it upon thy soul.

After this, several Scriptures, sweet and precious to my taste, sprang up in my heart to lay before thy view; that thou also mightst suck sweetness, and reap benefit through the living sense of them, and the bowing of thy spirit to what the Lord shall please to make manifest to thee thereby.

The first Scripture that sprang up in me to thee, was

that of Rom. xii. 2, not to be conformed to this world, but to be transformed by the renewing of thy mind, that thou mayest prove that good, that acceptable, and perfect will of God. Thou must stand at a distance from the spirit of this world, thou must not touch the unclean thing, but be a chaste virgin in heart, in word, in conversation; if thou expect to be married to the Lamb, to become one spirit with him, to know his mind, and to enjoy the love and be the delight of his Father.

The next Scripture in my heart, was Rev. ii. 10, "Fear none of those things which thou shalt suffer." Upon which Scripture, this question rose in my heart to thee, Dost not thou fear the sufferings which may attend thee, in thy state and place, for Truth's sake? Dost not thou look out at them? If thou do, it will weaken thy faith, and be a snare to thee; and such a beam in thy eye, that thou wilt never be able to see that particular way and path of Truth, which is most proper for thy soul, till this beam be plucked out and separated from thee.

Unto this, was soon added that of Isaiah, li. 12, 13. "I, even I, am he that comforteth you: who art thou, that thou shouldst be afraid of a man that shall die, and of the son of man which shall be made as grass; and forgettest the Lord thy Maker, that hath stretched forth the heavens, and laid the foundations of the earth; and hast feared continually every day, because of the fury of the oppressor, as if he were ready to destroy? and where is the fury of the oppressor?" O take heed of distrusting the Comforter, *thy* Comforter! who is able and ready to help and comfort the souls of his, in the sorest distresses and oppressions that can befall them, either within or without. And, consider this also, that forgetting the Lord, is the necessary consequence of fearing man. It cannot be, but that, he that feareth man should in some measure or degree forget the Lord,— his love, his wisdom, his power, his goodness, his faithfulness to, and tender care over his children in their following him,— especially, in the midst of the cruel hardships and sufferings, which often befall them therein.

The next was Samson's riddle, Judges, xiv. 14, "Out of the eater came forth meat, and out of the strong came forth sweetness." It is everlastingly true, both inwardly and outwardly, to the children of the Most High, who live in his Spirit, and walk in his Spirit, and are guided by the power and virtue of his life. Every thing that would devour and destroy them, the Lord destroyeth, by the power and virtue of his life and Spirit springing up in them; and, out of that which is strong against them, which roars against them in the strength and power of darkness, the Lord brings forth sweetness in and to their spirits.

Then, that of Luke, ix. 23, 24, came before me, (which is said to all that hear Christ's voice and blessed counsel,) "If any man will come after me, let him deny himself, and take up his cross daily, and follow me. For, whosoever will save his life shall lose it; but whosoever will lose his life for my sake, the same shall save it." Now, I beseech thee, consider; dost thou take up the daily cross, and bear it faithfully for Christ's sake? Dost thou stand a faithful witness against the spirit of darkness, and works of darkness, where thou livest? Dost thou not comply with any worship there, which thy heart knoweth to be out of the Truth and Spirit of life, wherein all true, holy, living spiritual worship, can alone be performed? Oh! take heed of shunning the cross in any respect; for then, thou givest way to unbelief, and to that wisdom, thoughts, reasonings, and judgment, which are not of the Truth, but of the flesh: shunning that, which God hath appointed to crucify sin in the heart, and under which the seed is to spring up and live, which is the power of God unto salvation, to all that abide under it, and daily bear it.

The last Scripture, which at this time sprang up in me to thee, was that very sweet one in Solomon's Song of Songs, chap. i. ver. 7, 8, "Tell me, O thou whom my soul loveth, where thou feedest, where thou makest thy flock to rest at noon: for, why should I be as one that turneth aside by the flocks of thy companions? If thou know not, O thou fairest among women, go thy way forth by the footsteps of the flock, and feed thy kids beside the shepherd's tent." If thou wouldst come to the feeding-place of the flock, and to rest in the pure life, power, and righteousness of the Lord with them; thou must mind their footsteps, thou must go forth out of that, which God hath gathered and led them forth out of, thou must forsake whatever is not of the Father, but of this world, (and, in forsaking it, stand a witness against the world,) as God hath taught them to forsake it. Thou must wait for the same Spirit, for the same cloud and smoke by day, and the shining of the same flaming fire by night, to lead thee and preserve thee, which hath led and preserved them; see Isai. iv. 5. And this will lead thee out of the same Egypt and Sodom, and all the remainders of Babylon, wherein as yet thou mayest be held captive; and this alone must break the oppressing spirit and power which stands in thy way, through thy faithful sufferings under it. And, through the same wilderness and righteous judgments of the Lord, must thou pass, that they have passed. For, Zion and her converts must be redeemed with judgment and righteousness, and with the spirit of burning, and the pain of the cross; nor dost thou know, how thou standest in the way of thy own soul's good, while thou in any measure avoidest or escapest it. And, if thou be one of the called, chosen, and faithful, following fully after the Lord, in the same Spirit, and power, and banner of the cross, under which his called, chosen, and faithful ones have followed him; he will lead thee into the same land of life, rest, peace, and holy dominion over sin and Satan, into which he hath led those, who have faithfully followed the Lamb, whithersoever he hath pleased to go before, and lead them. So, thou must wait to have thy heart daily more and more opened, and guided purely, and livingly, and sensibly by the Lord, into what he hath led his children, servants, family, and redeemed heritage. For, of a truth, the Lord hath raised the seed of life in his people; and what his seed denies, what the life of the Son denies, what Truth in the heart denies, all that are of the Truth and in the Truth, will be taught by it, and learn of it, to deny also.

Thus, my dear Friend, in the most dear, tender, and true love, have I opened my heart to thee, as things sprang in me for thy sake: and the desire of my soul to the Lord is, that they may be serviceable to thee, and that thou mayest be led by the holy leading Spirit more and more into Truth, and live in Truth, and feel the life of Truth living and reigning in thee; being delivered from the enemy's temptations, and the subtle twinings of the serpent, which thy condition will often meet with: the Lord discover them to thee, and preserve thee from being ensnared with them.

Thy constant Friend, in the dear love and service of the Truth, I. P.

AMERSHAM, BURY END,
20th of First Month, 1675.

LETTER LXXX.

Observations on the Ministry.

TO A NEAR RELATIVE.

DEAR ——, — The gospel is the power of God unto salvation; it is the glad tidings of freedom from sin, of putting off the body of sin by the circumcision and baptism of the Spirit, of being delivered out of the hands of our spiritual enemies, that we may serve God, (without fear of them any more,) in holiness and righteousness all the days of our life.

The ministers of the gospel are those, who, in the Spirit of Christ, by the gift and inspiration thereof, preach these tidings to the poor and needy, to the captives, to those that groan under the pressure of the body of corruption.

This gospel, through the great mercy of God, I have at length heard preached; and I have not heard *man*, but the voice of my Beloved; whose voice is welcome to me, though in the meanest boy, or most contemptible female. For, in Christ, there is neither male nor female; nor should his Spirit, which is not limited to males, be quenched in any. And though thou, through prejudice, call this speaking of the Spirit through servants and handmaids, *prating*, yet the Lord can forgive thee; for surely, if thou knew what thou didst herein, thou wouldst not thus offend the Lord;—extolling preaching by man's wisdom, from a minister made by man, for gospel-preaching, and condemning the preaching of persons sent by God, in the immediate inspiration of his Spirit. I am confident, if, without prejudice, and in the fear of God, thou didst once hear such, thou wouldst not be able to forbear saying in thy heart, It is the voice of God, of a truth; — but, that which hath not the sheep's ear, can never own the voice of the true Shepherd.

As for those whom thou callest ministers, if I should speak concerning them, the very truth from the mouth of the Lord, thou couldst not, in that state wherein thou standest, receive it; yet, am I far from accounting them *the off-scouring of the earth;* for, I look upon them as wise and knowing, and as of great beauty in the earthly learning and wisdom; but surely, not as having "the tongue of the learned," "to speak a word in season to him that is weary;" nay, they are men unlearned in this kind of learning, and such as toss, and tear, and wrest the Scripture, in their uncertain reasonings and guessings about the sense of it, and in the various doubtful interpretations they give.

And, whereas I am blamed, for not putting a difference between the profane and scandalous ministers, and the reverend and godly sort; my answer is, They are united in one ministry: and the question is not concerning the persons, but the ministry; in which they are one, — their call one, their maintenance one, their way of worship and preaching one, their standing and power of government one; which is not by the power and presence of the Spirit, but by the strength of the magistrate. But, the true gospel and ministry is spiritual, and cannot stand, nor be upheld by that which is carnal, neither in its call, maintenance, government, or what else belongs to it. When Christ came in the flesh, the words he pronounced, were not so much against the profane and scandalous among the Scribes and Pharisees; but against those that appeared most strict, and were accounted among the Jews the most reverend and godly. And, were it not for the appearance of godliness in these men, the persecution of the present times had not been so hot, the good old cause so lost, and the work of reformation, (inasmuch as relates to men,) so overturned as at this day. O ——! there was once a good thing in divers of them, which my soul would rejoice to see revived; but, as the seat of government eat out the good that was in the bishops, so gaping after the seat of government hath sunk the good thing in others also; and made their eye so dim, that they cannot see the mighty breakings forth of the Spirit of Christ in his people. I. P.

LETTER LXXXI.

Of Love, Humility, and Order among Friends. Also of Persecution.

To a Near Relative.

Ah! Dear ——,—Why dost thou so often give me occasion of mourning before the Lord, on account of hard and unrighteous charges from thee! How often have I solemnly professed, that there was never any desire in me, or endeavour used by me, to draw thee to this way [of religious profession]. All that is in my soul is this,—that thou mightst have the true knowledge of Christ, that thou mightst indeed hear his sayings and do them, and not set up thy own or other men's imaginations and invented reasonings, instead of the sayings of Christ.

Now, though I am not for ways or opinions, but only for Christ, the substance, the living power of God in the heart; yet, because thou stumblest at these things, and, through prejudice, refusest the living testimony of God concerning Christ the Rock, building upon that which thou hast imagined concerning the Saviour,—in love and pity to thy soul, I cannot but say somewhat;—for, who knows, but God may at length give thee repentance to the acknowledgment of the Truth, and to the disclaiming of the way of error.

Thou layest down three reasons, why thou canst not believe this way to be of God.

First. *That God's way is a way of love, peace, and unity.*

Answer. If thou hadst that eye which can see the things of God, and didst apply thyself to look therewith, thou mightst see that peace, that love, that unity among this people, [Friends,] which other men do but talk of. But, if thou take things by the report of the enemies both to God and them, thou shalt be sure to hear and believe bad enough.

They have no war with anything but unrighteousness, and with that they cannot have peace, no, not in their dearest relations. They love the souls of their enemies, and think no pains or hazard too much for the saving of them; being persecuted, they bless, being reviled, they entreat, and pray for their persecutors. They are at unity with whatever is of God, but with the seed of the serpent they cannot be at unity; they know the "generation of vipers" in this present age, and can witness against them under their several painted coverings, as freely as ever Christ and his apostles did against the Scribes and Pharisees. For, the spirit of the Scribes and Pharisees is now in the world, as is also the Spirit of Christ and his apostles, and they cannot but fight, each with their proper weapons; the one with their stocks, whips, fines, prisons, &c., the other with the spiritual armour of Christ. Thus, the one of these wrestles with flesh and blood, fights with the creature, hurts that; the other loves the creature, seeks the saving of it, and fights only with the power of darkness, which rules the creature. Now, which of these are the ministers of Christ? These that stir up the magistrate to afflict the body, or these that use the sword of the Spirit to wound the conscience?

And this peace, this love, this unity they attain, not by their own strivings, but by receiving it from above. Indeed, all our religion lies in receiving a gift, without which we are nothing, and can do nothing, and in which nothing is too hard for us. Yea, being kept in that, up to God, we can do all things, we can believe all things, we can suffer all things. Never was there a generation brought forth weaker in themselves, more foolish, more ridiculous to the fleshy wisdom, more exposed to sufferings from the world and worldly professors; yet, being kept faithful to Him that hath called us, we sometimes feel strength and wisdom, even such, as the most zealous in the worldly ways of religion, have not an ear to hear the relation of.

Secondly. Thou sayest, *that God's way is a way of humility.*

Answer. If this people had not been humbled and broken by God, they could never have entered into a way, which the lofty, fleshly part abhors; nor is this a voluntary humility, but a humility which crosseth and breaketh the will all the day long. Thou judgest at a distance, and with that which is not to judge, but to be judged.

Thirdly. *That God is a God of order, and not of confusion.*

Answer. Blessed be the Lord, who hath recovered somewhat of the true church's order for us, and delivered out of the confusion of antichrist. We know order in the light, order in the Spirit, order in Christ the Truth; but that which man in his wisdom calls order, is but antichrist's order, which with God is confusion. To have man's spirit speak, and God's Spirit stopped, this is the order of all the antichristian congregations, and churches; but to have man's spirit stopped, and God's Spirit speak, this is the order of Christ's church. It is this order we know, and rejoice in, finding that raised in us, which teaches us to "cease from man," and *his* voice [as man] is not at all "accounted of;" but, the voice of the living God is heard, known, loved, and obeyed, by that which he hath quickened in us, and made to live to himself. The Lord is judging that which loved man's meanings and inventions, all that the human part in us could gather from the Scriptures, and is nourishing that which is of himself, that which can receive no food but from his hand.

Thou believest not, that Mr. Gurdon, (as the world calls him,) or any other godly man, doth persecute these people for the exercise of their consciences.

Answer. I know, no godly man can persecute; the lamb did never worry the wolf. But, the grossest persons will not acknowledge that they persecute for conscience, but accuse those whom they persecute for evil-doers, and say, they suffer as evil-doers. Canst not thou see the narrowness of this covering? Would the Scribes and Pharisees, and zealous among the Jews, confess, that they put Christ and Stephen to death for conscience? Did they not put them to death as evil-doers, as blasphemers, as speaking against the holy temple of God, the laws and ordinances of Moses? Ah! ——, the children of wisdom were never justified by that wisdom, wherewith thou judgest of things. The Scribes and Pharisees were as confident that Christ and his disciples were deceivers, and that they brought up a new way of religion contrary to Moses, as any can be that *these* people are deceivers, and that their way is new. The scene is turned; the same things that were then, are now; and the eye of that spirit is as blind now, as it was then; it cannot see its own deceit.

O pierce into the nature of things! set not up shadows instead of the Truth; wait for the gift; receive the true love, the true peace, the true unity, the true humility, which lies not in the will of the creature, but destroys it; —then, we shall soon know one another, and have comfort one in another. I. P.

14th of Twelfth Month, 1658.

LETTER LXXXII.

On the Danger of Self-complacency.

To Catherine Pordage.

Friend, — In truth of heart and tender love to thee, it is with me to return answers to the chief passages in thy letter, as briefly as I may.

It hath not been my work, to bring thee out of esteem or into esteem of persons. The Lord guide thee into true judgment, and keep thee out of judging, except so far as that is raised in thee, which the Lord maketh able to judge. But, I have known several, who have spoken most gloriously and ravishingly, as to the Scriptures, opening things even to admiration, who have been out of the mystery of Truth; and who have sparkled with the light and life of a wrong spirit, though they themselves knew it not to be so.

It is better with him who feels his unwillingness, and waits to be made willing by the Lord, than with him, who thinks he is willing, and, upon his own search, finds and judges himself to be so. I have thought I had been willing in several cases; and that, if the Lord would have showed me his will, I should have obeyed; which I found to be otherwise, when the Lord came to lay the law of his Spirit and life upon me. This I am sure of; there is that in thee, which is not willing to be impoverished, and I cannot say concerning thee, as in God's sight, that thou art yet separated from it. Now, while it is in thee, it will be working in a mystery of deceivableness, hidden from thy heart, which thou canst not possibly discern, but as the seed is raised, and the pure light shines in thee. Thou mayest easily think better of thyself than indeed it is with thee; but, it is hard for thee, in this thy present state, to know what and how thou art in the sight of the Lord.

Thou shalt know the tenderness and melting compassion of the Lord, when *that* is broken down in thee, towards which his tenderness *is not,* and *that* raised up in thee and thy mind joined to it, towards which his tenderness *is;* but great and subtle workings are there in thy mind, from the enemy, against God's Truth, which thou dost not discern and eschew, but rather embrace, as if they were true and precious. If that tenderness were ministered to thee, either from God immediately, or from us, which thou expectest and desirest, (perhaps, thinking thy state is wronged, in not being so dealt with,) it might soon destroy thee, and that forever.

Thus, in great plainness, have I written to thee, and beseech thee to be willing, or rather, to look up to the Lord to make thee willing, to have the wound kept open in thee, which the condition and state of thy soul needs; that it may be thoroughly searched, and that which is for judgment judged and destroyed; and so, thy soul everlastingly saved by the everlasting Physician, who is wise and skilful in ministering both judgment and mercy to every one, according to their need.

Thy Friend in true, faithful, and unfeigned love and tenderness. I. P.

25th of First Month, 1671.

LETTER LXXXIII.

Against Self-exaltation; and on the Cross of our Lord Jesus Christ

To Catherine Pordage.

Friend, — I observed yesterday, that thou didst own the light to be the principle of life; and that thou didst affirm, that those people with whom thou walkedst, also owned it, and directed to it. Now, it is one thing to own the principle in judgment; another thing to know it, feel its guidance, and be subject to it. It is a good step to own it in the comprehension, from the testimony without; but yet, they that go so far, may never come truly to know and own the thing itself. Now, nothing redeems, or can preserve, but the light and life itself. Therefore, how to meet with the thing itself, and be changed by it into its own nature, and therein to believe, know, will, understand, and judge,— that is a skill which none can learn, but those that are taught of God, and keep close to the foundation, not rising in the high elevations above it. Ah! the humility of the seed, and of that soul that is one with the seed! Ah! how low it lies, and how weighty its sense and operations are, and how pure and infallible is its judgment! The great danger is, in rising up above the thing itself, which whoso doth, miscarrieth, whatever he hath formerly known or enjoyed.

There now springs up in my mind a state since Adam, which I would have thee seriously consider of; and then tell me, if thou hast known or heard of such another. It is recorded in Ezekiel, 28th chapter, of one that was "perfect in wisdom and beauty." In what wisdom, in what beauty? Let thy soul, if it hath understanding, answer. For, he had "been in Eden, the garden of God," (what, had any been so since Adam?) "and had every precious stone for his covering." What a glorious temple then was he! yea, and he was created (by what creation?) unto this state. Yea, he was "the anointed cherub that covereth," and God had "set him so." (What is it, to be the anointed, covering cherub, and to be so set by God!) He was also "upon the holy mountain of God," and "walked up and down in the midst of the stones of fire." Yea, saith the Spirit of God further concerning him, "Thou wast perfect in thy ways from the day that thou wast" created. Yet, after all this, "iniquity was found in" him, and the hand of the Lord turned against him. Answer me, now; was this a state of mixture, or no? And if so perfect a state was liable to this, what is a state of mixture liable to?

Ah! many have had some touches of the light, some true appearances thereof, and tastes of the glory; but, who hath been so united to the light, as to keep out of all that corrupteth! There is somewhat still lives near, that would fain be mixing with it, and drawing higher than the pure light of life and truth: but this leads out of the way, above the pure, the true, the innocent, the simple; and then, there is a making haste to be rich and glorious, and a departing from that poverty of spirit, wherein is the safety and preservation. How have some that come among us, here split themselves by aspiring! Ah! what a foolish thing it is, to be found singing, before dominion is witnessed, and victory over that which captivateth; such songs will end in desolation, anguish, and confusion; for thereby, the lust of the mind goes forth, and that is fed, which keeps from the victory and the dominion. It is better to know the old bottle emptied, yea, broken, than filled with new wine. And, how many have taken themselves to be new made, who, when the Spirit of the Lord hath come to search them by his pure, eternal light, have been found and are found in the old nature and spirit!

Come, live no more, know no more of thyself; but wait to feel the pure seed raised to live and know in thee, and to feel its light enlightening thee, and creating a new capacity in thee; and that will give thee to bear the pain of dying, and taking up the cross, which will really slay every life, appearance, and power, that is not of its own nature. Thou hast formerly taken up crosses in a way of wisdom, and according to a comprehensive knowledge and judgment; come, now, learn to take up the seed's cross in the true foolishness. For, there is not another thing that gives life, than the cross of our Lord Jesus Christ, which truly and really slays; and to that which can discern and take up this cross, and live and walk under it, the yoke is easy and the burden light. But, that must first be brought under and destroyed, which counteth it hard, before it can be felt and owned to be so. If thou couldst come out of thy own wisdom and consideration of things, into the simplicity of the seed, thou wouldst soon recover thy lost ground again; and see, how the enemy with his subtlety hath gained upon thee, and into what great danger he hath brought thy soul.

The Lord searcheth and trieth the heart, and that is the true state thereof, which his light discovereth. That is not the state, which the mind out of the light apprehendeth it to be, as we have often had experience of, in ourselves. Therefore, be still; justify not thyself, nor condemn the judgment of others, till the Lord make things manifest to thee. If it then prove better with thee than others have said, that will be thy advantage; but, if thou then prove mistaken, and the judgment which thou in thy heart hast condemned should stand, it will be thy great loss and disadvantage.

This is in love and true friendship to thy soul, in a deeper sight of thee and sense concerning thee, than thou art aware of. I. P.

26th of Third Month, 1671.

LETTER LXXXIV.

To such as Drink of the Waters at Astrop Wells.

I entreat you to consider what is within written for your eternal good; and be not deceived by the enemy of your souls, in things of an everlasting concern.

Some queries propounded to your consideration, in the tender, melting love of my heart towards your everlasting welfare.

First query. Is not the great God, who created heaven and earth, light, pure light, spiritual light, eternal light, in whom is no darkness at all? 1 John, i. 5.

Second query. Is not man, in his natural, unregenerate, corrupt state, darkness? And can he possibly, in that state, have any union or fellowship with the great God and Saviour? See Eph. v. 8; 2 Cor. vi. 14; 1 John, i. 6.

Third query. Doth not the great God, in his tender love to mankind, cause his pure heavenly light to shine in man's heart, in this his dark and corrupt state? 2 Cor. iv. 6; John, i. 5.

Fourth query. What is the end of God's causing his pure light to shine in man's corrupt heart? Is it not, that man might be turned from darkness, and from the power of Satan, which keeps him in darkness, to the light which God causeth to shine in him, and to God from whom this light comes? Acts, xxvi. 18; that so, following Christ, and not walking in darkness, he might obtain the light of life? John, viii. 12.

Fifth query. Doth man, in his natural corrupt state, love this light, when it shines in him; or rather hate it?

And can he hate it, without hating God from whom it comes, and of whose nature it is?

Sixth query. Why doth man, in his natural corrupt state, hate this light? Is it not, because his deeds are evil; and because he would continue in his evil deeds, without being disturbed or reclaimed by this light? John, iii. 19 to 21.

Seventh query. What does this light of the pure God, and of his Christ, do for them that receive and obey it? Doth it not bring them out of darkness, and change their nature; so that they become children of the light, and no more darkness, as they were before, but light in the Lord? John, xii. 36; Eph. v. 8.

Eighth query. How shall it fare with those, who receive the shinings of this light of God and Christ in their consciences, hearkening to the reproofs of it, eschewing that which it shows to be evil, and doing that which God by it shows to be good? Shall not they receive the remission of their sins from God, and an inheritance among the saints in light? Acts, xxvi. 18; Coloss. i. 12, 13.

Ninth query. What will become of those, who do not mind the shining of God's light in their hearts, nor are turned to it, nor changed by it; but spend their time in what pleaseth the corrupt part in themselves? Will they not be separated, when they go out of this world, from God who is light, and have their portion with dark spirits, in utter darkness? 2 Thess. i. 6 to 10. See also Matt. xxv. 30.

O consider these things, while ye have time, for your soul's eternal good! that ye miss not of the holy way of life and salvation, and so perish; whom God would not have perish, but stretcheth forth his hand of love, by his inward "light of life," effectually to save your souls.

I. P.

ASTROP,
20th of Sixth Month, 1678.

LETTER LXXXV.

To one who sent a Message to him from Astrop Wells.

I HAD no end in writing or sending those papers, but true love to your immortal souls; that ye might seriously consider thereof, and be found in the practice of them, and so be happy forever. For, as Christ said to his disciples, so it is with me in this case towards you, "If ye know these things, happy are ye if ye do them." I have felt the sweetness and great benefit of the practice of them, which I heartily desire ye may also experience.

I here send enclosed a token of my love to thee in particular, which thy courteous message drew from me. It contains, in a few words, the true path-way of salvation; which, though thou mayest know already, yet the reading and serious consideration thereof, may not be unserviceable to thee.

I am thy Friend, in true love and desires for thee,

I. P.

THE PLAIN PATH-WAY OF SALVATION.

The Lord Jesus Christ is the only Saviour.

Grace and Truth comes by Jesus Christ.

The Lord Jesus Christ saves by the grace and Truth which comes by him.

For, it is the grace of God that brings salvation, and it is the Truth, as it is in Jesus, which makes free indeed.

He, therefore, that would be saved from sin and condemnation, must wait for the inward manifesting and revealing of the grace and Truth in his heart; and must receive it, and be subject to it, learning of the grace, to deny ungodliness and worldly lusts in every kind; and he must learn of the Truth as it is in Jesus, to deny whatever is contrary to the life, nature, and Spirit of Jesus. He must likewise learn of the grace and Truth, to fear God; to turn from all false, invented worships and ways of men, and to worship God, the Father of spirits, in spirit and in truth: and, as he learns and practises this, he will also learn of the grace and Truth, to live soberly and righteously in this present world, yea, and godlily also, even as the holy God would have him; for, God would have men live no otherwise, than as his grace and Truth teaches them. Now, God's grace and Truth, and the law of the Spirit of life in Christ Jesus, which is written in the inward parts, do not only teach that which is good, and to deny and depart from that which is evil, but give ability so to do. "My grace is sufficient for thee," said God to Paul. And the Truth of Jesus, revealed inwardly, hath virtue and power in it; insomuch, that they who receive the grace and Truth which comes by Jesus Christ, receive power to become sons of God. For the grace, the Truth, is not a notional thing, but hath the virtue and power of life, and mortification in it; and they that truly receive it, partake of its virtue and power in operation and exercise of it in their hearts, and are thereby really made dead unto sin, and alive unto God.

So, then, he that knows the grace and Truth which comes by Jesus Christ, receives it, learns of it, is subject to it, and partakes of its virtue and power, he knows Christ unto salvation; but, he that knows not, receives not, is not subject to the grace, doth not experience the sufficiency of the grace, nor witness ability and power through it to become a son to God, and to do the will of God,—he doth not yet at all know the Lord Jesus Christ unto the salvation of his soul, notwithstanding whatsoever he may profess or believe concerning him. I. P.

Astrop,
28th of Sixth Month, 1678.

LETTER LXXXVI.

Acknowledgment of Christ's Manhood.

To Richard Roberts.

R. R.—Thou didst acquaint me, that Timothy Fly, the Anabaptist teacher, did charge me with denying Christ's humanity, and also the blood of Christ, which was shed at Golgotha, without the gates of Jerusalem; and that I own no other Christ but what is within men.

Sure I am, that neither T. Fly, nor any other man, did ever hear me deny, that Christ, according to the flesh, was born of the Virgin Mary, or that that was his blood, which was shed without the gates of Jerusalem. And the Lord, who knoweth my heart, knoweth, that such a thing never was in my heart; nay, I do greatly value that flesh and blood of our Lord Jesus Christ, and witness forgiveness of sins and redemption through it. Yet, if I should say, I do not know, nor partake of his flesh and blood in the mystery also, I should not be a faithful witness to the Lord. For, there is the mystery of God and of Christ; and that is the soul's food which gives life to the soul, even the living bread and the living water. For, there is living bread and living water; and the flesh and blood in the mystery, on which the soul feeds, is not inferior in nature and virtue to the bread and water. There is a knowing Christ after the flesh, and there is a knowing him after the Spirit, and a feeding on his Spirit and life; and this doth not destroy his appearing in flesh, or the blessed ends thereof, but confirm and fulfil them.

The owning of Christ being inwardly in his saints, doth not deny his appearing outwardly in the body prepared; unless T. F. can maintain this, that the same Christ that appeared outwardly, cannot appear inwardly. "Know ye not your own selves, how that Jesus Christ is in you, except ye be reprobates?" 2 Cor. xiii. 5. "And if Christ be in you, the body is dead because of sin," &c. Rom. viii. 10. "Christ in you, the hope of glory." Col. i. 27. "Behold, I stand at the door and knock; if any man hear my voice and open the door, I will come in to him." Rev. iii. 20. "I will come again," saith Christ: Ye are now in pain, as a woman in travail, full of sorrow for the loss of my outward, bodily presence; but I will come to you again in spirit; see John, xvi.; and, John, xiv. 17, "He," that "dwelleth with you, shall be in you:" and then, when the Bridegroom is inwardly and spiritually in you, and with you, "your heart shall rejoice, and your joy no man taketh from you," John, xvi. 22. And so, the apostles and primitive Christians did "rejoice with joy unspeakable, and full of glory," 1 Peter, i. 8, because of the spiritual appearance and presence of the Bridegroom. And yet, there is no other bridegroom, who now appears in spirit, or spiritually in the hearts of his, than He that once appeared in the prepared body, and did the Father's will therein.

I. P.

LETTER LXXXVII.

Postscript to some Considerations respecting the Gospel Church.

ADDRESSED TO THE INDEPENDENTS AT CANTERBURY.

I HAVE been a seeker after God, and a worshipper of him from my childhood, according to the best of my understanding; and, at last, sat down in that way, which is called Independency, believing it to be the way of the gospel, and entering into it with much fear and seeking of God. In which way, the Lord had regard to the uprightness and tenderness of heart, which he had formed in me.

But, at length, the Lord's hand fell upon me, breaking me all to pieces therein, as to my inward state; for what cause, I had then no knowledge at all of; but mourned before him unutterably, night and day, and lay panting and languishing after him, who was the only Beloved of my soul. Many pitied me, but none could reach my state, but, after much serious discourse with me, greatly wondered: and some said, it was a prerogative case, and would, questionless, end in good-will and mercy from the Lord to me. I parted from that people in great love and tenderness; they expecting my return to them again, (the love between me and them being so exceeding great, and I having let in no prejudice against them,) and I knowing nothing to the contrary.

But, it pleased the Lord, after many years, when my hope nearly failed, to visit me in a wonderful manner, breaking my heart in pieces, giving me to feel his pure, living power, and the raising of his holy seed in my heart thereby; insomuch, that I cried out inwardly before him, "This is He, this is He whom I have sought after, and so much wanted! this is the pearl, this is the holy leaven! do what thou wilt with me, afflict me how thou wilt, and as long as thou pleasest, so that at length I may be joined with this, and become one with this!" So, the eye of my understanding was from that day anointed, and I saw and felt the pure life of the Son made manifest in me; and the Father drew me to him, as to a living stone, and hath built my soul upon him, and brought me to mount Zion, and the holy city of our God; where the river of life sends forth its streams, which refresh and make glad the holy city, and all the tabernacles that are built on God's holy hill. And indeed, from this holy hill and city, the law and word of life doth issue, and the inhabitants of the rock of life hear it, and are friends to the Bridegroom, and glad of the Bridegroom's voice, and follow the Lamb, the Shepherd and Bishop of their souls, whithersoever he leads; who leads them into the pastures of life, and folds of pure rest, and gives them eternal life to feed on, and his peace and patience to possess their souls in.

O ye Independents! whom I have loved above all people, and never had thoughts of rending from you, but was forcibly taken by the hand of the Lord out of your Society; — yet, not without a desire to return to you again, if the Lord pleased to make any way thereto; — I say, O ye Independents, above all professions the one most dearly beloved by me! — O that ye could hear the sensible, experienced testimony, that is on my heart to you concerning my Beloved, concerning his appearance, concerning his church, concerning his way, his Truth, his kingdom. It is nigher than ye are aware, and above all that ye can comprehend concerning it. O that ye might inwardly know these things! Turn in, turn in: mind what stirs in your hearts; what moves against sin, what moves towards sin. The one is the Son's life, the Son's grace, the Son's Spirit; the other is the spirit and nature which is contrary thereto. If ye could but come to the sense of this, and come to a true, inward silence, and waiting, and turning at the reproofs of heavenly wisdom, and know the heavenly drawings into that which is holy and living; ye would soon find the Lord working in your hearts, to stop the issues of death, and to open the issues of life there; and ye would find yourselves anointed daily by the Lord, (for there is not a day but we need to see, nor a day but the Lord gives sight,) and an understanding also would be given you to know Him that is true, and the "eternal life," 1 John, i. 2, and an abiding in him that is true. And, abiding here, ye cannot fail of receiving power, (from him who ministers according to the power of the endless life,) not only to overcome sin and your soul's enemies, but to become sons to God, with delight performing his will. And that yoke which yokes down and subdues sin in you, will be easy, yea, the ease, pleasure, and joy of your souls.

The Lord open an ear in you to hear as the learned, that ye may become experiencers and possessors of these things; for, of a truth, the Lord is arisen to shake terribly the earth, and to build up his Zion, and to give unto his people "a peaceable habitation, and sure dwellings, and quiet resting-places" upon mount Zion. Isai. xxxii. 18.

I. P.

LETTER LXXXVIII.

The Way to Life Narrow; Hard Things Made Easy to the Obedient. Also, Some Answers to Objections on Prayer, &c.

To Catherine Pordage.

Friend,—It is true, the way to life is so difficult and intricate, that none can find it, but such as are lighted by the Lord, and follow the guidance of his Spirit.

Christ, who preached the kingdom, and bid men seek it, yet said, "Strait is the gate and narrow is the way which leadeth unto life, and few there be that find it." In a race, many run, but one obtaineth the prize. Canst thou read what Christ said, "Except ye eat the flesh of the Son of man, and drink his blood, ye have no life in you;" that seemed a hard saying to some of his own disciples, many of whom left him. And truly, Friend, as it is not an easy thing to come into the way, so neither is it an easy thing to abide in the way; for, many are the by-paths, many and great the temptations, both on the right hand, and on the left. The way was always the same, full as difficult and hard formerly as now; but, the states and conditions of some make it harder to them, than it is to others; yea, it is easier now, than it hath been in many foregoing generations, being prepared and cast up by the Lord.

It is sad, indeed, that any should be convinced of Truth, and not come into subjection to it; yet, it is very easy and common. For, men cannot withstand conviction, when it comes in power; but, they may deny obedience to that, which they are convinced of; nay, some in the apostles' day went further, even to taste of the heavenly gift, and powers of the world to come, and to partake of the Holy Ghost, and yet fall away. Was not this very sad? and yet, this was no well-grounded objection against the Truth and way of God then. Indeed, I make little of the illumination of the understanding, without subjection to him that illuminateth, in those things wherein he illuminateth. But, that is a great mistake, to suppose I did condemn any waiting or praying, that is according to a true illumination and leading of God's Spirit; for, the true light and spirit are not separated; but, the exceptions I have against the prayers of professors is, that they are so much out of the true illumination, in a light of their own apprehending, forming, and conceiving. Now, these are but the limits of the fleshly birth, out of which comes nothing that is pleasing to the Father.

Did I, or any of us, ever affirm, that the forbearance of the means was the way to attain the end? But, the setting up or using a false means, is not the way to attain the true end. "So run," said the apostle, "that ye may obtain;" did he not forbid all running, but the right running? The praying of the fleshly birth, or in the will, and according to the wisdom of the flesh, is not the means or way to obtain the everlasting kingdom; but the prayers of the true birth are. And, if I should say thus again and again to thee, So pray, as that thou mayest obtain what thou prayest for,— I should not be thine enemy therein; for, it is easy asking amiss, not so easy to ask aright. Prayer is a gift: and he that receiveth it, must first come to the sense of his own inability: and so, wait to receive; and, perhaps, begin but with a groan or sigh from the true Spirit, and thus grow in ability from the same Spirit, denying the ability which is after the flesh: this latter abounds in many, who mistake and err in judgment, not waiting on the Lord, to be enabled by him rightly to judge and distinguish between flesh and spirit, but are many times willingly ignorant in this particular,— it will cost so dear to come to a true understanding therein.

Hath not all flesh had some manifestation of God's Spirit allotted it? was not that which might be known of God manifest in the Gentiles? and ought not all flesh, in that, to call upon the Lord, as the true sense is given them therefrom? But because of this, might the heathen pray according to their own imagination? Is there not a rule of prayer? Is not God's light, God's gift, God's Spirit, the rule to all? Is any prayer required or accepted out of this? Indeed, he that hath the sense of being but a dog, as I may say, and not worthy to be counted a child, yet, may pray for crumbs, and be heard, and receive them. But, what are prayers, out of the light and life of God's Spirit? are they not prayers of the fleshly birth, fleshly will, fleshly wisdom? can they that are in the flesh, or pray in the flesh, please God? O forsake thy own wisdom, reasonings, will, and desires! that thou mayest come to true understanding in this particular.

As to stirring up the gift, 2 Tim. i. 6, Paul knew to whom he wrote: Timothy had a great understanding, and both knew the gift and how to stir it up; but, he that hath not a true understanding, may stir up somewhat else, instead of stirring up the gift, and so, kindle a fire of his own, and offer up his own sacrifice, with his own fire, neither of which are acceptable to the Lord.

The troubled soul is not only to go to the Lord, but, it must be taught by him, *how* to go to Him. The Lord is the Teacher; and *this* is a great lesson, which the soul cannot learn of itself, but as it is taught by him. Men abound in their several ways in religion, in that which God is arising to scatter and confound; so that, it is not the great and main work to be found *doing*, but to be found doing *aright*, from the true teachings, and from the right Spirit.

In the time of great trouble, there may be life stirring underneath, and a true and tender sense, and pure desires, in which there may be a drawing nigh and breathing of heart to the Lord; but, in the time of trouble and great darkness, may not a man easily desire amiss, and pray amiss, if he have not his Guide? A little praying from God's Spirit, and in that which is true and pure, is better than thousands of vehement desires in one's own will, and after the flesh. For, as long as a man prayeth thus, that which should die in him, lives in his very prayers; and how shall it ever be destroyed, if it get food and gain strength there? But, life and virtue may be felt, and that which troubleth be near too, and greatly troubling. Did Christ feel neither life nor virtue, in the time of his great trouble?

We neither lay weight on outward things, as considered in themselves, nor take off from the inward. Ah! consider what spirit this charge comes from; and if thou discern it, take heed of joining to it, and bringing forth the fruits of it any more. What, if God hath chosen weak and foolish things to the eye of man's wisdom, now, as formerly? Do we, in so testifying, lay any more weight thereupon, than God layeth? And what, if God hath thrown by all preachings, prayings, singings, (yea, inward,) which are not in his Spirit, but from the transforming spirit and birth. Do we herein debase, or testify against, any thing that is inwardly of God? The *outward* which is right in God's sight, must come from the *inward*, but not from the inward will or wisdom of the flesh, but from the inward light and Spirit of God; but, it is a great matter to receive singly and go along with the inward light, and avoid the inward, deceitful appearance of things.

There is one thing hath been with me all along, still, throughout thy letter, even a cry to thee for obedience, obedience to the Spirit and power of the Lord; and to consider, whether disobedience hath not drawn this darkness and power of the enemy upon thee. It is not thy proper work to look out at the way, or think it hard, (for, it is not so to the true seed,) but, to be travelling in faithfulness, as thou art drawn and led; and this will save thee much sorrow.

As for Christ being a Mediator and Reconciler, it is by his death and life; both of which are partaken of, in the light which comes from him, even in the grace and truth which he dispenseth. For, as God wrought all in him by the fulness which he bestowed on him, so, he works all in his by a measure of the same Spirit, life, and power. But, why dost thou so desire to be able to comprehend and reason about these things? — that is not thy present work, but to feel after and be joined to that, whereby Christ reneweth and changeth the mind, and wherein he gives the knowledge of his good, and acceptable, and perfect will. Take heed of being exalted above measure, or desiring to know the things of the kingdom after the flesh, for, it is better to lie low, and as a child to enter the kingdom, and to receive the knowledge of the things of God there, than to be feeding that knowing mind, which is to be kept out and famished.

Ah! watch, that thou mayest not lose thy Leader, and meet with the deceiver, instead of Him that is true; and so, go back from light, life, truth, and power, instead of going forwards toward them. Indeed, this letter of thine makes me afraid, as Paul speaketh to the Galatians, lest I have bestowed labour on thee in vain; for, there seems to me to be in thee, a strengthening of thy mind towards returning back to that, from which the Lord in his mercy hath been redeeming and gathering thee. If thou feel the right seed, and come to be of the right seed, the way of the seed will not be too hard for thee; otherwise, it will.

This is to thee, in love and grief, from thy soul's true Friend, I. P.

21st of Sixth Month, 1671.

LETTER LXXXIX.

The Scriptures Exceedingly Precious. The Gospel a Ministration of the Spirit of Life in Christ Jesus. The Liability of Losing the Sense and Savour of this.

Professors have long known the name of Christ, and what the Scripture relateth concerning him so named; but, O that they could once know Christ [himself,] and receive him into their vessels, and feel life flowing from him into them. Then, would they indeed know Christ according to the Spirit; which knowledge quickeneth, but the literal knowledge killeth. For, he that *hath* the Son, he that is in true union with Him, and really changed by him, so as to become one nature and Spirit with Him, *he* hath life; but, he that hath not the Son, hath not the life of the Son, nor the liberty of the Son, but is in the death of sin, and in service unto sin.

The directions from God's Holy Spirit in the Scriptures, are exceedingly weighty and precious in themselves, and very proper to the several states to which they were given forth; and, blessed is he, who is found in the practice and observation of them. And it hath been the desire of my heart from my childhood, and still is, that I might be found walking with the Lord, according to what is there taught and prescribed to the children of God, in the several foregoing ages and generations; which things were written, and are useful, for *our* instruction also, being read by us, and heeded, in that which gives the true understanding of them.

But, though this was my desire, yet, in my way to attain this, I missed; for, I thought, that by getting the directions of Scripture into my mind, and applying myself to the strict observation of them, and praying for God's Spirit and help, I might obtain what I desired. And truly, the Lord was merciful to me, and did help me in a great measure, to walk uprightly and lowlily with him, and inoffensively before men; yet not so, but that I often felt the temptations and darkness of the enemy nearer me than my rule, and in many cases knew not what to do, nor how to be resolved from the Scriptures.

At length, the Lord greatly distressed me, and brought me to a fuller sense of my want of his Spirit and power, and dashed all my religion in pieces; that I was just like Babylon, for in one hour judgment and desolation came upon me, Rev. xviii. 10; and I knew not what to do without the Lord, nor which way to draw nigh to him — but, then was the Lord preparing for me that day of mercy, which since, in his tender goodness, is broken in upon me. And now, the eye which he hath opened in me seeth, that the gospel is a ministration of the Spirit and power of the Lord

Jesus Christ; and that he who would be his disciple indeed, must be turned to His Spirit, and receive the immediate light and shinings of His Spirit into his vessel; and must feel the law of life, the holy laws of the new covenant, not comprehended outwardly in his mind, but written inwardly in his heart by the finger of God's Spirit. And, being written in his heart, they have power over his heart, and cause him to obey them; so that, being here, he cannot possibly but fulfil the holy directions of the Scriptures, he being in that from which they came, which reveals the substance of them unto him, and makes them living and powerful in him. For, indeed, the law of sin and death hath power over a man so long as he liveth; but, when he meets with that, which kills sin and death in him, and maketh him alive to God, and he receives life in abundance in and through the Lord Jesus Christ; then, the fruits of life become easy and natural to him, and the fruits and ways of sin, unbelief, and disobedience unnatural: and here, the yoke is easy and the burden light, and none of the commandments of our Lord Jesus Christ grievous. But, take them merely out of the letter, not feeling the Spirit leading into them, and quickening and enabling to the performance of them, O how heavy, how hard are they! How impossible to believe aright, hope aright, pray aright, walk aright, watch aright over the heart, fight against the enemies, lusts, and corruptions aright! &c. On the other hand, how pleasant is the way of life in the covenant of life, in the power and virtue of life, and ministered from the Spirit of our God! and here, he is praised, and victory over his enemies witnessed, and peace with him enjoyed in the pure seed of life; blessed be the name of our God forever! For the letter, or description of things, is not the way; but the life is the way, the Spirit the way, the power the way, the Truth as it is in Jesus the way, which none can truly and rightly know, but as they are ingrafted into and formed in him, and he formed in them; — this is only obtained, witnessed, and preserved, in the soul's union and communion with, and obedience to his Spirit and power inwardly revealed and made manifest.

Friend, there is somewhat further in my heart towards thee, which I have the true and certain sense of, which is this: the Lord, who is near thee with his Holy Spirit and power, hath been begetting life in thee, and hath at times given thee a true sense and discerning, in some measure; but, there is also somewhat near thee, which watcheth to destroy and devour what the Holy Spirit of God begets in thee, and to beget another sense and belief in thee, different therefrom, and indeed contrary thereto. Now, it behoveth thee exceedingly to watch, and to pray to the Lord for help; for, the life of thy soul depends upon the one of these, and death and destruction will inevitably break in upon thee, and have power over thee, if thou hearken to the other. Whom doth the enemy so much strive to devour, as the sheep and inheritance of the Lord? And, they are only preserved in the Lord's way, and in subjection to his Spirit. O how many hath the enemy betrayed and deceived of the life of their souls! how many men's spirits are now cankered, and the good long ago eaten out of them, who had once some tenderness and upright breathings after the Lord! but now, their silver has become dross, and their wine mixed with water, so that the very nature and property of it is changed; the salt having lost its savour, — wherewith shall it be seasoned? I mention this to thee, that thou mayest watch and pray; that thou thyself do not lose thy savour, and sense, and tenderness, which the Lord at some times kindleth in thee, by hearkening to the subtle reasonings and suggestions of another spirit, either in thyself or others.

This is in the nakedness of my heart, as in the Lord's sight, and in the truth of friendship towards thee.

27th of Ninth Month, 1670. I. P.

LETTER XC.

On Abiding in the Root of Life.

FOR MY DEAR FRIENDS, BRETHREN, AND SISTERS IN THE TRUTH, IN AND ABOUT THE TWO CHALFONTS.

FRIENDS,— The Lord will wonderfully teach his people, and wonderfully help them! he will pour of his life and virtue into them, and cause his strength to appear in them, and break forth through them, to the glorifying of his name, and making glad the hearts of those that have breathed after him, and waited for him. Therefore, let us lift up our heads, and "fear the Lord, and his goodness in the latter days!" And, let us wait to be made able by him to receive of his riches, and drink in of his fulness, that we may become rich and full in him, and kept empty and poor in ourselves; that the more the life ariseth in us, the more we may feel our own nothingness, and be to the praise of the riches of his grace and mercy, wherein and whereby he hath made us accepted in his Beloved.

And, dear Friends, mind the principle, mind the root, into which the Lord hath ingrafted us; that we may abide and grow up therein, and daily find and feel the sap thereof springing up in us, and quickening us more and more to God. Ye know how ye entered; even so, ye must abide and grow up,— even, in the light, in the life, in the power, which gathered, preserveth, and causeth to flourish. So, my dear Friends, let us all dwell in our everlasting habitation, and no more go forth, but sink into the kingdom, and wait to feel the dominion, righteousness, holiness, power, and purity thereof, daily revealed more and more in our hearts. For, there is no other root or spring of life, than that into which the Lord hath gathered us, no other true life and power in any vessel upon the earth, besides that which springs therefrom. Therefore feel, O! feel that which establisheth, and that wherein the establishment is, and your union, life, and strength therein; that ye may not be bowed down or overborne by whatever happens, either from within or without; but, may feel and enjoy the rest and peace of your souls, in that which is over all, and orders all to the good of those who fear him, and in uprightness of heart wait upon him! I. P.

AYLESBURY GAOL,
23rd of Fourth Month, 1667.

LETTER XCI.

The Unsearchable Riches of Christ. Believers may partake thereof through obedience, and be preserved from every harm.

TO FRIENDS OF BOTH THE CHALFONTS.

OH! the treasures of wisdom and knowledge, the riches of love, mercy, life, power, and grace of our God, which are treasured up for the soul in the Lord Jesus; and are freely dispensed and given out by him, to them that come unto him, wait upon him, abide in him, and give up faithfully to the law of his life,—whose delight it is, to be found in subjection and obedience to the light and requirings of his Spirit.

Feel, my Friends, O! feel your portion, and abide in that wherein the inheritance is known, received and enjoyed. For, there is no knowing Christ truly and sensibly, but by a measure of his life felt in the heart, whereby it is made capable of understanding the things of the kingdom. The soul without him is dead: by the quickenings of his Spirit, it comes to a sense and capacity of understanding the things of God. Life gives it a feeling, a sight, a tasting, a hearing, a smelling of the heavenly things, by which senses it is able to discern and distinguish them from the earthly things. And, from this measure of life, the capacity increaseth, the senses grow stronger; it sees more, feels more, tastes more, hears more, smells more. Now, when the senses are grown up to strength, then comes settlement and stability, assurance and satisfaction. Then, the soul is assured of, and established concerning the things of God in the faith, and the faith gives assurance to the understanding; so that doubtings and disputes in the mind fly away, and the soul lives in the certain demonstration, and fresh sense, and power of life. It daily feels the eternal Word and power of life, to be, in the heart and soul, what is testified of it in the Scripture. It knows the flesh and blood of the Lamb, the water and wine of the kingdom, the bread which comes down from heaven into the vessel, from all other things, by its daily feeding on it, and converse with it in spirit. What heart can conceive the righteousness, the holiness, the peace, the joy, the strength of life that is felt here!

For, Friends, there is no straitness in the Fountain. God is fulness: and it is his delight to empty himself into the hearts of his children; and he doth empty himself, according as he makes way in them, and as they are able to drink in of his living virtue. Therefore, where the soul is enlarged, where the senses are grown strong, where the mouth is opened wide, (the Lord God, standing ready to pour out of his riches,) what should hinder it from being filled? And, being filled, how natural is it to run over, and break forth inwardly, in admiration and deep sense of spirit, concerning what it cannot utter! saying, O the fulness, O the depth, height, breadth, and length of the love! O the compassion, the mercy, the tenderness of our Father! How hath he pitied, how hath he pardoned, beyond what the heart could believe! how hath he helped in the hour of distress! how hath he conquered, and scattered the enemies! which, in the unbelief, the heart was ready often to say, were unconquerable, and that it should one day die, by the hand of one or other of its mighty enemies, lusts, and corruptions. How hath he put an end to doubts, fears, disputes, troubles, wherewith the mind was overwhelmed and tossed! and now, he extends peace like a river; now, he puts the soul forth out of the pit, into the green pastures; now, it feeds on the freshness of life, and is satisfied, and drinks of the river of God's pleasure, and is delighted! and sings praise to the Lamb, and Him that sits on the throne, saying, Glory, glory! life, power, dominion, and majesty, over all the powers of darkness, over all the enemies of the soul, be to thy name for evermore!

Now, my dear Friends, ye know somewhat of this, and ye know the way to it. O be faithful, be faithful!—travel on, travel on; let nothing stop you; but, wait for and daily follow the sensible leadings of that measure of life, which God hath placed in you,—which is one with the fulness, and into which the fulness runs daily and fills it, that it may run into you and fill you. O that ye were enlarged in your own hearts, as the bowels of the Lord are enlarged towards you! It is the day of love, of mercy, of kindness, of the working of the tender hand,—of the wisdom, power, and goodness of our God, manifested richly in Jesus Christ! O! why should there be any stop in any of us? The Lord remove that which stands in the way; and, in the faithful waiting on the power which is arisen, the Lord will remove, yea, the Lord doth remove; and growth in his Truth and power, is witnessed by those that wait upon him. So, my dear Friends, be encouraged to wait upon the Lord in the pure fear, in the precious faith and hope which is of him; and ye will see and feel, he will exalt the horn of his Anointed in you, over the horn of that which is unanointed, and will sweep, and cleanse, and purify, even till he hath left no place for the impure: and then ye shall become his full dwelling-place, the place of his rest, the place of his delight, the place of his displaying his pure life and glory; and he will be your perfect dwelling-place for evermore!

May the Lord God in his tender mercy, and because of his deep and free love unto us, guide our hearts daily more and more in the travel, and into the possession of this; that every soul may inherit and possess, notwithstanding all its enemies, what it hath travelled into, and may also daily, further and further, travel into what is yet before. I. P.

AYLESBURY GAOL,
2nd and 3rd of Sixth Month, 1667.

POSTSCRIPT.

FRIENDS,—Be not discouraged because of your soul's enemies. Are ye troubled with thoughts, fears, doubts, imaginations, reasonings, &c? yea, do ye see, yet, much in you unsubdued to the power of life? O! do not fear it; do not look at it, so as to be discouraged by it; but look to Him! look up to the power which is over all their strength; wait for the descendings of the power upon you; abide in faith of the Lord's help, and wait in patience till the Lord arise; and see, if his arm do not scatter, what yours could not. So, be still before him, and, in stillness, believe in his name; yea, enter not into the hurryings of the enemy, though they fill the soul; for, there is yet somewhat to which they cannot enter, from whence patience, faith, and hope, will spring up in you, even in the midst of all that they can do.

Therefore, into *this* sink; in *this* lie hid in the evil hour; and the temptations will pass away, and the tempter's strength be broken, and the arm of the Lord, which brake him, be revealed; and then ye shall see, that he raised but a sea of trouble to your souls, to sink himself by; and the Lord will throw the horse and his rider, which trampelled upon and rode over the Just in you, into that sea; and ye shall stand upon the bank, and sing the song of Moses to Him that drowned him, and delivered you from him! and, in due season, ye shall sing the song of the Lamb also, when his life springs up in you in his pure dominion; triumphing over death, and all that is contrary to God, both within and without.

Now, Friends, in a sensible waiting and giving up to the Lord, in the daily exercise, by the daily cross to that in you, which is not of the life, this work will daily go on; and ye will feel, from the Lord, that which will help, relieve, refresh, and satisfy, which neither tongues nor words can utter. And, may the Lord God breathe upon you, preserve and fill you with his life and holy Spirit; to the growth and rejoicing of your souls in him, who is our blessed Father, and merciful Redeemer — in the Lord Jesus Christ, our Head and King forever and for evermore!

And then, as to what may befall us outwardly, in this confused state of things, shall we not trust our tender Father, and rest satisfied in his will? Are we not engraven in his heart, and on the palms of his hands, and can he forget us in any thing he doth? Shall any thing hurt us? Shall any thing come between us and our life, between us and his love, and tender care over us? What, though the fig-tree should not blossom, neither there be any fruit in the vine; what though the labour of the olive should fail, and the fields yield no meat; what, though the flock be cut off from the fold, and there be no herd in the stalls; may we not, for all this, rejoice in the Lord, and joy in the God of our salvation? And what, though the earth be removed, and the mountains carried into the midst of the sea; what, though the waters thereof roar and be troubled, and the mountains shake with the swelling thereof; is there not a river, the streams whereof make glad the city of God? Is not the joy, the virtue, the life, the sweet refreshment thereof, felt in the holy place of the tabernacle of the Most High? And He that provides inward food for the inward man, inward clothing, inward refreshment; shall he not provide also sufficient for the outward? Yea, shall he not bear up the mind, and be our strength, portion, armour, rock, peace, joy, and full satisfaction, in every condition? For, it is not the condition makes miserable, but the want of him in the condition: he is the substance of all, the virtue of all, the life of all, the power of all; he nourisheth, he preserveth, he upholdeth, with the creatures or without the creatures, as it pleaseth him; and he that hath Him, he that is with Him, he that is in Him cannot want. Hath the spirit of this world content in all that it enjoys? No: it is restless, it is unsatisfied. But, can tribulation, distress, persecution, famine, nakedness, peril, or sword, come between the love of the Father to the child, or the child's rest, content, and delight in his love? And doth not the love, the peace, the joy, the rest felt, swallow up all the bitterness and sorrow of the outward condition?

The seed, the godliness, the uprightness, the true nature and birth, hath not only the promise of eternal life; but, also whatever is necessary for the vessel wherein it dwells, in this life too. So, dwell in that to which is the promise, and live upon the promise; yea, live upon that, which cannot miss of the promise, but feels the presence and power of the Father, in all and over all. The just lives by his faith; and he that is in union with the just, lives by the faith of the just, and takes no more care than the lilies, but leaves the care of all, to Him to whom it properly belongs, and who hath taken it upon him;

who nourishes, clothes, preserves, and causes the lilies of the field to grow and flourish in beauty and glory: and shall he not much more clothe, nourish, and take care of his own lilies, the heavenly lilies, the lilies of his garden?

Let us, then, not look out, like the world, or judge or fear according to the appearance of things, after the manner of the world; but let us sanctify the Lord of hosts in our hearts, and let him be our fear and dread; and he shall be an hiding-place unto us in the storms, and in the tempests, which are coming thick upon the earth.

Thus, my dear friends, let us retire, and dwell in the peace which God breathes, and lie down in the Lamb's patience, and stillness, night and day, which nothing can wear out or disturb: and so, the preservation of the poor and needy shall be felt to be in his name; and glory shall be sung to his name over all, which is a strong tower, a mighty, impregnable rock of defence, against all assaults and dangers whatsoever; — which, they that have trusted therein, have already experienced it to be; and they that continue trusting therein, shall always experience it so to be, in all trials and dangers, whatever may happen, of what kind soever, even to the end. Amen.

LETTER XCII.

On the Fear of God.

To those Persons that Drink of the Waters at Astrop Wells.

There is a great God, the Creator of all things, who gave man a being here in this world; to whom every man must give an account, when he goes out of this world.

This great God, who loves mankind, and would not have

them perish, is nigh unto man, to teach him the fear, which is due from him to God. The man that learns this pure fear of God, is daily exercised by it in departing from evil, both in thought, word, and deed, and in doing that which is good in his sight.

There is likewise another teacher near man, who is also ready to teach such as do not know God, or fear God, that which is dishonourable to the great God, who made man a vessel of honour, and to be to his glory. They that learn of this teacher, learn not to fear God, or to do good, but to please themselves in doing evil, both in thought, word, and deed. O! what account will all such give, when they go out of this world, and come to be judged by the great God, (who is of pure eyes, and cannot behold iniquity,) when all their sins are set in order by him before them, and just judgment proportioned by him thereunto! O! why do men forget God their Creator, days without number, hearkening to him who first deceived them, doing the will of the deceiver and destroyer of souls, and not the will of the blessed Creator and Saviour!

O! hearken to wisdom's counsel, when she cries in the secret of your hearts against that which is evil, and contrary to the nature, life, and will of God; lest a day of calamity from God come upon you, and then ye cry unto the pitiful and tender God, and his face be turned against you, and he refuse to show mercy to you! Read Prov. i. 20, to the end of the chapter; and the Lord give you the weighty consideration and true understanding of it for your soul's good, and for the reclaiming of you from anything that is evil, and destructive to your souls.

This is written in tender love unto you, from one who pities and loves you, and desires your prosperity in this world, and your everlasting happiness with God forever.

I. P.

ASTROP,
15th of Sixth Month, 1678.

LETTER XCIII.

Some Doubts Answered Respecting Prayer.

To Widow Hemmings.

Friend,—Well may there doubts and scruples arise in the minds of persons concerning prayer, as they come to any sense or touch of Truth from God's Holy Spirit; that duty having been performed and practised so long from the fleshly mind and nature, and not in the leading will and compass of God's Holy Spirit and power. And those who doubt therein, cannot be satisfied, till the Lord open their spirits, and make the thing manifest to them! yet, this is most certain, that all prayer, all true prayer to God, is in and from his Holy Spirit; and whatsoever is otherwise, is not accepted of the Father. The promise, indeed, is to the prayer in faith and to the Holy Spirit; but not to the prayer of the fleshly birth, will, or wisdom. Therefore, the great care and concern in prayer is, that that which is of God pray unto the Father, in the quickenings and motions of his own Spirit. For, the dead cannot praise God, nor can the dead truly pray unto him. And truly, in the forbearing praying, there can be no peace, for we are to pray continually; nor in praying in a formal way without life, without God's Spirit, (who gives to pray, and who makes intercession,) can there be any peace within; rather accusation and anguish to that mind, which, desiring to pray aright, yet knows not how so to do. But it is manifest, prayer is not in the time, will, or power of the creature; for, it is a gift of God, and the ability lodges in his Spirit; it is not ours, but as given of his Spirit,—which, therefore, is to be waited upon, when it will move and breathe in us, and so give us the ability of calling upon the Father, and the power of prevailing with the Father, in the name and through the life of the Son.

Now, as to thy queries, I shall answer in plainness, as the Lord shall please to open my heart.

As to the first. Whenever the creature finds breathings to the Father from a sense of its wants, these are not to be stopped, but to be offered up in that, from which the breathings come. For, there is no true sense of one's condition, or of one's wants, but from the Spirit of the Lord; and the Lord gives this sense, that the soul might feel its need of him, and cry to him; and every sigh and groan, that is thus offered up to him, is accepted of him, and prevails with him for good towards that soul, which it shall certainly receive, as it comes to know the Lamb of God, and follow him in the leadings of his good and Holy Spirit. And, in particular, it ought to pray for the appearance of God's Spirit and power; and, if it do already taste somewhat of it, it ought to pray for more of the Spirit, and that it may distinguish the requests that rise up in the heart, whether they come from God's Holy Spirit and will, or from the fleshly nature and will. For, the wrong birth also desires the kingdom, and would have the kingdom, and prays for the kingdom, and strives for the kingdom; but it prays amiss, and it strives amiss, even so, as it never shall obtain, the kingdom being appointed for, and given to another.

To the second. Those that do not know, nor are sensible partakers of the Spirit, yet feeling their want thereof, and true desires after it, ought to offer up those desires to God; and keeping in that which begets those desires, they shall not long be ignorant of God's Spirit, but find that God is more willing to give it, than a parent to give necessary things to his children. But those that have prayed long for the Spirit, yet have not hitherto received it, have just cause to question the nature and ground of their prayers; since God is so ready to give the Spirit to his children. For, doth a child ask bread of his father for many years, and not receive it? O consider this thing! If the child ask the Spirit aright, it is impossible but he should receive some proportion of it from the Father, so much as is necessary to his present state. God doth require his children to perform every thing to him in and with his Spirit, knowing they can do nothing right without it; and surely, he will not require duties of them, and withhold that from them, without which, they cannot acceptably perform these duties to him.

To the third. A notion that all the soul's supplies are from the Father, is not a sufficient ground of prayer; for the false birth may, and often doth pray so; but, a true feeling of the thing, is a sufficient ground, if the heart and mind keep within the limits of the feeling, and offer up no more than what ariseth there; for, truly, that is from the Spirit, of the Spirit, and in the Spirit, wherever it is found. And, O! that every one who hath any true sense of God, might wait on him, to savour *this little* which ariseth from God, from [amidst] the multitude of his thoughts, words, and desires, which are from another root, — even from the flesh, and are of a fleshly nature, neither are of value, nor avail with the Lord: but, the birth of life, the sensible breathings of his own life, in the poorest and weakest babe, are always of esteem, and prevail with the Father.

To the fourth. The creature may misapprehend its duty, may have a wrong sense, apprehending *that* to be its duty which is *not,* and may not apprehend *that* to be its duty which *is;* and so, if the sense be wrong, then the act of obedience, (according to this wrong sense,) is wrong also, and is not accepted with the Father. It is true, prayer is of God, and is a duty; not *all* prayer, but prayer after that manner that the Lord requires, which is in the true sense, and within the limits of the true Spirit and power — praying always in the Holy Ghost. The pure prayer, the pure breathings of God's child, of the true birth, is always within the limit which God hath prescribed. Therefore, watch unto prayer, watch unto God's preparing the heart, by the motion and virtue of his good Spirit, and offer up the breathings that then arise; and wait to distinguish between the desires which arise from the fleshly part, and the desires which arise from the spiritual and heavenly part. For, the first nature is earthly; but the second nature, the nature which is from the second Adam, the quickening Spirit, is pure and heavenly; and such are all the desires and breathings, that spring from that nature in the vessel. And, as thou comest into that nature, and into that Spirit from which the nature proceeds, thou wilt truly distinguish concerning prayer, concerning faith, concerning love, and all other spiritual things; and wilt know Him who is Truth and no lie, who deceives not, but preserves that mind which is given up to him, and abides in him, out of all error and deceit.

Thou seemest, also, to be disturbed about some other duties, as well as prayer. If the Lord have begun to put a stop to the workings of flesh in thee, and thou be subject to him therein, and cease from thy own willings and workings, and wait on him to be taught to perform things aright,— this is his love to thee; and, if thou come to feel the leadings of his Spirit further, and follow him, thou wilt have cause to bless his name, as many others have, whom in this day he hath thus led. Indeed, flesh should be silent before him. Alas! what room is there for his Spirit and power, when there is such a multitude of thoughts, and workings, and reasonings, such a noise of flesh in many hearts and spirits? Happy is he, who feels flesh silent, who comes to an end of his own willing and running, though that is a time of great distress, when the full mind is emptied and brought low; but then, He that shows mercy is near, and the day of mercy is not far off to that soul.

The Lord raise up that in thee, which is of him; and so guide and order thy heart, that it may long and cry after him, and be heard and satisfied by him. I. P.

28th of Ninth Month, 1670.

LETTER XCIV.

On Drinking of the Fountain of Living Waters.

To Widow Hemmings.

There are two or three Scriptures now on my heart to lay before thee; and it is the desire of soul, that thou mayest so know the Lord, and so receive his Son, as that thou mayest experience them.

The first is in Prov. v. 15, "Drink waters out of thine own cistern, and running waters out of thine own well."

The second is the words of Christ, John, vii. 38, "He that believeth on me, as the Scripture hath said, out of his belly shall flow rivers (or streams) of living waters." For, "there is a river the streams whereof make glad the city of God."

The third is that of John, iv. 14, where Christ signifies, that whosoever drinketh of the water which he giveth, shall never thirst more after water from without, but shall forever thenceforward be satisfied with the springings up of the well of life from within.

To these I may add, the precious promise of the sweet

state of the gospel, Isai. xii. 3, "Therefore, with joy shall ye draw water out of the wells of salvation:" the outward Jew drew the outward water from the outward wells: they had the upper springs, and the nether springs outwardly; but the inward Jew, in the light of the gospel day, draws inward water out of the inward wells with joy. The thirsting after it, when the soul could not meet with it, was a time of great sorrow and perplexity; but, when the river of life is found, when the well of life is received, and the water springs up, the soul draws it from the spring, and drinks it with unspeakable joy. This metaphor or similitude is explained by the evangelist John, at ch. 7, v. 39. The receiving of the Spirit, the receiving of the substance, belongs to the Christian's state, as the receiving of the figures did to the Jew's state. When the Spirit is received — the river, the well of life is received; and then, the waters thereof flow, and are drawn and drunk of. Now, the primitive Christians did receive the Spirit, not only in gifts and manifestations, but as a fountain of life and heavenly virtue dwelling within them. Rom. viii. 9. And, as He dwelt in them, so life sprang up from him, peace, joy, knowledge, virtue, wisdom, power, &c.; even the peace which passeth all man's understanding, and joy which is unspeakable and full of glory. The presence of God was with these, and they knew the times of refreshment, even the times of consolation from the holy Comforter.

These things are witnessed now again, in the preaching of the same everlasting gospel, by the same eternal Spirit and power, which preached it at first. For, though the vessels in which the power appears are contemptible *now*, to the professors and wise ones of this age, as they were *then* to the professors and wise ones of that age; yet, it is the same treasure of life which is hid, and at times is made manifest, revealed in and through the earthen vessels: — blessed be the Lord! of whom is the excellence of the glory, and not of us, who are but instruments and vessels in his hand. Now, seeing the Lord hath given us to partake of the riches of his grace, and of the precious treasures of life in his Son, and of his everlasting kingdom, we cannot hold our peace; but, are required of him to proclaim the day of the Lord, the day of the gospel, even the everlasting day, which never shall have an end; and invite to the waters of life, the pure, still streams of Shiloh, which our souls drink of, and are satisfied with; — especially to such as now thirst after them, as *our* souls once vehemently did, and were near failing through the extremity of thirst; — which thirst or desire, for the nature of it, (blessed be the Lord!) is not lost or extinguished, but satisfied. And so, the spouse having heard the Spirit inviting to the waters, being taught by Him to come to, and drink of the living streams, daily also enjoying life and sweetness therefrom; now, she cries also to her fellow-travellers, to the weary and thirsty ones, — O come, saith she, to the fountain of life, which I mourned after, and languished for want of! O taste the sweetness of my Beloved, for whom my soul fainted, when I could not find him! So that, not only the Spirit of the living God saith, Come; but the bride also saith, Come; for, the fountain is not now sealed any longer, but open, through the tender mercies of our God, for every thirsty soul; that whoever hath a will kindled in him by the Lord, may come to drink of the water of life freely.

O! drink, then, no longer at the muddy streams of your own conceivings and imaginations, with which, that which inwardly thirsts after the living God, and his pure streams of life, cannot be satisfied; (it is not the true seed, it is another birth which is satisfied with these things, before the fountain of life comes to be opened in the heart;) but, wait on the Lord, retire in spirit to be gathered into his light, which he causes to shine in the heart, and into his Son's life and Spirit, which he manifesteth and revealeth there; that ye may eat that which is good, and be satisfied with the fatness of his house, and drink of the river of his pleasures! For, indeed, the Lord, in this his gospel day, doth make to his children a feast of fat things, and of wines on the lees well refined, on his holy mountain, even in the kingdom which cannot be shaken; and the Beloved doth not only knock at the door of the heart, but comes in, and sups with his, and they with him. I. P.

16th of Eighth Month, 1672.

LETTER XCV.

Considerations relative to the Church; with some Cautions to Christian Professors.

To my Friends at Horton and thereabouts.

There hath been a cloudy and dark day, wherein God's church and building hath been laid waste, and his holy city (according to his decree and purpose) trodden under foot by the Gentiles; all which time, his church hath been as a desolate widow, mourning in the wilderness. Yet, during this season, God hath not left his people; but, there have been breathings and stirrings of life in and from the precious seed; in which breathings of life, they have seen somewhat of the beauty of the built state, and have had true desires and longings after it: but, in the midst of these desires, the enemy hath struck in upon their spirits, and put them upon pressing more forward towards it, than they have been truly led. So, reading in the Scriptures of a Church state and church orders, &c., they thought it was their duty to set on building; and so, have thrust themselves into these things, in which they have not been accepted of the Lord; though, in their breathings and true desires, they were accepted. And, what hath been the issue of these buildings? Ah! the pure seed hath been buried in them — they have been as a grave to it; and their own imaginations, and wrought out knowledge, and way of worship, hath been of high esteem.

O Lord my God! raise again, I beseech thee, the pure life, and those pure breathings which have been drowned, lost and buried in these buildings!

Now, dear Friends, the Lord alone built his church at the first. The Lord also laid the buildings waste, and carried his living temple, out of the shell of it, into a wilderness. And the Lord alone can lead his church out of the wilderness, (leaning upon her Beloved,) into her built state again. Ah! dear Friends, all must be scattered, all must be scattered,— all the gatherings, all the buildings, which are not of the Lord, that *his* gathering, *his* building may be known and exalted in the earth: so that, I would not have you hold up any thing, in this day of the Lord, (it is so, indeed,) against the light and power of the Lord. The Lord is able, and will maintain his building, however weak and low of esteem it be in the eye of man; but, man shall not be able to maintain *his* buildings, however high and strong in his own eye; yea, every high tower, and every fenced city shall fall before the dread of His presence, who hath now appeared among his poor, desolate people, and gathered them within the verge of his power: blessed be his holy name forever!

And, since my spirit is at this time thus unexpectedly opened, in love and in life, towards you, I shall mention one or two great snares, which I see professors entangled in; that you may wait on the Lord, to escape the evil and danger of them. — One is this: they look too much at *outward time* and *outward things*, and their expectations are too much that way. O let it not be so with you! but wait for the inward day, wherein, the things of God are wrought in the heart. And take heed to your steps, thoughts, and ways: for, the Lord, who hath long tenderly visited, is now laying stumbling-blocks; and not only the world, but even professors also, shall be hardened, snared, fall, and be taken; and this word shall be fulfilled, even among them, "He taketh the wise in their own craftiness." But, wo unto him that hath stumbled at the living appearance of God's precious Truth in this our day, and in his wisdom hath been exalted above that, which he should have fallen down before! O that none of you, (whom I have dearly loved, and still love, and whom I have truly sought in the Lord, and still seek,) ever prove sad examples and spectacles of what I now write, in a living, feeling sense! O that that, which hath mourned and is oppressed among you, might live and rise up in the power of life, over that which hath grieved and oppresseth it! for, of a truth, I feel among you a wisdom and knowledge, which is not of the seed, but oppresseth it. O what plainness of speech doth the Lord give me towards you! indeed, I am melted in concern for you; and, in the strength of that love which searches into your bosoms, desire, that the abominable thing among you might be discovered and purged out, and that which is indeed of God might spring up, live, and flourish among you.

A second thing, wherein professors grievously mistake, is, about *praying in the name of Christ;* in which name, he that asketh, receiveth; and, out of which, there is no right asking of the Father. They think, that praying in the name of Christ, consists in using some outward words, as, "Do this for thy Son's sake," or, "We beg of thee in Christ's name;" whereas, *that* in the heart, which knoweth not the Father, may use such words; and that which is taught of the Father to pray, and prayeth in the Son, may not be led to use those words. *The name,* wherein the asking and acceptance is, *is living;* and he that prayeth in the motion of the Spirit, and in the power and virtue of the Son's life, *he* prayeth *in the name*, and his voice is owned of the Father; and not the other, who hath learned in his own will, time, and spirit, to use those words relative to the Son.

Another thing, wherein professors exceedingly err and mistake, is, about the applying of Christ's righteousness, which is only rightly done in the Spirit, where the application hath its true virtue. But, man's misapplication hath no virtue; for, notwithstanding *that*, his sins remain; and so, the comfort, hope, and joy in his heart, that his sins are pardoned, is only a pleasing dream, which will deceive him when he awakes, and finds his sins not blotted out by God, but only in his own apprehension.

Ah, Friends! that ye might travel into Truth, and meet with the unerring substance of things, that ye might live and not die; and then, ye will see, how man hath erred and errs,— yea, even the man in *you;* and that the seed only, and they that are born of the seed, know the living Truth, and walk in the living path, where there is no error, no deceit, but a perfect preservation out of them. There, it is my desire to meet and embrace you, in the dear bowels of love, where we may unite and know one another, in the spiritual birth and life, inseparably, forever; if we daily mourn after, and faithfully wait upon, the true Guide and leader thereunto.

I remain your imprisoned Friend, according to the wisdom of God, and in his pure content and fear; though the wisdom of man might easily have avoided these bonds.

I. P.

Aylesbury Gaol,
22nd of Eighth Month, 1665.

LETTER XCVI.

Hints on steadfastness in the Truth and its Testimony; on Forsaking Assemblies for Divine Worship, and on Slighting Gospel Ministers.

To Thomas and Ann Mudd.

Dear Friends,— Of whose love to me, I have been and am sensible, and to whom I bear true love.

When I was last at Rickmansworth, it was on my heart to visit you; and, while I was there with you, true and living breathings did spring up in my heart to the Lord for you. Since, I have often thought of you, and in my desires have wished well concerning you, as concerning my own soul.

Your days here cannot be long; and what ye sow here, ye must reap, when ye go out of this world. O that ye may now so sow to the Spirit of God, as that ye may then reap of him life everlasting!

Last first day, my wife had a letter of George Fox's sent her, which I heard read that night. In the reading of it, I had many thoughts respecting you, and a desire that ye might sincerely and uprightly, without prejudice, peruse it; which I sent unto you, the next day, for that end.

Now, this morning, ye were upon my heart; and two or three things rose up in me in reference to you as very necessary for you, that ye may be safe, and that it may go well with you forever.

One was, that ye keep steadfast in that holy testimony of Truth, which was given forth among us at the beginning. For, *this* Truth is the same, and the testimony of it doth not vary or pass away, but shall last throughout ages and generations, to redeem all that receive it and are faithful to it. The testimony was, to draw from outward dead knowledge, and out of dead practices and worships, after men's own conceivings, into an inward principle, and into worship in spirit and truth, both inwardly in the heart, and outwardly in the assemblies of God's gathering.

The second was, that we keep in the sense, esteem, and sanctified use of those holy instruments, which God hath made choice of, both to gather and build up his called and chosen ones. It was never well with Israel, when they slighted Moses, (though they many times had exceptions against him;) nor when they despised the prophets, whom God sent afterwards, (though they were often prejudiced against them also;) nor was it well with any of the churches, when, by the subtlety and seeming simplicity of those that endeavoured to betray them, or by any other means, they were drawn to think meanly of any of the apostles or ministers of Christ, in their day. And the Lord, who preserved Moses in *his* day, and the prophets in *their* day, and the apostles and holy ministers of Truth in the first promulgation of the gospel, is the same God still; and doth, and will preserve those, whom he hath in this age sent forth to publish his everlasting gospel, and to gather his lambs and scattered sheep into holy gatherings and assemblies.

The third was, that ye be daily exercised, guided, and your hearts opened and quickened, by the principle and Spirit of Truth; that so, ye may know what it is, to walk with the Lord, and to feel the power of the Lord, and enjoy the presence of the Lord; and be led by him out of, and away from, the mysterious workings of the power and spirit of darkness, inwardly. For if, through grievous mistake, ye let this into your minds and spirits, instead of the Spirit of Truth, ye must needs call darkness light, and light darkness; truth error, and error truth; and so will err from that, which is indeed the way, into somewhat, which in God's sight is not so. For, there is a spirit of delusion, as well as of truth; this works in the heart as a minister of righteousness, in a seeming light, and, warming the heart with a wrong fire, brings it into a wrong bed of rest, and administers to it a wrong peace, hope, and joy; setting up there a wrong sense, belief, and judgment concerning itself and others. This leads to separate from them that are true, and joins to them that are false; draws from the assemblies and worships of God's gathering, and begets prejudices against and hard thoughts of those, who are owned by the Lord, and are kept in their habitation by him, who dwells in them, and they in him.

O my Friends! the Lord give you the true discerning of this spirit, and of his own Spirit; and deliver you out of the snare of the enemy, and open that eye in you, to which he gives the sight of what is, and who are of him, and what is, and who are not of him: that ye may be disjoined from all that is not of God, and joined to the Lord, abiding and walking in him; and may know, that God doth not cast off his holy people, gatherings, and assemblies, but constantly appears in the midst of such as truly and humbly wait for him; glory be to his name!

God knoweth in what sense, in what understanding, in what love, in what desire, in what fear, in what knowledge from him, I write this to you; who am a true Friend to you both, (in true and faithful love, as in God's sight,) and an hearty desirer of your everlasting happiness.

I. P.

19th of Twelfth Month, 1672.

LETTER XCVII.

On hating Reproof.

To Catherine Pordage and another.

Friends, — Take heed of that spirit, which will be stirring up hard thoughts in you of God and his way, and the faithful testimony thereof, when, in the tender mercy of the Lord, it is given forth to you; for, that spirit is your soul's enemy. Wait, therefore, to know in yourselves that which is to stumble, and fall, and be snared, and broken, and taken; for, it cannot receive God's Truth.

And, take care of that spirit which hateth reproof; for, the reproofs of instruction are the ways of life, and, whom the Lord loves, he rebukes and chastens. And truly, Friends, this is God's Truth in my heart to you both, this morning: — the ministration of conviction and reproof, is that which ye are to come under: and, it is your proper state to wait daily, not for comforts, not for refreshments, (that day is to come afterwards,) but, for convictions and reproofs of that in you, which is contrary to God. And, if ye walk faithfully in this dispensation, ye shall in due time know another, when the work of this is over; for really, Friends, ye must be emptied of that wherewith ye are now filled, before ye can be filled with that which is true and living. If I should say one word to you, could ye bear it? and yet this counsel is with me towards you: O! wait for, receive, embrace, be glad of that which reproves you, and be afraid of that which comforts you in your present state; for, ye are to come through the trouble, judgment, breaking down, plucking up, consuming, and burning of the contrary nature and spirit, which yet deceives you; and to witness all the knowledge, profession, practices, beliefs, hopes, that are founded there, and spring up thence, confounded and destroyed, before ye can possibly come into the true ministration of life and power. (Ye must die to your own wisdom, if ever ye will be born of, and walk in the wisdom of God.) Yea, ye must die to that part, that is so active from and in that wisdom, and which would be labouring in the very fire for what is but vanity; if ye will receive the knowledge, which springs out of truth and life itself, which indeed flows over, and covers the earth of God's heritage, as the waters cover the sea, in this day of his great goodness and plentiful redemption.

When we were in desolation and great distress, indeed, unutterable, we had none of these helps and instructions, which abound towards you. O what a day of mercy have you met with? and how great will be your condemnation, if ye become as deaf adders to the Spirit of the Lord, and so miss of his salvation. And, if ye will ever know the Spirit of the Lord, ye must meet with him, as a searcher and reprover, in your own hearts; yea, the merciful God must ye meet with, as a severe Judge, and unquenchable, consuming fire against that spirit, wisdom, knowledge, and faith in you, which is but of a chaffy nature. Truly, Friends, it is far better to be stripped of it, than to find any rest or pleasure in it.

O hear the voice of the living God! His word is nigh, nigh you; and his word hath a voice that speaks. O that the ear that *can* hear, might be opened in you! and the ear stopped, which *will* not, *cannot* hear the voice of the Shepherd! O wait for the Reprover! and turn the ear to him, letting in his reproofs, and turning from what he reproves for, without murmuring, without disputing; and the exercise of that ear, will open it more and more: so that, ye will come to know the voice more and more; which, though it prove very bitter to that which is of a contrary nature, and would not hear the voice, yet will be sweet, yea, sweeter and sweeter daily, to the true birth. And here, ye will witness true death to that which is to die; and true life, ministered by Him who lives forever, to that which is to live.

But, while ye are striving to comprehend, and to begin obedience after that wisdom, ye will find the power, which opens to others, shutting you out from that which is true; and yourselves liable to be tempted, and persuaded to esteem and take up that which is false, instead of that which is true.

What spirit is that in you, which prejudices your hearts inwardly against, and makes you so apt to cry out [because] of destroying? Is it not that spirit, which would save alive what is to be destroyed in you, that your souls might live in and to God! The Lord discover to you, how the enemy works in you, against the life and salvation of your souls; for he knows what will be the issue of this destroying work, if it have its thorough course and effect upon you; and that none of his kingdom will be left standing in you. I. P.

7th of Seventh Month, 1671.

LETTER XCVIII.

Of "Fleshly Wisdom."

To Francis Pordage.

Friend,—There is a mind, which can never know nor receive the things of God's kingdom; and yet, this mind is very busy in searching and inquiring after them.

The Scribes and Pharisees were still questioning Christ, and desiring satisfaction about the kingdom, and about his doctrine and miracles, and the practice of his disciples, but could never receive satisfaction; yet, the disciples themselves were many times afraid to ask Christ questions, there being a dread of God upon their spirits, and a limit to the knowing and inquiring part in them; for indeed, the true birth learns under the yoke.

This, therefore, is precious; to come to feel somewhat to limit that mind, which is forward and inquisitive out of the true nature and sense, and to receive the yoke, and to be limited by it and famished; for famine, not food of life, is appointed for that mind and birth. It is written, "I will destroy the wisdom of the wise, and bring to nothing the understanding of the prudent." Now, this is precious and greatly needful: for a man to know, and discern, and watch against that wisdom and understanding in himself, which God will destroy and bring to nothing; for, to be sure, while he is learning and striving to know with that, God will never teach him, but rather hide the mystery of life and salvation from him. And what is all man's knowledge worth, that he learns of himself without God's teaching; and which he receives into that understanding, which is to perish and be destroyed? In the new understanding, God sets up the true light; but, in the other understanding, are false lights set up, which do not give a true distinction of good and evil, but they call good evil, and evil good, and put darkness for light, and light for darkness, and cannot do otherwise; because, the light in them is darkness, it not being the gift of grace whereby they see and judge, but a light of their own forming, according to their own comprehension of things, in the dark and fallen understanding.

Now, the Lord hath taught us the difference between all these lights, and the light of his grace, which purely teacheth, livingly teacheth, not in the reasonings of the mind, but in the evidence and demonstration of God's Spirit in the soul and conscience. When we came to see in this light, we found, that that which we had called good, according to our former apprehension of things, was not so in the true balance; and what we thought had pleased God, was abominable in his eyes. And, truly, all that are not come to this light, they offer that which is abominable to God, and yet think it pleaseth him; and what a gross and dangerous mistake is this! indeed, all are no better than will-deeds, which are done out of the light, life, virtue, and power of God's Spirit. For, the root must be good, or the fruit cannot be good. The mind must be renewed, or the knowledge is but old, dead, literal, and fleshly; such as the fleshly understanding comprehends and receives, which can neither know nor receive what is spiritual.

Truly, the Lord hath led us a great way in our journey, nd done great things inwardly for and in our spirits; yet, if we were not kept under the yoke, but that part in us had liberty to know, and live, and act, and worship, we should yet perish, and be cut off from the land of the living. I. P.

LETTER XCIX.

Advice on Church Discipline.

To the Women Friends that meet at Armscot in Worcestershire.

Dear Friends,—In your meetings together to do service for the Lord, be every one of you very careful and diligent in watching to his power, that ye may have the sensible, living feeling of it, each of you in your own hearts, and in the hearts one of another; and that ye may keep within the limits of it, and not think, or speak, or act beyond it. And know, O! wait more and more to know, how to keep *that* silence, which is of the power: that, in every one of you, what the power would have silent, may be silent. O! take heed of the forwardness of the flesh, the wisdom of the flesh, the will of the flesh, the talkativeness of the flesh; keep them back, O! let them forever be kept back in every one of you, by the presence and virtue of the power.

The power is the authority and blessing of your meetings, and therein lies your ability to perform what God requires; be sure ye have it with you. Keep back to the life, keep low in the holy fear, and ye shall not miss of it. You will find it easy to transgress, easy to set up self, easy to run into sudden apprehensions about things, and one to be of this mind and another of that; but, feel the power to keep down all this, and to keep you out of all this; every one watching to the life, when and where it will arise to help you, and that ye may be sensible of it when it doth arise, and not in a wrong wisdom oppose it, but be one with it. And thus, if any thing should arise from the wrong wisdom in any, ye may be sensible of it, not defiled or entangled with it, but abiding in that which sees through it and judges it; that so, life may reign in your hearts and in your meetings, above that which will be forward, and perking over the life, if ye be not very watchful.

So, the Lord God of my life be with you, and season your hearts with his grace and Truth, and daily keep you in the savour thereof; that ye may be blessed by him, and a blessing in his hands; all that is evil and contrary to Truth, being kept down in your own hearts, ye will be fit to keep down evil in the minds and hearts of others; and, if any thing be unsavoury anywhere, it will be searched into, judged, cast out, and the recovery of the soul which hath let it in, sought, that, if possible, it may be restored; and then, ye will know the joy of seeking out and bringing back the lost sheep. And, be tender to others, in true compassion, as ye would be tendered by others, if ye were in their conditions.

There is that near you, which will guide you; O! wait for it, and be sure ye keep to it; that, being innocent and faithful, in following the Lord in the leadings of his power, his power may plead your cause in the hearts of all his tender people hereabouts: and they may see and acknowledge, that your meetings are of God,— that ye are guided by him into that way of service, in his holy fear, in which he himself is with you, and by the movings of his Holy Spirit in your hearts, hath engaged you. Be not hasty, either in conceiving any thing in your minds, or in speaking it forth, or in any thing ye are to do; but, feel him by his Spirit and life going along with you, and leading you into what he would have any of you, or every one of you do. If ye be in the true feeling sense of what the Lord your God would have done, and join with what is of God, as it riseth in any, or against any thing that is not of God, as it is made manifest among you; ye are all in your places and proper services, obeying the blessed will, and doing the blessed work, of the Lord your God.

I had somewhat upon me yesterday to you, but my weakness was great. This morning, this lay as a weight upon my spirit to lay upon yours; may the weight of it come upon you, to weigh down whatever is light or chaffy in any of you, that the seed of life may come up over it, and ye may be weighty before the Lord, in the weighty seed of life. The Lord make you rightly serviceable to him, and truly glorious in your meetings, and in your several places. Ye will find a great work to keep one part down, that that which is pure and living of God may come up in you, and ye act only in it, not exceeding the limits of it. I. P.

Written at JOHN HAWFORD'S,
7th of Seventh Month, 1678.

LETTER C.

An Expostulation and Warning.

TO THE EARL OF BRIDGEWATER.*

FRIEND,—It is the desire of my heart to walk with God, in the true fear of his name, and in true love and good will to all men, all my days here upon the earth. For this end, I wait upon God night and day, to know his will, and to receive certain instruction from him, concerning what is acceptable in his sight. After he hath in any thing made manifest his pleasure, I wait upon him for strength to perform it; and when he hath wrought it by me, my soul blesseth him therefore. If this be a right course, I am not to be condemned herein: if it be not, and thou knowest better, show me, in love, meekness, and tenderness; as I would be willing to make any thing known to thee, for thy good, which the Lord hath shown me.

But, this I am fully assured of, that God is higher than man: and that his will and laws are to be set up, and obeyed, in the first place; and man's only in the second; and, in their due subordination to the will and laws of God.

Now, Friend, apply thyself to do that which is right and noble, and that which is truly justifiable in God's sight; that thou mayest give a comfortable account to him, when he shall call thereunto. That which thou hast

---

* See the Life of Isaac Penington, by J. G. Bevan.

done to me, hath not made me thy enemy; but, in the midst of the sense of it, I desire thy welfare, and that thou mayest so carry thyself in thy place, and actions, as that thou mayest neither provoke God against thee in this world, nor in the world to come. Hast thou not yet afflicted me enough, without cause? Wouldst thou have me bow to thee therein, wherein the Lord hath not given me liberty? If I should give thee outward titles and honours, might I not do thee hurt? O come down, be low in thy spirit before the Lord! honour him in thy heart and ways, and wait for the true nobility and honour from him. Thou hast but a time to be in the world, and then eternity begins; and what thou hast sown here, thou must then reap. O that thou mightst sow, not to thy own will and wisdom, but to God's Spirit; and know his guidance, who is only able to lead man aright. Indeed, thou shouldst be subject in thy own heart to that, which thou art offended at in others,—even that in the inner parts, which testifies for God and against the thoughts, ways, and works of corrupt man; that thou mightst feel a principle of life from God, and good fruit brought forth from that principle to him; and that the evil nature, and the evil works thereof, might be cut down in thee; that thy soul may escape the wrath and misery, which attends the works and workers of iniquity.

I have sent thee this enclosed, in love. Read it in fear and humility, lifting up thy heart to the Lord, who giveth understanding, that it may be a blessing to thee; for, in true love was it written, and is of a healing and guiding nature. I have formerly written to thee; but my way hath been so barred up, that I have not found access easy; and how or whether this will come to thy hand, I know not; but, this I truly say to thee, I have felt the Lamb's nature, under my sufferings from thee, whereunto I have given thee no provocation, neither for the beginning nor continuance of them; and if thou canst, bring that thing to the trial of the witness of God in thy heart, that will deal truly with thee, blaming what God blames, and justifying what he justifieth. And, though the Lord beholdeth, and will plead the cause of his innocent ones, (who the more helpless they are, the more they are considered and tendered by him,) yet, I do not desire that thou shouldst suffer, either from God or man, on my account; but, that thou mightst be guided to, and preserved in, that which will be sweet rest, peace, and safety, to all that are sheltered by it, in the troublous and stormy hour; in which, the Lord will distress man, and make him feel his sin and misery.

This is the sum of what I have at present to say; who have written this, not for any by-end, but, in the stirrings of true love towards thee; and from a true desire, that thou mightst feel the power of God forming in thy heart aright and bringing forth the fruits of righteousness in thee; — that thou mightst be made by him of the seed of the blessed, and inherit the blessing, and find the earthly nature consumed, and brought to naught in thee. For, to [this nature] is the curse, and it must feel the curse, as God brings forth his righteous judgments in the hearts, and upon the heads of the transgressors. And, knowing there is a certain day of God's calling transgressors to account, also the terribleness of his wrath and consuming pleasure in that day,— I warn thee in tenderness, and in love beseech thee, to consider thy ways, and make thy peace with him; that thou mayest not be irrecoverably and eternally miserable; but, mayest be transformed by his life and nature, and sow to him the fruits thereof, that thou mayest reap, and receive of him that which is the soul's joy.

And, Friend, know this assured truth, — it is not a religion of man's making or choosing, (neither the Pope's nor any other man's,) but only that which is of God, which is acceptable to Him: and, what will become of that man, whose very religion and worship is hateful to God? Where will he stand, or what account will he be able to give, when he appears before him?

Thou hast not often met with such plain dealing as this. These things very nearly concern thee. O! wait upon God for his true light, that thou mayest not be deceived about them; because thy loss thereby, will be so great and irreparable.

I am thy Friend in these things, and have written as a true lover and desirer of the welfare of thy soul.

I. P.

FROM AYLESBURY GAOL,
24th of Sixth Month, 1666.

LETTER CI.

Faithful dealing between Brethren Recommended.

DEAR FRIEND,— I have heard that thou hast somewhat against W. R., whereupon thou forbearest coming to meetings at his house: this thou oughtst seriously to weigh and consider; that thy path and walking herein, may be right and straight before the Lord. Is the thing, or are the things, which thou hast against him, fully so, as thou apprehendest? Hast thou seen evil in him, or to break forth from him? and hast thou considered *him* therein, and dealt with him, as if it had been thy own case? Hast thou pitied him, mourned over him, cried to the Lord for him, and in tender love and meekness of spirit, laid the thing before him? And, if he hath refused to hear thee, hast thou tenderly mentioned it to others, and desired them to go with thee to him? that, what is evil and offensive in him, might be more weightily and advantageously laid before him, for his humbling, and for his recovery unto that, which is a witness and strength against the evil. If thou hast proceeded thus, thou hast proceeded tenderly and orderly, according to the law of brotherly love; and God's witness in thy conscience will justify thee therein. But, if thou hast let in any hardness of spirit, or hard reasonings against him, or hard resolutions as relating to him, the witness of God will not justify thee in that.

And if, at any time hereafter, thou hast anything against others, O learn, from that of God in thee, to show compassion towards them, even as the Lord has had pity on thee! And keep to his witness in thy heart. Wait to feel the seed, and to keep thy dwelling therein, that thou mayest abide in the peace and rest thereof, and not depart out of thy habitation, out of the sense of Truth; for, that will let in temptation upon thee, give the enemy strength against thee, and fill thy soul with anguish and perplexity.

So, the Lord God of infinite tenderness renew his mercy upon thee, and keep thee in that, wherein his love, life, rest, joy, peace, and unspeakable comfort of his Holy Spirit, (which keeps the mind out of all the snares and temptations of that which is unholy,) is felt and witnessed, —by those, who are taught and enabled of him, to abide and dwell in that, into which he gathered them,—and in which he hath pleased to appear unto them.

This is, in the love and tender goodness of the Lord to thee, from thy Friend in the Truth, and for the Truth's sake. I. P.

13th of Tenth Month, 1667.

LETTER CII.

On Dwelling with the Lowly Seed of Life in all Conditions.

To M. Hiorns.

Dear Friend,—I received two letters from thee lately, whereby the sense is revived in me of thy great love to me, and the Lord's great goodness to thee, in administering that which rejoiceth and refresheth thee.

Now, this advice ariseth in my heart. O! keep cool and low before the Lord, that the seed, the pure, living seed, may spring more and more in thee, and thy heart be united more and more to the Lord therein. Coolness of spirit is a precious frame; and the glory of the Lord most shines *therein*,—in its own lustre and brightness; and, when the soul is low before the Lord, it is still near the seed, and preciously (in its life) one with the seed. And, when the seed riseth, thou shalt have liberty in the Lord to rise with it; only, take heed of that part, which will be outrunning it, and getting above it, and so, not ready to descend again, and keep low in the deeps with it.

O my Friend! I have a sense, that this hath been the error of that people, thou hast formerly walked with: and I observe in thy spirit yet a liability thereto; which the Lord give thee to watch against, that thou mayest come to a pure observation and discerning of the everlasting, unchangeable seed in thy own heart, and mayest daily feel thy mind bowed down and worship in it, becoming wholly leavened into it, and perfectly changed and preserved by it.

POSTSCRIPT.

We are here but a while in this world, for the Lord to make use of us, and serve himself by us; and so, by his ordering of us, to fit us for the crown of glory, which he will give us fully to wear in the other world. Now, feel the child's nature, which chooseth nothing, but desires the fulfilling of the Father's will in it. I cannot desire to enjoy any thing, (saith the nature of the true birth,) but as the Father, of himself, pleaseth to give me to enjoy. There is a time to want, as well as to abound, while we are in this world. And the times of wanting, as well as abounding, are greatly advantageous to us. How should faith, love, patience, meekness, and the excellency and sufficiency of God's grace shine, but by, in, and through the many exercises and varieties of conditions, wherewith the Lord visiteth his? Yea, the greatest in the life, power, and glory of the Lord, have the greatest trials and exercises, which is to their advantage, as also for the good and benefit of others, and to the great honour and glory of the Lord. O! at all times, and in all conditions, take heed of a will, take heed of a wisdom, above the seed's will, and above the seed's wisdom.

Let the Lord alone be all in thee, and make thee every day what he pleaseth; and, in due time, thou shalt know a life,—even the seed's life, the Son's life,—whom all the angels are to worship,—and the mystery of whose life, the angels desire to look into, as it is revealed and brought forth! So, be still and quiet, and silent before the Lord; not putting up any request to the Father, nor cherishing any desire in thee, but in the seed's lowly nature and purely springing life; and the Lord give thee the clear discerning, in the lowly seed, of all that springs and arises in thy heart.

Thou didst read precious things of the seed, when thou wast here, written outwardly; O that thou mightst read the same things, written inwardly in thy own heart; which that thou mayest do, become as a weaned child, not exercising thyself in things, too high or too wonderful for thee. Every secret thing, every spiritual mystery, but what God opens to thee, is too high and wonderful for thee. And, if the Lord at any time open to thee deep mysteries; fear before the Lord; and go no further into them, than the Lord leads thee. The error is, still, in the comprehending, knowing mind, but never in the lowly, weighty seed of life; — whither the Lord God of my life more and more lead thee, and counsel thee to take up thy dwelling-place there, daily instructing thee so to do. For the greatest, as well as the least, must be daily taught of the Lord, both in ascending and descending, or they will miss their way; yea, they must be daily taught of him to be silent before him, and know [what it is] to be *still in him*, or they will be apt to miss in either.

This from thy Friend, I. P.

AMERSHAM, WOODSIDE,
4th of Fifth Month, 1679.

LETTER CIII.

On Prejudices against Anointed Ministers.

TO HIS BROTHER.

DEAR BROTHER, — This morning, as I was going out to walk, somewhat sprang up in my heart freshly and livingly to thee; whereupon, I consulted not, but immediately turned back so to do. Now, if the Lord make it useful to thee, thou wilt have cause to bless his name; and so shall I also, who heartily desire the life and welfare of thy soul in the living God, and thy avoiding all such snares as the enemy lays to betray, and to keep it in death and bondage. The thing that rose up in me, was this.

God gave some apostles, some prophets, &c., for the

work of the ministry, for the building up of the body, for the perfecting of the saints. This was God's gift, in mercy and love, to them in that day, of which gift they were to walk worthy, and to be thankful for it.

And, in these days, the Lord hath given gifts to some for this work, which the body hath need of; and the body is to wait on the Lord in the use of his gift, in fear and humility. For, those that gather the soul to the Lord, they also are appointed to watch over the soul, in the same power and authority that gathered. Now, that which is of God in any heart, being heeded, will teach to make use of the gift and ministry which is of Him; and it cannot be despised, but God is despised; nor can it be neglected, without loss and danger to the soul that neglects it. For God is wise, and his ordinances, his ministry, his gifts are weighty, and his blessings go along with them. Who have been gathered to him in these days, but by his ministry which he hath appointed and sent to gather? and who have been preserved, but those who have waited on the Lord, and been subject to his Spirit in the same ministry which hath gathered? Mark, Brother, in every age, God's ministers have been despised. Moses and all the prophets were despised in their day. What! [said the despisers,] hath God spoken only by Moses? hath he not spoken also by us? The apostles were despised in their days, by those that kept not to the anointing; for this always teacheth to reverence, in subjection to the Lord, the ministry which is of the anointing. "He that despiseth you," said Christ, "despiseth me." He that despiseth them in their gathering, or in their building up, despiseth Him that sent them. They were earthen vessels, in presence contemptible, and very liable to be despised. It is easy still, to despise God's messengers and servants; but, he that will truly and rightly esteem them, must lie low, must dwell in the pure fear, and in the sense of life, that he may be taught of God so to do. It is an easy matter to have objections enough against them; but, to see through all prejudices and objections, to the pure and precious life in them, and to the gift and spirit and power of the Lord, wherein and whereby they minister,—this requires a true eye, and an heart opened by the Lord.

Ah Brother! this is a snare, wherein many have been caught in former ages, and in this age also,—which it is easy falling into,—but the preservation out of it, is not easy, but only by the power and mercy of the Lord. And blessed are those, whom the Lord so favours as to preserve out of it, and to remove from them those prejudices and devices, whereby they are entangled. Dear Brother! when I am in the pure sense before the Lord, and my spirit opened by him, and *thou* presented before me; I could even beg most earnestly of the Lord, that he would open thy eye, and give thee a true sight of thy state, and cause thy spirit to bow before him; and to know and honour what is of him, and not, by any device of the enemy, be hindered from receiving therefrom, what he, in tender love and mercy, holds out to thee.

And, dear Brother, mind this advice which just springs in my heart: pick out some of the faithful ones of the Lord's servants, and open thy heart to them, as, in the leadings of the Lord and waiting upon him, thou findest freedom thereunto. Indeed, Brother, I have had, for a long time, a deep sense of danger towards thee: the Lord prevent it, that thy soul may live to him, and not die from him! There is a wisdom, a will near thee, which will destroy thee, unless the Lord destroy it in thee.

O that thou mightst come to wait aright for the motion of his Spirit! and mightst be kept by him in that which knows the drawing; then wilt thou hunger and thirst after the righteousness of his kingdom, and long after times of meeting and assembling with his people; and find thy sense of them living, and thy life refreshed therein. For, God is with his people, of a truth, and they meet not without him; but, his presence is in the midst of them, causing his life to flow into every vessel, that stands open to him. And, death has not come over his people, whatever the enemy suggests, where he gets an ear open; but, life grows more and more in freshness and into dominion in them. O Brother! the Lord fully gather thee into and preserve thee in that, wherein thou mayest feel this in *thy own* particular,— wherein thou mayest feel the freshness of life, and the power thereof in *them;* that *thy* heart, also, may be as a watered garden, and as a living temple, wherein the pure, living God dwells!

I am satisfied in my heart, that not only my love, but my life speaks to thee. O that thou couldst hear, and feel, and fear, and bow down before the Lord! that he might, in his due season, raise thee up in his life and power among his people, purifying thee, and preserving thee pure and living to him forever.

POSTSCRIPT.

Dear Brother,— The desire of my heart to the Lord for thee is, that he would open and keep open in thee the eye which sees, and the ear which hears, and the heart which understands his truth; and that he would prevent the enemy from raising up another thing in thee, instead of the seed of life and holy witness.

Great hath been the subtlety, and deep hath been the error from the Truth; and many who seem to be Jews are not, but have erred from the Spirit, life, and power, wherewith they were at first convinced, and whereby they were at first led. And, in these, the enemy hath raised up a seat of prejudices, and strong holds, against the ministry and power of the living God; but, those that are of the right seed, bless the Lord, beholding his work, while others slight it, and are expecting somewhat else; they bless also the church which the Lord hath built, and the ministry which he hath sent forth to gather and build it.

O Brother! there is an high-mindedness in *some* which takes upon it to judge beyond its growth and capacity; and there is a fear in the hearts of *others*, lest any thing in them should get up, or judge, or be any thing, beyond or beside the pure Truth; — *this* teacheth to honour and prefer those, whom the Lord hath preferred, *the other* hath accusations and pleas against them; *the one* of these witnesseth preservation from God, *the other* is left to fall. Dear Brother, believe a traveller in the path of life,— (the Lord God raise up in thee that which can believe,)— the enemy with great subtlety hath laid his snares,— hath taken many in his snares,— even in the snares which he laid by his instrument, J—— P——; and many did let in his spirit before they were aware, and are at this day (unknown to their own hearts) entangled therein. The Lord God will terribly appear against such, (indeed, it is truth,) unless they bow to his light, acknowledge their error from the Truth, and come back to the body by repentance, and turning from that, wherein this spirit hath entangled them.

Dear Brother, it is my desire that thou mayest not perish, but feel the carrying on of the work of salvation in thee; travel on in the pure, holy, living, powerful path, and receive the crown of fidelity to the Truth! Ah Brother! mourn to the Lord; fear before him; converse and consult with those that abide faithful; and they may help thee to see, (through the guidance, presence, and power of the Spirit of the Lord with them,) what of thyself, thou art not able to see. Remember this counsel; thy life is wrapped up in it; for thou hast need of the helps, which the Lord in his tender mercy hath provided, and canst not be safe without them.

Thy dear Brother, in the unity of nature, longing after perfect sense of thee, and unity with thee, in the pure life.
I. P.

AYLESBURY GAOL,
7th of Eighth Month, 1667.

LETTER CIV.

Of the Church and Ministry.

IN REPLY TO AN ANSWER OF I. H. TO SOMEWHAT WRITTEN ON BEHALF OF TRUTH.

—— INDEED, to speak properly, the church of the gospel, or new testament church, is invisible. The persons in whom the church is, are visible; yet, the new testament church is not a society of men, but rather, of the invisible life in men. It is a fellowship in the faith, in the spirit, which is the bond of their unity and of their peace.

The life is breathed invisibly into the hidden man. John iii. 8; it is there nourished and built up invisibly into a spiritual invisible temple, house, or church, and in *that* is the unity and fellowship. So that, the church is a mystery, and the fellowship a mystery, which is hid from every eye but the eye of life; and there is no having fellowship one with another, but by coming to that, and keeping in that, wherein is the fellowship. 1 John, i. 7. It is of inward Jews the church is built; it is of such God seeks to frame his new house of worship, under the gospel. John, iv. 23. Now, of such stones as these, the Lord builds up a temple for his Spirit to dwell in, a house for his life and presence to manifest itself in,—even a church for the living God. This building is by the Spirit, in the Spirit, and of that which is spiritual; this building is one with the foundation, and therefore is the pillar and ground of Truth, which none is but Christ, and that which is married to him, and so one with him. 1 Tim. iii. 15. Consider the place well, and see whether it relate to that, which thou callest the *invisible*, or to that, which thou callest the *visible church.*

It is the candlestick in persons, that is the church; not any outward meeting of persons, or joining together by covenant, or receiving or practising of ordinances, can make a church; but, the eternal life in believers, formed by the Spirit into a candlestick, to hold the eternal lamp or light, with the everlasting oil of salvation. The light thus shining in this candlestick, continually refreshed by this oil,—here is a flourishing temple, wherever it is found; here is the church of the living God, here is the spouse married to the Lamb, her Husband. But, grieve the Spirit, quench the Spirit, despise the prophesyings thereof, (and light up a candle of the fleshly wisdom and knowledge of the things of God, instead of these,) the oil soon fails; the oil failing, the lamp goes out; the lamp, or light being gone out of the candlestick, the Lord soon removes the candlestick; and the candlestick being once removed, the very same persons may meet together often, and hold up the form, (performing things mentioned in the Scriptures concerning a church, and observing such things as they may call the institutions and ordinances thereof,)—but they are far from continuing to be a church. Take away the faith, what is left of a Christian? and take away the candlestick, what is left of a church?

It is the Spirit alone that can square stones, and fit them for building a church of; and He alone can build them up into a house, when he hath squared them. Eph.

ii. 22. And, after he hath built, He can pull down again, and bring into a wilderness state; for, there is a wilderness state of Christianity, as well as a built state, Rev. xii. 6; and as, in the built state, it is dangerous to be out of the church, so, in the wilderness state, it is dangerous remaining in that building, which the Spirit of the Lord hath forsaken. Now, if the Spirit be the builder, then, surely, he will take in no stones, but such as he hath first squared and fitted for the building. And, after the church is built, it is he alone who addeth to the church; who will be sure to add none, but those whom he hath first converted. Acts, ii. 47.

The church is a body gathered in the Spirit, and watching to the Spirit; who is present there with His pure, searching, discerning eyes; so that, nothing that is impure can enter, (they watching to the Spirit, according to the order of the gospel;) no, not one counterfeit Jew, no, nor so much as one false apostle, though they clothe themselves ever so like angels of light. Rev. xxii. But if they be negligent, and from off the watch, not waiting for the guidance of the Spirit; then, that which is corrupt may creep in, and endanger the body. Jude, 4.

AN ACCOUNT OF LADY CONWAY.

[*Forming a Supplementary Note to Page* 195 *of this Volume.*]

THE preceding sheets were nearly printed off, when, through the kindness of a friend, the editor at length obtained a sight of a small work, in which some account is preserved of the Lady Viscountess Conway. It is entitled, "The Life of the learned and pious Dr. Henry More, late Fellow of Christ's College, Cambridge; &c., by Richard Ward, A. M.—London, 1710."

This excellent lady appears to have been at one time a pupil of the above named Henry More, and between them there subsisted from first to last a great degree of friendship and esteem. While the circumstance of her having attached herself to the Society of Friends, would render some mention of her character highly interesting to that class of readers; it was thought, on the other hand, that the high standing of her encomiast, as a member of the Established Church, and his public opposition to the religious principles of the Friends,* would not fail to add weight to his testimony in her favour. Much allowance must, however, be made on this latter account, for the imperfect exhibition of this lady's views and motives, in the humiliating preference, which she gave to "Quakerism." With this proviso, a faithful abstract shall be given of the particulars recorded of her by Henry More and his biographers.

She was sister to "Sir John Finch," some time Ambassador from the English Court to that of the Ottoman Empire. Her understanding was singularly quick and apprehensive, her judgment sound and solid, and her sagacity and prudence in affairs of moment, were such as surprised all those, who had occasion to consult with her. Her friend, Henry More, would

---

* See several of his publications.

say of her, that he scarcely ever met with any person, man or woman, of better natural endowments. With regard to the cultivation of these extensive powers, we are told, she was mistress of the highest theories, whether of philosophy or religion; having the greatest facility for physical, metaphysical, and mathematical speculations; and was qualified to search into, and judiciously sift the most abstruse writers of theology. In the company of others, she never, upon the fairest occasion, made the slightest display of her superior ability or acquirements; nor did it appear, that she indulged in these studies out of any vanity of mind or fond curiosity; such pursuits seeming to be as the genuine food of her natural genius, notwithstanding the distressing impediment, under which they were usually engaged in. For she had the affliction to be exercised, from her very youth, with extreme and continued pains in her head, which at length extended over her whole frame, and, at times, accompanied with such severe paroxysms, as might nearly be said to be insupportable. In hope of relief or recovery from this malady, she submitted to many very painful remedies; and, having tried the medical skill which this country at that time afforded, she went to France for the same purpose; but, without receiving any benefit or alleviation.

There was nothing in the character of this "incomparable Lady," (as Henry More was accustomed to call her,) which so called forth the admiration of the serious, among those who had known her from her youth, as this,— that she had such a timely sense and high relish of that, which is infinitely beyond all other attainments,— even, the saving knowledge of "Christ (that is, of his power, life, and Spirit) in us, the hope of glory." It was by virtue of *this*, as her learned friend justly remarks,— in comparison of which, she esteemed all things else but as loss, that she was endued with such marvellous patience, composure, and fortitude, to bear the constant, tedious, as well as more agonizing conflicts of the flesh. And, it seemed to him to be not without providential wisdom, that all means of mitigation proved so ineffectual; in order that this glorious power of God, in its operation on an obedient soul, might the more fully appear. Thus it was, that, in a close pursuit after Truth and knowledge, the Christian graces so eminently shone forth in her, as even to obscure the lustre of other accomplishments, at least, with those who could behold and appreciate them.

Something of the pious resignation of her spirit is discovered in the following expressions, which occur in a letter. "From the redoubling of my afflictions. the continuedness of my great pains, increase of weakness, with new additional distempers, I might fancy my release not far off, from those weighty sufferings I have groaned under so many years. But, life and death are in the hands of the Almighty; and what he designs for me, I desire I may be enabled to give myself up to willingly, without murmuring; who only knows, what measure of suffering is most necessary for me." Her mind was not so fastened down to her own personal concernments or situation, as to render her conversation ungrateful to others; but meekness, disinterestedness, uniform kindness to all around, condescension and forbearance towards the failings of others, together with a provident solicitude on behalf of relations and friends, continued to be the frame of her mind up to the very close. And though her pains of body increased, the clearness of her intellect was not in any wise impaired, nor the tranquillity of her soul molested; for, at the last, she went off as one asleep, drawing her breath shorter and shorter, and thus yielding up her spirit to God, who gave it, and had redeemed it to himself through much tribulation.

One of her earliest friends, on being made acquainted with the manner of her departure, made this remark: "I perceive, and bless God for it, that my Lady Conway was *my Lady Conway* to her last breath; the greatest example of patience and presence of mind, in highest extremities of pain and affliction, that we shall easily meet with: scarce any thing to be found like her, since the primitive times of the church."

Several of Henry More's learned treatises were composed at Ragley Hall, the family seat, and expressly at the desire of the Lady Conway; and, in an Epistle Dedicatory to his "Antidote to Atheism," he gives a great character of her. After her decease, it was designed, that something of her own experience should have been printed, by way of Remains or Pious Fragments; and, with this view, her valued friend essayed an account of her, by way of preface, from which, some parts of the present brief memorial are taken. This document winds up with the succeeding reflection.

"These things, which I have communicated to thee, concerning our friend, this excellent Lady, I have not done out of any partial or carnal boastings; but, that God may be glorified, and that thou mayest the more fully understand, that that religion, which availeth any thing in the time of distress, is not opinion, ceremony, talk, or fancy; but the power of God in the inward man, in virtue of the new birth, or real regeneration; which is the true and saving knowledge of Christ in us, the hope of glory. Which mystery, she being acquainted with from her youth, and growing up therein, it made her such an invincible champion, and enabled her to bear up with that stoutness and constancy, either against the buffetings of Satan, or sad incumbrances of afflictive nature; in which, by the divine power in the new birth, she hath proved herself more than conqueror."

It does not appear at what period she began to attach herself to the Society of Friends, nor at what time she expressed the following sentiments connected with that subject, in a letter to Henry More. "Your conversation with them [the Friends] at London, might be, as you express it, charitably intended, like that of a physician frequenting his patients, for the increase or confirmation of their health; but, *I* must profess, that *my* converse with them is, to *receive* health and refreshment *from* them." And, towards the close of the same letter, she further adds, "I pray God, give us all a clear discerning between melancholy, enthusiasm, and true inspiration; that we may not be imposed upon, to believe a lie. The great difference of opinion in this point, amongst the learned and experienced, occasions much perplexity in minds less exercised, and thus not so well fitted for judging." Her learned friend said of her, that she would not give up her judgment entirely unto any; which makes it the more remarkable, that she should have cherished such a leaning towards this people, as she is known to have done. He attributed this change to the height of her virtue, and said, "It was the greatness of her mind which betrayed her to it; who, looking upon some pretensions of the Quakers to be very excellent, all the external considerations of her quality and of the world, availed nothing with her, for the hindering of those regards which she showed towards them." She preferred such servants as were of this persuasion, because of their seriousness and quietness, which indeed were qualifications very desirable in her tried state. Hence the inference was drawn, that the melancholy circumstances, under which she so long laboured, gradually inclined her towards Friends and their opinions. This, however, is clear; she chose the company of some of the best and most eminent among them, as Robert Barclay, William Penn, &c.: her physician, also, Baron Van Helmont, who lived long in her family, is said to have been "a frequenter of the Quakers' Meetings." She acknowledged, she was never in love with the *name of a Quaker*, nor with their *rusticity;* but regarded only their principles and practices, so far as they were good and Christian. In the same letter, she particularly takes notice of the pressures and sufferings they had lain under, and that she was much refreshed by the accounts of their trials and consolations; and that they were fitted, from the various and heavy exercises they had themselves experienced, and their supports under them, to administer comfort to others in great distress.

Henry More was much affected with the change wrought in the Countess, so that, at length, he received the account with tears; and laboured all that a faithful friend could do, to set her, as he thought, right, with regard to her judgment in these matters. But, when he saw, that he could not sufficiently prevail, he desisted; and thought fit to leave that great person to enjoy, in her extremities, the company and the ways she most approved. How far her peace of mind was concerned, with regard to the humiliating path she must often have had to tread, while espousing a cause so misrepresented and despised, as that of the Society of Friends then was — how far she was satisfied in the course she adopted, may be fairly estimated from the sincerity and piety of her character through life, and from the consolation and support she was favoured with in death.

THE END.

www.ingramcontent.com/pod-product-compliance
Lightning Source LLC
LaVergne TN
LVHW010229110826
845151LV00004B/1233
9781425525958